AF210284

© Christophe Carreau, 2025
Cover: Claire Carreau
Corrections: Fred de Leau, Arvind Parmar
Publisher: BoD · Books on Demand GmbH, In de Tarpen 42,
22848 Norderstedt, bod@bod.de
Print: Libri Plureos GmbH, Friedensallee 273, 22763 Hamburg

ISBN : 978-3-7693-2322-1
Legal Deposit: February 2025

CHRISTOPHE CARREAU

The Netherlands : Another way of life in Europe

The life of a French resident for 30 years

Cultural differences between the Netherlands and France

Second Edition

Citations

★ « *Whoever wants to succeed must learn to suffer.* »

★ « *One only has the good we do for ourselves.* »

★ « *God created the world, but the Dutch built the Netherlands.* »

Dutch sayings

★ « *If you want life to smile at you, first bring your good humour to it.* »

★ « *What we cannot prohibit, we must necessarily allow.* »

Baruch Spinoza

★ « *Every disadvantage has its advantage.* »
Johan Cruyff

★ « *Violence is the last refuge of incompetence.* »

Isaac Asimov

★ « *France is a paradise populated by people who believe they are in hell.* »
Sylvain Tesson, French writer

★ « *We are an unhappy people collectively.* »

Frédéric Lenoir, French philosopher

★ « *We must affirm what makes this country great: the freedom to be yourself.* »

Lodewijk Asscher, Dutch Minister of Social Affairs, 2013

★ « *What other place could we choose in the rest of the world, where all the amenities of life (..) are so easy (..)? What other country where we can enjoy such complete freedom, where we can sleep with less worry, where there are always armies on foot expressly to guard us, where poisonings, betrayals, slanders are less known, and where more remains of the innocence of our ancestors?*»

René Descartes, 1631, Amsterdam

★ «*There, everything is order and beauty, luxury, calm and pleasure.* »

Charles Baudelaire, The evil flowers, 1857

★ « *A true land of plenty, where everything is beautiful, rich, peaceful, honest; where luxury takes pleasure in being reflected in order; where life is rich and sweet to breathe; from which disorder, turbulence and the unexpected are excluded; where happiness is married to silence; where the cuisine itself is poetic, rich and exciting at the same time.* »

Charles Baudelaire, The Spleen of Paris, The invitation to travel, 1869

★ « *Ultimately, if I chose to live in the Netherlands, it is precisely for this search for the good life.* »

Océane Dorange, Petites chroniques des Pays-Bas, 2019

Prologue

★ *Without needing to change continent, it is possible to experience another life in Europe, by crossing a border a few hundred kilometres from France.*

★ *Despite the wars, religions, industrial and technological revolutions that all European countries have shared, despite this common history, Dutch society has developed a unique way of life.*

★ *Observing others is observing ourselves in a mirror that reveals our mutual differences as much as it connects us in diversity.*

★ *No, the Dutch are neither benign nor naïve!*

Another life in Europe

The Netherlands is indeed a country in northern Europe with a Protestant background which shares similarities and affinities with the Scandinavian countries. There we find these same societies that are easy to access without a pronounced hierarchy, a relaxed and almost stress-free atmosphere, a high level of satisfaction and happiness felt, high social protection, claimed equality between men and women, autonomy and empowerment of individuals, the practice of local and associative democracy, a less burdensome but effective State and administration, high taxes and strong involvement of citizens in the affairs of society. However, in this Nordic area, the Dutch are distinguished from their neighbours by a unique culture and mentality, which are not found anywhere else. We will not mention here the history that this country has shared with its European neighbours, by allying or confronting themselves since the time of the Roman Empire, with nations in Europe for two thousand years.

This great European history, animated by the same springs and the same motives everywhere on the continent, has nevertheless seen the birth and strengthening of unique cultures and mentalities specific to each people, deeply rooted, that neither the disappearance of religious practice, neither the erasure of borders nor globalisation have been able to begin.

Knowing and understanding the life and mentality of the Dutch, our European neighbours, of Protestant and Nordic background like Germany and the Scandinavian countries, will give you access to another life, to another way of considering life in society for greater happiness.

After more than 25 years living in the Netherlands, I became a French and Dutch European at the same time, with a new, expanded and enriched identity. You too can discover the European within you to understand the keys to a happiness felt in society that is higher than in France.

Whether you are employed in a Franco-Dutch or multinational company and wish to better understand your Dutch partners, whether you have to do business with them, or simply whether you would like to know what separates you from this high felt happiness which characterises Nordic societies, this book will take you to the roots of the cultural and behavioural differences that separate France from the Netherlands.

The postcard is true indeed

The preconceived ideas that we bring with us when arriving in the Netherlands are not unjustified. Of course, we immediately see that the country is immensely flat and that its towns and countryside confirm the postcard views of tourist guides. One can cycle absolutely everywhere on cycle paths along the canals where ducks splash and where white swans, emblems of the national airline KLM, sail gracefully. The quaint villages boast their red brick houses, their windmills and the bell towers of their Protestant churches. The towns line up their tall mansions along wide canals spanned by a multitude of bridges crossed by multitudes of cyclists. Despite the excitement, the water, wisely channeled and domesticated, makes the landscape serene and idyllic.

Welcome to the land of the happy people

A life in a harmonious society, a liberal, even libertarian spirit, a tranquility and a lack of stress completely unreal for a Frenchman, a repetitive urban architectural model, a society which seems normalised by dint of being perfect, an unfailing good humour bathed in a good-natured atmosphere, people who do not seem to take themselves seriously while paying the greatest attention to the quality of their way of life, tolerance defended and erected as the pinnacle of life in society, the cleanliness of the interiors open to the view of all passers-by through large windows without curtains, the domestic sense of the Dutch who love to enjoy the simple things of everyday life, all this is absolutely true.

> *A few hundred kilometres from France, there exists in Europe a completely different society, another way of life, a joy of living together that is unimaginable for many French people. And yet.*

Without bragging about a French art of living, without claiming to have refined cuisine, a brilliant culture, universal human rights or a humanism nobler than commercialism, the Dutch nevertheless achieve a higher level of happiness than in France. Studies have proven this undeniably for several decades. In the ranking of the 147 happiest countries in the world established by the United Nations[1], the Netherlands remains in 5th position, behind the Scandinavian countries. France, which had just risen to twentieth place in 2022, its best score since the creation of the ranking, has just lost one place in 2023. As for the quality of life index[2], the Netherlands are the first of the ranking, while France is relegated to 30th position.

Is individual liberalism happiness?

What in France is considered a derogatory and frowned upon word, is interpreted in the Netherlands as a synonym for freedom and well-being.

It is believed that the freer people are, the happier they are[3]. The freedom of the Dutch is clearly much less hampered by strict teachers and peremptory authority, by an authoritarian hierarchy and bosses, by a paternalistic and restrictive state. The inhabitants of this country enjoy a freedom to undertake which is combined with the freedom to exist and feel happy.

---

[1] *World Happiness Report, ONU, 2023*

[2] *Indice de Qualité de Vie 2023, NUMBEO*

[3] *Gaël Brulé, sociologue, Université de Genève en Suisse et de Rotterdam aux Pays Bas.*

The Dutch have the self-confidence to make their own choices, they are empowered and have autonomy, which French citizens are deprived of. More autonomy would undoubtedly make them happier.

It is an individualism in the noble sense of the term, which protects as much as it allows the individual to flourish in their life, while investing in the community for which they are responsible. The Dutch are notoriously known for their developed community life, and their involvement in the political life of their society. Dutch society is the very illustration of autonomous and responsible individuals who invest more in the group, the happiness of the greatest number thus passing through the collective. This type of society and associative life better protects individuals against the trials of life and traumatic events.

Another look

This text aims to present to the French the cultural and political differences of our Dutch neighbours. In no way does it seek to make value judgments, to say what is good or what is not. What is mentioned there differs, from the way of doing and thinking in France, and denotes cultural particularism. For the Dutch, this will also be the way to know what distinguishes them from the French. They will be interested to know how they are seen by a foreigner whose interest in their culture and mentality has only grown over the years.

The aim is not to change the French into Dutch, or the other way around. Nevertheless, awareness of our own French identity will come through awareness of the diversity of the other European cultures that surround us. This may also create the awareness of what can bring us together and what we share at a global scale in our own modern era.

There are also people like that in France...

As you read this book, you will be entitled to consider that there are also people like that in France, people who never get angry with their children, who respectfully follow the waiting line at the stores, who speak informally to their boss without being jealous, who discuss politics without aggression while listening to others, who do not complain constantly, who are disciplined, who feel responsible for the well-being of the community, who take initiatives, who speak languages without apprehension and without feeling judged, who are not afraid of the future... And there are also Dutch people in the Netherlands who lack civility, who get angry quickly, who cook well and who do not interfere in what does not concern them. The Dutch are known for their business pugnacity, which can make them tough to negotiate, even unpleasant. These individual characteristics, which are to be attributed to people who are seen stubborn in their work, do not, however, corrupt a welcoming and caring society, which enjoys social relations, even in negotiation and political discourse, that are peaceful and balanced, certainly respectful of the well-being of the community. We will find exceptions everywhere, in the Netherlands as in France, which will only confirm the general rule. This book will restore to you the atmosphere which permeates life and society in the Netherlands as a whole, and which is the fruit of my daily personal experience, accumulated during two decades of immersion in my host country. It will offer you an overall painting made up of small scenes, like a Bruegel painting, from which an overall style and atmosphere will emerge, typical of northern paintings. It will also provide you with reflections and points of view with more height to bring out what makes the soul, not to mention genius because arrogance is not well seen, of this singular people.

No, the Dutch are neither benign nor naïve!

This book addresses harmonious life in society, erected as a fundamental principle, social relations devoid of aggression, the empowerment of individuals and the trust granted a priori, the spirit of compromise that ultimately prevails in any negotiation, as well as the practice of the government coalition in a proportional electoral system and a parliamentary regime. All these aspects, intrinsically natural for the Dutch but improbable for the French, will inevitably give rise to skepticism among the latter. It is indeed doubtful that such a state of mind is achievable, except by dealing with naive, docile and indoctrinated individuals.

And yet, no. One must admit this reality rather than denigrate it out of bad faith chauvinism. The Dutch are far from being nice teddy bears. On the contrary, their way of life and mentality allow discussion and protest to be expressed before they have to turn into confrontation to be heard. Reading this book, you will realise that they dare to protest and negotiate more naturally than the French, without false shame. They possess the culture of counter-power that each citizen, fundamentally autonomous and free to act, has the duty to exercise on their own initiative in the name of the community. The society they have built results from their atavism to defend their interests with stubbornness and to immediately open negotiations to obtain what they want.

Which means that things are rather the opposite of what one believes. It is the French, generally kinder and more measured, who do not appreciate rubbing shoulders with the Dutch in work, the latter not hesitating to take on the role of the bad guy to defend themselves. Only the French of Protestant faith seem to get used to it...

The mirror to cultures

When leaving for abroad, we unknowingly take the homeland culture of our country deep within us. Without having understood it by living among our compatriots, we become bearers of our own national sensitivity which is revealed through contact with differences. Only flying fish, which experience air and water alternately, can realise the existence of the environment in which they live. For others, the question will never arise, incapable of suspecting the other world which marks the limits of theirs. The sea will remain indefinable, since nothing can reveal and identify it in a uniform universe, without difference and without reference.

The boundaries are there to be crossed, in one direction then the other, in order to play with the reflections of the worlds on either side of the mirrors which reveal them. It is here that cultures can be figured out, it is from there that they draw their substance to live and enrich themselves.

> *Without borders to read, without awareness of its own identity, a culture cannot integrate and transform into original expression the currents of the world in which it evolves.*

A culture can only survive by welcoming travellers who prove its difference and bring into it its material. The proper development of one requires the flourishing of the other, without which hegemony marks the end of the contrasts and creations that arise from the complex interplay of confrontations of ideas.

> *Learning to know others means first learning to know yourself.*

Diversity as a reason for being

Today, Europe is a reason for being and living in a connected continent made of exchanges, confrontations and beneficial reciprocal stimulation, of fertile cultural diversity.

This diversity is not only the wealth of Europe, but above all its energy and its own functioning. It has drawn from it its values and its principles, it draws from it the strength to adapt to the world and to move with history.

> *Europe is not an end in itself, it is the means to evolve and progress.*

Everyone has a European identity, often hidden. Everyone has the right to access this additional identity without denying their origins and their native culture, on the contrary by enriching it.

Europe is not foreign, everyone should feel at home there. Everyone must have the opportunity to experience it and make it their own.

What have I become? French or Dutch?

After more than 30 years spent in the Netherlands, with frequent exchanges and trips to France with friends and family, with children attending the Van Gogh French high school in The Hague, but also at the international school in The Hague (ISH) and at Leiden University, having worked in a European international environment at the European Space Agency, with children now living in Berlin in Germany, Edinburgh in Scotland and Lund in Sweden, residing in once again in the Netherlands near The Hague, but also in the Bordeaux region in Aquitaine, what have become of me? I have become a European from France living at home in the Netherlands, having acquired another identity which is not limited to an exclusively French or Dutch civil status, but rather an additional identity made of the living and lived synthesis of the two cultures.

Testimony of a French woman living in the Netherlands, married to a Dutchman and having recently adopted Dutch nationality in 2024, while retaining her nationality of French origin. Océane Dorange keeps a fresh look at Dutch society, which she observes in her Chronicles with a lively and humane style, often touching.[4]

"No longer quite French, I will never be Dutch. Being between two cultures is not a handicap, but a wealth, a gift.

---

[4] *Petites chroniques des Pays-Bas, Plus totalement française, pas non plus néerlandaise, des chroniques de l'entre-deux, Océane Dorange, www.petiteschroniquesdespaysbas.com*

When you live between two cultures, making a choice is impossible. You are both. You are neither one nor the other. Dual nationals are a homogeneous solution whose components have become inseparable."

During his last stay in Paris, René Descartes, who had lived longer in the Netherlands (the United Provinces at the time) than in France, where he produced all his philosophical and mathematical works, was looking forward to returning there soon, to his home in Egmond.:

> *"Standing as I am, with one foot in one country and the other in another, I find my condition very happy, in that it is free.»* [5]

Roots or wings in Europe?

Younger generations, by easily studying throughout Europe, naturally adopt this broader identity, so much so that the questions I asked my children "Are you French? Or do you feel Dutch? Which country are you from? What are your roots? » no longer makes sense to them. "But from no country exclusively, I myself am where I want to live in Europe, in the manner of the young generations of our time.". Morals and mentalities change more quickly among younger generations, wherever they live in their countries of origin, or elsewhere in Europe. These young people, who are moving around more and more, are developing a culture which is not "international", nor American, nor Asian, nor African, but indeed European. This culture is revealed both in the light of major global phenomena, such as migrations, terrorism, extremism or populism, but also and above all, in everyday life when we work and live together as Europeans.

> *Seen from the outside, our European culture and its values clearly distinguish Europe from the rest of the world. We often forget how easy it is to live together in Europe and how much we have in common.*

---

[5] René Descartes, Lettre à Elisabeth, juillet 1648

I.   Another way of life

★ *I swore to myself never to live in the Netherlands. I finally returned there to feel at peace, and to raise my family of four children in real family happiness.*

★ *Visitors returning home to France often regretted having to leave what they had experienced, what they called "the bubble" of happy people.*

★ *First impressions are always sharp. Immediate immersion as if you were there.*

I will never live in the Netherlands!

In the early 1990s, I'm travelling for work to the Netherlands in The Hague. It is a dreary winter day, and after morning meetings followed by a cold lunch on the go, made of bread and ham, I find myself in the street under a fine rain that insidiously chilled my bones. I notice the passers-by who are crowding together, dripping, under the bus shelter. The cobbled street is a wet mirror reflecting the gray sky. No light emerges from this desolate scene, and I say to myself that "I will never live in this country! ". At this moment, I only ask to quickly return to Italy where I live with my young children under the sun and the blue sky of the "Castelli Romani", pretty green hills on the heights of Rome.

It's the end of the war

A few years later in 1995, I found myself again in the Netherlands in a rental house that I had to prepare to soon move my family there, following my new job assignment. With remarkable and surprising efficiency, the craftsmen begin and finish the work within a week. Just after leaving my frenetic life in the Mediterranean south of Europe, I find myself in the heart of a northern village where people take things efficiently and calmly without ever getting angry, greeting you in the street while they don't know you, honestly give you the exact amount of your change, show respect and welcome you with ease and kindness. "It's the end of the war," I thought without thinking. I was preparing to live more than 25 years of my life in a happy and comfortable bubble.

First and second impressions

I didn't have to go through hard work to assimilate into the Netherlands. Effortlessly, the country opened up to me in a natural and spontaneous way. Long after my arrival, I often felt impressions which resembled like little lights which punctured daily life, like first impressions which kept sparkling over the years, and whose accuracy was never to be denied subsequently. I am giving you now, as a way of making first contact with this country, some of these first and second impressions, which will be developed further in the book, without filter as they came to me, in an attempt to restore their spontaneity and authenticity. Immersion without « a priori » and without « a posteriori ».

Guard down

I have just arrived in the Netherlands from Italy a few days ago, alone as a scout to prepare for the arrival of my family. I meet Dutch people with whom I begin to communicate, rather easily in English. Suddenly I realise that everyone has their guard down, that no one is on alert, that everything is done easily without duplicity, without malice or bad motives. Everything is done with ease, honesty and simplicity.

A life on a bicycle

I look in astonishment at the people around me on their bikes, who find nothing extraordinary there. I insert myself, as discreetly as possible like the regular that I am not, into the flow of bicycles going briskly in urban traffic which turns out to be quite dense and rushed, while I am still assimilating the cycling as a distraction. When stopping at a red light on the path, I notice a woman pulling up next to me with her young child sitting in the back on a small seat. Of the size and robust build of a Batavian woman, she is visibly pregnant at an advanced stage, her legs touch her belly when she pedals. All this perched on a bicycle seems precarious to me, I move away discreetly so as not to bother her and let her pass. The light turns green, and in a few pedal strokes, the vigorous young mother literally leaves me behind her. I realise that all these people on bikes are not on vacation strolling with their noses in the wind, that they travel efficiently to nursery, school or the office, and that they have forged calves of steel since their earliest childhood.

The organised confrontation

I am arriving at the office at the European Space Agency to take on the role of project control, meaning that I will have to monitor the development costs of large industrial projects such as scientific satellites, which are also extremely demanding in advanced technologies. I realise that the word "cost control" is understood in the restrictive sense of the term, in order to constrain and limit expenses, otherwise they will always tend to slip away like sand through the fingers. And I realise that, within the same team and the same project, the confrontation of interests is not only taken into account from the start of the development of the spacecraft, but also organised in functions and meetings whose aim is to put differences on the table and negotiate openly between colleagues. The most surprising thing for me, a young Frenchman fresh out of the « grandes écoles » who never exposed me to this state of mind of bargaining and control, is that all this is done without causing personal resentment or embarrassment. Here, budgets are treated as resources that must be constantly scrutinised and preserved. Here, we negotiate and confront each other between colleagues without harming the people who are, all at the same time, responsible for the same project. It's a job like any other to bring the balance of power into play. This is done in a calm and relaxed manner, without ever getting angry around the negotiating table. Nobody wins, nobody loses. The project is moving forward thanks to this. Then we go to eat together in the canteen, on very good terms in a relaxed atmosphere.

Saint Nicholas arrives

It is mid-November and we go out in the afternoon to welcome Saint-Nicolas with his family who, after long weeks of waiting, is arriving in town. I carry one of my young children on my shoulders and we head towards the canal which serves as a harbour in the middle of the village, where the holy man will disembark, as in all the villages in the Netherlands on this November afternoon, at the same time. He is surrounded by a flock of young servants and "Black Peters", all dressed like servants from the Middle Ages, and who move around him like trash-talkers. He wears a white beard and a red miter on his head, a long red garment, white gloves and an episcopal crosier. Far from inspiring solemnity and fearful respect, the sight of His Holiness disembarking from his boat with great pomp after weeks of waiting, provokes cries of joy and delirium from the laughing children who crowd around his white horse. We are immersed in a carnival party, specially organised for these children, but which also delights parents, amazed by so much joy and candid exaltation. The brats who are the "Black Peters" with their faces blackened by the soot from the chimneys through which they passed to place the gifts at the feet of the slippers, gesticulate like crazy, distribute treats on the fly, and, to top it all off, climb and jump on the roof of police cars! I am amazed to witness a pure delirium of childish exaltation in the heart of the village transformed into a playground for all the children, and for all the parents who are treating themselves to a memorable family celebration.

Shall we have a drink, or a cup of coffee?

When I arrived in the Netherlands, I signed up for an evening course in Leiden to practice life drawing. It's 10:30 p.m., class is over, it's time to take leave to go home, when one of the students asks the question loudly and clearly: "Who's coming for a drink?». The question, so natural, does not expect an answer as it would be obvious: everyone here has a drink or a cup of coffee after an activity in a club, whatever it is. Whatever the activity practiced, painting, chess, skating, sport shooting, fencing or tennis, there is often a bar area at the club where you can socialise over a cup of coffee, an infusion or a beer. If there is no bar, we will then go to the local café in town. Collective activity is inseparable from taking a break to relax and talk about anything and everything, which in Dutch is "talking about cows and calves" ("over koetjes et kalfjes praten"). In the Netherlands, the group life does necessarily pass through these endless talks around a drink or a cup of tea or coffee, through these moments of relaxation which are appreciated for what they are, moments outside of time where one pays attention to the other, a break from the daily hustle and bustle reserved for good human relations. It is said in Dutch "chillen", and could be translated as a mixture of "hanging out, relaxing, chatting and listening".

Aggression curbed

During one of my first outings one evening in a bar with my colleagues from the art club, one of the customers, visibly drunk, began to insult those around him and threatened to come to blows. Immediately, and without any consultation or signal, a few fellows spontaneously get up from their table and come to surround the troublemaker. Firmly, but without any force, they control him and lay him on the ground to calm him while waiting for the police, who quickly show up. Without being surprised by anything, while saying hello to the owner, the police took our man away without vehemence and without breaking the atmosphere. The incident will have gone unnoticed by many. In this country, he who loses his nerve, loses. Without this triggering a crisis, just a trivial incident.

American preference

We take possession of our new accommodation, a small typical Dutch house next to the others along a charming canal. We happen to be on the edge of a small military airport serving as a base for maritime patrol planes, which provides us with a vast green space in front of our windows. As a fan of planes and aeronautics, I watch the large four-engine aircraft at the end of takeoff fly heavily over the neighbourhood before turning towards the nearby sea. These are American made P3-Orion planes, which were also sold to Germany and Portugal, to the detriment of the competing French plane Atlantis. My neighbours express their satisfaction at having their country equipped with American planes, which places their small country alongside the leading military power in the world, with which they also share certain cultural affinities. It was the first time that I was confronted with this American preference which was openly displayed, and which was never subsequently denied.

French 2 CVs and US jeeps

When the sunny Spring days arrive, one can see friendly processions of vintage cars which travel through the region with slowness and delight. Among the most represented models are the timeless Citroën 2CV, and the essential US jeep, straight from the landing beaches of D-day. We once again find the affinity for American material and culture, in particular for everything relating to the significant era of the Second World War and the liberation.

This is also complemented by the love that the Dutch have for French Citroën cars, in particular the legendary 2CV and DS. My French colleague Hubert, an engineer keen on French automobile mechanics, has no less than 3 2CV models which he purchased in kit and which he had assembled by a mechanic specialising in this type of model in our own village in Wassenaar.

Still, you speak French well!

We arrive in France at the hostel in our car which displays its beautiful Dutch license plate, an unusual yellow and clearly foreign to our owner who eyes it with a suspicious look, wondering in what language we are going to address him. We try to put him at ease straight away by starting the discussion in our native French without any accent. The conversation progresses slowly, while explaining to him that we are French living in the Netherlands. Visibly still disturbed, our man can't help but compliment us half-heartedly: "Still, you speak French very well"!

Without understanding where this blockage comes from, I have often noticed that it is difficult for a French person to imagine that a compatriot can go abroad without losing his soul, that it is difficult to understand foreigners and to consider cultural differences without it being disruptive, or even threatening. In fact, I have come to think that it is complicated, if not impossible, to put oneself in one another's shoes, to grasp that a foreigner may have a different way of thinking. It seems difficult, if not impossible, to adopt this new mentality in turn, if only for the time of an exchange. Inevitably, one will fall, often before the end of a sentence, in one's own shoes.

II. Cultural paradoxes

★ *You have to live there to believe it. The Dutch are difficult to understand because they are so different from France and its spirit.*

★ *Society, individuals, police, taxes, drugs, rising water levels... everything in this country is paradoxical.*

One has to experience it to believe it

What will be revealed in this book will undoubtedly surprise any French reader, conditioned by their French mentality and culture. It is difficult, almost impossible, to extricate oneself from the matrix of a society without having to leave it and emigrate. You have to live there to believe what you see. The characteristic of a culture is to pass off as natural and normal behaviours which elsewhere seem contradictory or improbable, and whose strangeness makes one doubt whether they can be practiced by another people in a way as natural as one breathes. Foreign is what is not proper or natural to someone, and which becomes an apparent contradiction.

« We do not see things as they are, but as we are. »[6].

Beyond the hasty and difficult-to-understand clichés, this book will offer you an experience lived inside the country, which will make things less abstract, less foreign, and ultimately, who knows, almost acceptable for French people who would like to be inspired by it. After all, these Batavians are renowned for being a generation ahead of all social issues compared to France, whether it is women's right to vote, the abolition of the death penalty, the right to vote for women, foreigners in municipal elections, the supervision and control of drugs, that of prostitution, end-of-life support, homosexual marriage... They are especially known for experiencing a happiness felt significantly higher than in France, what everyone aspires to.

"Both" or "Cultural Paradoxes"

Certainly, the Dutch will be difficult to understand because it is so different from France and its spirit. There, education, population behaviour and public policies seem to be made up of improbable associations and combinations that would be difficult to envisage in France.

---

[6] *Anaïs Nin*

*« In all my long and adventurous life I have not seen
a people so full of contradictions as the Dutch »*[7].

However, seen from the Netherlands, French culture has its own
inconsistencies and paradoxes that are just as improbable and
inconceivable for the Dutch.

Cultural paradoxes in France

Art of living: both delicacy and animosity

The Dutch are often surprised by the anxiety and chronic
nervousness of the French, while the latter claim to have an art
and a refined gentleness of living, but are apparently incapable of
living together in a harmonious way, without complaining,
without contesting, without criticising, without confronting and
confronting each other relentlessly.

1789: both the revolution and anxiety for the future

In 1789, the French broke the chains of an old regime by
releasing the principles of freedom, republic and democracy
which would change their future and that of the European
continent. Since then, they have liked to claim this revolutionary,
pioneering and universalist spirit.

But on the other hand, French society is characterised today by a
strong resistance to change which arises at the slightest attempt at
reform with strikes and systematic defensive protest. The French
show excessive anxiety in the face of a future that terrorises them.

School: both distinction and supervision

The French education system is entirely focused on the
search for individual excellence. Its stated objective is to bring as
many people as possible to the Baccalaureate, then to university,

---

[7] *Duc of Baena (Spain)*

in the name of the laudable principle of equal opportunities. It values individual talents. Egos are encouraged to express themselves without being framed by a group spirit and collaborative work.

But on the other hand, the entire French educational system demonstrates formal rigidity by establishing a strong hierarchy between teachers and students, by erecting a master teaching system which subjects and disciplines students to the hierarchy of functions in society. In doing so, this system deprives individuals of any autonomy and sense of responsibility within the community, while it highlights individual excellence..

Character: both excellence and "French bashing"

Proud of their culture, the French are often rightly proud of the richness of their heritage, their cuisine, their fashion and their haute couture.

But, on the other hand, this quest for excellence and distinction is contaminated by their famous critical spirit, erected as a national culture. The French then begin to openly criticise in public their negative points and their failures, from which they derive a certain satisfaction, thinking that they are thus enhancing their individual value by criticising others and their own society, an attitude that remains incomprehensible to foreigners.

Cultural paradoxes in the Netherlands

On the Dutch side, seen from France, these "improbable amalgames" which are characteristic of a culture, are as numerous as they are confusing.

Society: both more social and liberal

Dutch society as a whole combines policies that are both more social but also more liberal than in France, more collectivist while being very liberal on a personal, economic and societal level.

Individual: both subject to the group and autonomous

The education of Dutch children instills in them from an early age the primacy of the group over the individual and the need to conform to the interests of the community. We format individuals for normality by repeating to them "Behave in an ordinary way, it's crazy enough!.." ("Doe maar gewoon, dan doe je al gek genoeg..").

But on the other hand, everyone must be autonomous and take their share of responsibility. Everything will be done to help the individual develop to maintain their autonomy and maintain their mobility for as long as possible. The individual must be active through paid or voluntary work, meet their financial needs, and be responsible for their actions. We will be able to participate in the interests of the group and help the public authorities who make TV broadcasts available to help the police in their research, or who call on citizens to improve the situation, through investigations, alerts, evaluations, contributory networks... You will first have to try to solve your problems yourself by asking for help from your loved ones if necessary, before asking for help from the State.

> *Autonomy and individual responsibility within the community are the keystone that underpins the entire Dutch society.*

Individuals: both serious and funny

The Dutch have this Calvinist background which can make them austere and serious when they are at work, talking about money or negotiating fiercely. They are also when they go straight to the point to address subjects without false shame, or without unnecessary modesty in their eyes.

But on the other hand, they are the champions of the good joke, the lovers of the big joke which they practice on any occasion, particularly in groups or in clubs where we also go to relax and have a good laugh, whatever the activity carried out. Much more than the French, the Dutch like to be made fun of and laughed at, to the point of becoming crazy.

Police: both local and uncompromising

The police play proximity, they are close to fellow citizens with whom they communicate directly without arousing fear. She is close to the population who feel protected by her police and who are ready to help her.

But on the other hand, the police will have no qualms about applying the law, issuing fines for the slightest violation of authorised limits, immediately repressing violence or excesses, regulating behaviour with an efficiency that plays on a certain brutality, to enforce the law with an intransigence that can send shivers down your spine.

Society: both friendly and hardworking

This is the country where the coffee break is king, every morning and every afternoon, where bistros and tea rooms are legion, where each sports club or association has its bar, where the moment of relaxation and conviviality is established as a a pillar of corporate culture and life in society.

But on the other hand, we quickly get back to work by rolling up our sleeves, without pretending and without hanging around. The Dutch tackle the task with hardness, without complacency towards themselves, without complaining, and until the end. In a country of Calvinist culture, everyone earns their bread by the sweat of their brow, works hard and gives birth in pain.

Taxes: both suspicious and convinced

The expression "The State will pay" cannot exist in this country where all fellow citizens consider the State budget as theirs, and on which they keep a close eye in order to monitor expensive policies which would ultimately cost them dear.

But on the other hand, there is within this population a consent to heavy taxes on income, on assets and on inheritances. Through transparent organisation and management of public funds, the population is aware of a "return on investment" of the sums allocated in taxes. It can judge the effective services and organisation of the administration that taxes finance. Above all, she appreciates the harmonious development of life in society in which she invests.

Drugs: both tolerated and banned

Although illegal and uncontrolled like cigarettes or alcohol, soft drugs are nevertheless tolerated in the Netherlands. Moderate personal consumption is permitted and tolerated.

But moreover, its consumption, or only its possession even in reduced quantities, is strictly prohibited within middle and high school educational establishments, which are intractable on the issue: any student caught with hashish or other drugs on them, will be expelled immediately and will have to finish his studies elsewhere.

Rising waters: both threatened and confident

At a time of great current fear of rising ocean levels which threatens urban concentrations along the planet's coasts, in particular flood-prone areas at the mouths of major continental rivers, the Dutch, whose land was formed on the delta of the Rhine and the Meuse, draw from their ancestral struggle against the waters a calm which seems Olympian in the face of the catastrophe which threatens humanity. This country is certainly on the front line facing rising water levels due to global warming, which could swallow up to half of the territory. The population and the younger generations are not mistaken. The media, although less alarmist than in France, as well as environmentalists and activist associations, are at the forefront of the debate and occupy center stage. The Dutch have a traditional sensitivity to ecology that no longer needs to be demonstrated. Far from burying their heads in the sand of the North Sea, they speak openly about the major risk threatening the country.

> *However, the threat of rising waters has existed for them for centuries. This threat is even at the origin of the constitution of their territory as well as their proactive temperament as builders. They keep talking about it, while showing their confidence in the ability of their civil engineering to continue to resist it. It is a trait of their national genius: They fear the threat of water with confidence.*

III. Youth, education and the Dutch temperament

★ *Very early on, little Dutch children must learn to fly on their own to become independent. Very early on, children are considered adults in society.*

★ *The Dutch are fearless, never stressed and always happy. They are definitely not French!*

★ *Their temperament and culture lead them to travel, learn and speak foreign languages easily. They do not possess a particular gift or gene, but a culture, a relationship with others and a frame of mind of which the French seem deprived.*

★ *Education is naturally "positive" since society as a whole is.*

Neighbourhood schools, the beginning of the group

Naturally, parents will enroll their children in the nursery and primary school located nearby in their neighbourhood. These are so widespread that one is spoiled for choice, but in any case, the question will not arise: the choice is already implicitly made; one will go to the school closest to one's home.

The avowed aim of this proximity is to mix the children of the neighbourhood and to initiate their social development within their group. There are so many nursery schools that it is not uncommon for there to be only one class per level up to primary school. This is the early and founding emergence of a spirit of promotion by generation, of the group by age group.

As much as possible, students will follow each other throughout their schooling, then throughout their professional career.

> *The group by age group is an essential component of Dutch society. It will accompany the student throughout their schooling, up to university, then in their adult life through associations that will remain active throughout their lives.*

Neighbourhood life will then develop, thanks to the comings and goings of mothers and fathers who will go on foot to accompany their little ones to kindergarten, while picking up the little neighbours who will join their boyfriend or girlfriend, thus already arriving as a group at school.

Parents will take advantage of this to get to know each other, share out the accompaniments and entrust their little ones to each other, that is to say that they will also form their neighbourhood group. Children will continue this "public transportation" to primary school, but by bike this time and without their parents, stopping by each other's houses to pick up their friends and form huge clusters of cyclists who crisscross their neighbourhood to go to school.

These groups of young people, who manage the feat of riding in compact groups on narrow urban tracks without breaking their necks, are part of the life of the neighbourhood, which they bring to life with their joyful rides every morning and afternoon of the week.

From kindergarten, responsible in the group

As in all countries, everything starts very early in primary school. But in the Netherlands, this beginning is unlike any other. Young children must enter their class by first greeting and shaking the hand of the teacher who receives them individually, looking affectionately into their eyes, one after the other. Each morning, they are thus considered individually and are invited to consider their mistress as an equal. The child exists in the eyes of the teacher. Then they form a large circle (the "kring") with their teacher and their classmates in the classroom and will all take turns speaking. They will listen to all the others, including their mistress, who will not distinguish herself from anyone in this exercise.

> *From their earliest childhood, children experience life as recognised and autonomous people, acting as equals with their teacher, with respect for others, within the group to which they belong.*

The same attention will be given to new arrivals during the year. The whole class will take the time to welcome them and integrate them into the group. For a foreign child, if the language barrier is too great, we will provide linguistic assistance.

The little ones are assigned small responsibilities in turn for their small community, such as watering flowers, taking care of pets or growing plants, or distributing milk and cleaning the classroom by end of the day. Throughout their childhood at school, they will be allowed to play as much as possible, especially outside.

From a very young age, children are part of a community for which they are responsible, which they must maintain and preserve. They are not the subjects but the responsible actors.

4 years, day of induction into society

Each child returns to primary school on their 4th birthday, and not on the start of the school year for everyone. Throughout the year, the kindergarten class will welcome new arrivals on this specific day, and celebrate together both their integration into the community and their individual birthday. All their lives, the Dutch will celebrate their birthday as their true social birth.

This anniversary day of the fourth year when each child joins their nursery class, constitutes the induction of each child into Dutch society. The social definition of individuals is entirely contained in this founding event: a unique person recognised as such and responsible within the community.

The difference is striking with France, where each individual joins society on the same day of the start of the school year, and will have to conform to a framework which will define and maintain them as a subject. The definition and conception of the individual in society are radically different here in the Netherlands.

Team building at school

For children who will stay with the same classmates throughout each primary and secondary cycle, the importance given to class cohesion is crucial. From primary school onwards, they will be able to debate social issues that concern their school community, such as suicide among bullied children, bicycle safety or classroom heating. They generally do this by watching films, then by discussing among themselves, which is also the beginning of the unifying palaver in society.

Parents: responsible and involved at school

The nursery school immediately calls on parents who will without hesitation be entrusted with the responsibility of looking after the children during the lunch break ("Overblijfmoeder"), or when they leave class. For new arrival parents, it is, as for their children, an integration into the local community. They will be given complete confidence to look after the children of other parents whom they do not yet know, without requiring diplomas or previous experience in kindergarten. Likewise, French or foreign mothers will be asked to give language lessons to other children or adults, without requiring references or any diplomas. Adults, like their children, are responsible from the outset.

> *The welcome given to parents, the open trust given to them and their participation in school tasks, will facilitate relationships with teachers, who no longer belong to a distinct body, but to the same community of which all take care of each other.*

> *"If this is kindergarten, I'm glad I put my son there," my wife said when we took our little ones there.*

This trust is practiced between the parents themselves, who leave their little ones at their friends' birthday parties, and who accept that they are taken home by other parents they do not know. It must be admitted that French mothers will have a hard time not picking up their children themselves after the birthday party.

A definitive orientation test

At the fateful age of 11 (group 8 in the Netherlands, CE2 in France), all students are subject to a test, the famous "CITO toets", which aims to decide between those who will be able to continue towards the university sector, which is thus strongly regulated upstream of training. Around a third of students will be eligible. There are of course bridges to cross along the way from the general sector or apprenticeship, towards the university sector. In any case, parents have no recourse to influence or modify this orientation which is strictly dependent on the child's results on the CITO test. The results are clear.

At the age of 12, the courses are classified in order of decreasing level [8]:

1. VWO, with its options "Gymnasium" (Latin, Greek), "lyceum" and "Atheneum": baccalaureate at 18, which gives access to university
2. HAVO: baccalaureate at 17, which gives access to the previous VWO sector or the "Hogeschool / hbo-opleiding" schools corresponding to a BTS in France
3. WMBO: "pro" baccalaureate at 16, which gives access to the previous HAVO sector or to "mbo-opleiding" apprenticeship training

Alpha, Beta, Gamma, the best of all worlds

Without this corresponding to an organisation or a course officially established by the Ministry of Education, the Dutch often use in informal discussions the categories "Alpha", "Beta" and "Gamma" to designate affinities and qualities with which nature has endowed human beings. Alpha individuals are those inclined toward the "products of human action," such as history, linguistics, and literature. Beta individuals are those gifted in "non-human disciplines" such as physics, biology, mathematics, and computer science. Gamma individuals are those who prefer the "humanities" of psychology, sociology and above all, economics.

Far from referring to a segregation of individuals for a selective and coercive organisation of life in society, described by Aldous Huxley in his dystopian anticipation book "Brave New World" (1932), the Dutch accept differences in principle between individuals to recognise them as qualities intrinsic to each, as gifts

---

[8] https://stichtingnob.nl/artikelen/het-nederlands-onderwijssysteem

to be developed during schooling, so that each can be in harmony with their deep nature.

"If you judge a fish by its ability to climb trees, it will live its whole life believing it is stupid."[9]

This acceptance at the societal level does not exclude an undisguised aspiration of parents for their children to access the best educational pathways. Everyone will then try to put all the chances on their side by preparing their children as best as possible for the CITO test, in order to obtain the best possible ranking. Our neighbour, like a good Dutch father, spared no effort to make his three daughters work diligently before their test. Whether it was my wife's language teacher, or our neighbours, mothers did not miss an opportunity to tell those around them that their children had had access to the prestigious high-level course, particularly its famous "Gymnasium" option.

Teaching that is primarily practical

Before the famous "CITO toets" orientation test, education during primary school will refrain from providing theoretical knowledge, and will be mainly limited to the teaching of calculation and writing. We provide concrete knowledge that goes to the essentials to enable any child to get by from the age of 10, in a practical and efficient spirit. We also cover history, geography, in particular topography, sport, drawing, and music. There will be many cultural outings, to the museum, the library, the theatre, as well as day trips to the beach "strand dag", in the woods, "bos dag", or to do sport "sport dag" .

In the Netherlands, education is not, as in France, a socio-political tool which aims to educate the masses through knowledge and the inculcation of republican principles, which disciplines individuals in a system and which pushes students towards excellence. Instead of instilling a heavy educational program,

---

[9] *Albert Einstein*

the Dutch school advocates primarily practical teaching, as well as individual autonomy with respect for all.

No homework

Unbelievably for French children, little Dutch children do not have homework to do at home, all knowledge must be acquired in class. From the age of 10, they will timidly start to do it with 30 minutes per week!

Homework is replaced by research work on a free theme from the age of 5, then presentations to prepare from the age of 7, and the writing of a report as well as the presentation of a newspaper article from the age of 9.

Sex education from primary school

From primary school onwards, children are invited to anonymously submit their questions about sexuality in a special box. From the age of 6, they will learn that one can be homosexual and that one can get married. From the age of 10, they will observe a tampon in a glass of water and how to put a condom on the handle of the class broom. Very early on, they will be told about pedophiles and "Lover Boys" who seduce vulnerable young girls and then push them into prostitution.

And to make it all official, in a humorous, burlesque and schoolboyish tone, the actress "Doctoresse Corie" addresses all these subjects, often based on questions asked by listeners who are none other than children, in shows broadcast on television[10] for a young audience. Humour and comedy complete the demystification of the subject by systematically flushing out all the taboos.

---

[10] *Dr Corrie Show, https://schooltv.nl/programma/dokter-corrie/afleveringen*

A la carte courses

Society does not impose the establishment of the college according to the neighbourhood in which the family lives. The choice is open, it is up to the schools to be attractive to the students, who can choose according to their skills, motivations and affinities. In short, each establishment must sell itself, knowing that the baccalaureate will be the same for all. But the methods and formulas to achieve this may be different.

Some establishments may offer particular languages earlier than elsewhere. Others will offer reduced hours of presence in class in subjects that the student masters with at least an average of 14, provided that he devotes this freed up time to other areas that interest him more and that his average in the reduced subject does not decline. This is a first empowerment of the student, who accepts this contract of trust and will spontaneously provide additional personal work. Other institutions offer classes in English or additional "research and development" subjects to develop technical projects such as an ecological city or a water treatment system. These institutions instil in young people the spirit of innovation in the face of the problems of our time and the new needs of users.

All these offers are presented during open days, which allow young people to think, from the age of 12, about their future and how to commit to it.

The ritual of passage into secondary school

The transition from primary to secondary school is an important and emotional initiation rite for the children in group 8 (12 years old), but also for the parents, in a society whose stated goal is to make young people autonomous and independent as early as possible. In the Netherlands, parents must start to consider their children as young adults from the age of 12, which is quite early for loving parents.

The last weeks before the end of school will have been entirely devoted to preparing the children for their new environment at middle school. The teachers then take on the role of subject teachers and transform themselves into English, biology or mathematics teachers. The students will start to change classrooms to attend different teachers depending on the subject. Since families are not assigned to a school based on their neighbourhood, other group 8s from other schools join the children divided by future middle school. The last months will have been devoted to the preparation and rehearsals of the show for the closing night.

When the day came, the flag bearing the names of all the students in group 8 was hoisted to the top of the mast, at the foot of which they gathered with their parents. Then those in group 7 joined them, lowered the flag and hoisted theirs in its place, the new flag that succeeded them with the names of group 7. The symbolic handover took place. It was then that the hundreds of students from all the groups came out in turn to form a guard of honour for the passage of group 8. The show, prepared for months, followed by the closing ceremony, could then begin.

Here is the testimony of a mother, a French woman married to a Dutchman and living in the Netherlands, who discovered this ritual of passage with emotion.

« In the evening, they paraded on the red carpet, dressed and made up for their role. They played and sang with all their hearts. At the end of the performance, all the children on stage sang "For the Last Time." In the chorus, they gave thanks for the wonderful years that had passed. I then got up from my seat, moved closer to the stage to take a video and zoomed in on my son. I saw this big boy fighting back tears in a fit of laughter. I couldn't hold back my own. Children, parents, grandparents, everyone was crying. I was overwhelmed by the power and beauty

of the moment. We then told ourselves that this was the last time they were "little ones."[11].

We are not looking for excellence

Students are assessed by their ability to follow a university course, and by their ability to work in a group. It is not a question of pushing them towards excellence if they do not have the capabilities, nor of opening the doors of universities to as many people as possible out of republican principle. Students are generally satisfied with a score of 7 out of 10, following the principle "A 7 is better than no (festive) life." ("Beter een 7 dan geen leven"), unlike France where a student must excel to stand out to the detriment of the group.

> *The education system does not seek excellence but normality, recognition and respect in the community. The main role of the school will not be to pull everyone towards greater perfection, but to ensure the fulfilment and social development of individuals. In doing so, individuals accept that they will not be the best at everything, a preparation for their spirit of compromise.*

My eldest daughter practiced classical dance throughout her childhood in the Netherlands. Then, arriving in France where she wanted to continue her lessons at the age of 20, she was told that she absolutely did not have the required level, because she simply lacked the basics of the art. She then came face to face with a style of course which was the opposite image of what she had known in the Netherlands. The quest for excellence in France involves conditioning, bringing students into line, through discipline and respect for authority, through a certain harshness and a lack of empathy for students who have to sweat hard to be able to extract the quintessence from themselves. One cannot better describe in contrast the educational principles of Dutch society whose objective, whatever the activities, is to ensure the

---

[11] *Petites chroniques des Pays-Bas, Océane Dorange*

social development of individuals so that they can achieve their autonomy. That is to say, becoming adults.

Not standing out in society

Society itself is built on the principle that the individual is inferior to the group. Ostentatious behaviour, which highlights a superior title or function, is frowned upon. On the contrary, notables or men of importance will have to do their best to appear "normal" like ordinary people. Another saying is to "do it normal"[12] and not try to stand out. This certainly makes life and social relationships more pleasant, in a less distant, less competitive and more relaxed atmosphere.

No competitive elitism

There is no competitive entrance exam for Grandes Ecoles like in France, for which one must prepare strenuously for 2 or 3 years, to confront other candidates through an exam which will decide between the best and eliminate the worst, even if their level was excellent. This elitist confrontation which puts individuals in competition for access to prestigious positions in the State and large companies does not exist in the Netherlands, nor elsewhere in Europe.

No elite in society

In the Netherlands, everyone's ego is held within the strong and uniform social norms of the group. However, and this is one of the "cultural paradoxes" that this society succeeds in producing, this normalisation in the group preserves and teaches the autonomy, personal development and responsibility of each person. This system therefore does not generate submissive individuals devoid of personality like what science fiction novels describe in imaginary and dystopian societies governed by a totalitarian power formatting brainless individuals. What this

---

[12] « Doe maar gewoon »

system does not generate is elites who stand out in society and who place themselves above the basket.

The group and the association for life

The Dutch are integrated into their group from their social induction at the age of 4 in kindergarten, then remain linked and affiliated to the group throughout their lives. First at school, in their group of friends and buddies, then at university, in student bodies, sports or cultural associations, "fraternities", "houses", then, in adulthood, in alumni associations and professional associations linked to their field of activity.

The groups remain active until retirement and can sometimes manifest themselves unexpectedly. My neighbour, comfortably settled in his peaceful retirement, received, at the age of 70, an invitation from his former rowing club at the University of Amsterdam to celebrate the return of the Dutch rowers, who won medals at the Paris 2024 Olympic Games, who are now active members of the same club. It was natural to invite all the old-timers to the celebration, even those who, like my neighbour, had rowed there more than 50 years ago! He had trained there half-heartedly, had drunk beers with more vigour and, incidentally, had met his wife there, also a member of the club.

Speaking languages is a priority

The Dutch place great importance on teaching foreign languages from an early age. They encourage children to learn several foreign languages during their schooling. Although efforts have been made in France to introduce language teaching earlier and earlier in school, it is perhaps not as intensive or as early in the school career.

Across the country there are primary schools that offer their students extra hours of foreign language teaching (Vroeg Vreemdetalenonderwijs VVTO) and secondary schools that have a bilingual education program (TweeTalig onderwijs TTO). In addition, the government funds Dutch international schools, which are comprehensive English-language courses within a Dutch establishment. [13]

> *The Dutch education system emphasises the learning of foreign languages, up to three, while in France education will favour mathematics and logic.*

Foreign languages are practical and essential learning that is quickly assimilated and can be used more easily than in France.

Speak languages naturally

> *Above all, it is the state of mind that reigns in primary and secondary classes that allows children to progress naturally and peacefully in their learning of foreign languages. Students in the Netherlands are not put in a testing situation every time they speak. They do not feel judged or devalued publicly in front of their classmates. Children in class, or in their lives outside of school, are not afraid of ridicule or criticism when they try foreign languages. Speaking foreign languages is as natural as chatting, it's even fun.*

Language is primarily considered as a collection of words frequently used to allow people to socialise. We will then try to expose children to it as frequently as possible through fun activities, corresponding to real life tasks. The approach therefore does not focus on the analysis of the language itself, its grammar rules and vocabulary lists, but rather on the repetition and construction of phrases in a more implicit way than inductive or reasoned. We use stories in primary school and texts, videos in middle school and reports in high school, and films released in cinemas at university. Students use learning software like FluentU at high school and university to be able to learn with films and dialogues about modern life. The progress specific to each student will be monitored by software such as SlimStampen which

13 https://stichtingnob.nl/artikelen/het-nederlands-onderwijssysteem

measures memorisation and then suggests revision based on gaps. The idea is that students identify vocabulary in a situation, and take quizzes several times a week until this vocabulary is memorised. The software remembers words that are not acquired and reintegrates them into the exercises during the next work sessions until they are acquired. In class, the activities are varied and mainly focused on oral production.

The aim of these activities is firstly to reduce the anxiety linked to speaking by playing down the students' attempts, and by working on repetition and automation.

The activities are mainly done in groups, at the beginning even in song, so that the students develop a certain self-confidence. By focusing on the meaning of language and not its form, each student can use their own linguistic repertoire and learn from the repertoire of others. At the same time, everyone can work individually on the linguistic aspect they lack to express themselves. This requires guided autonomy and personal reflection – skills which are encouraged in Dutch schools. [14]

Another role for teachers

This way of working implies that the teacher is not only the one who transmits or evaluates knowledge, nor is he a model. He is the one who offers sources of knowledge, organises activities as motivating as possible, promoting repetition and automation of language. He is the one who creates an environment conducive to practice, to collaboration between students. He ensures that the foreign language is practiced as much as possible. He is also the one who detects the individual or collective needs of students and who offers activities to meet them.[15]

---

[14] *« Teaching languages differently: what the example of the Dutch teaches us. »* Grégory Miras, Audrey Rousse-Malpat

[15] *« Teaching languages differently: what the example of the Dutch teaches us. »* Grégory Miras, Audrey Rousse-Malpat

The teacher is not there to count the mistakes the students make. He takes into account the practice, communication and socialisation that language must allow as a whole.

Little Dutchman will become independent

Children are very early placed in a situation of autonomy, in an equal relationship with adults. In Dutch culture, there is no need to show respectful submission to authority and teachers.

Until the age of 18, meetings between parents and teachers will always be held in the presence of the student who will be the main protagonist. It is always to him that the teachers will speak directly during the interview, the parents being present only to be informed. After the age of 18, there will no longer be a meeting between parents and teachers, but only between the students themselves and their teachers.

Very early on, it is up to the students, and them alone, to take charge of themselves, to make their choice and to assume the consequences. They decide their own future through their actions, without their parents being involved, or even informed.

It's up to the students to take charge of themselves, to understand that they have to work to give themselves a future. It is not up to parents to push them to study, even less if the children are not willing to do so.

Troublemakers are out of date

Children understand well how to behave to conform to the group. Like everywhere, they will do anything to be accepted and well regarded by their friends, boyfriends and girlfriends. Posing as a troublemaker, questioning the authority of the teacher, who otherwise does not use it, will not give them any additional consideration in the eyes of other students.

On the contrary, they will feel out of place for breaking the good atmosphere, they will see themselves adorned with "the red cap" of those who are ready to degrade or poison the lives of others for selfish reasons.

We will have already explained to them that punishment is not the solution to behavioural problems, however they will not be tempted to punish themselves by distinguishing themselves from the group and being poorly seen by others.

Do not pit parents and students against each other

In the event of harassment ("pesten") between students, which social networks amplify these days, the children will be summoned to discuss it among themselves. We will avoid confronting the parents, which would inevitably lead to conflicting positions. Through discussion and compromise, children will be asked to resolve their problems among themselves, because they have an obvious interest in doing so. We do not want to pit parents and students against each other. At each difficulty, even in the presence of the parents, the child will be the main interlocutor and will remain at the center of the debate.

One changes schools due to an integration problem

When she settled in the Netherlands, a French friend had schooled her young son Vincent in the Dutch system, while leaving her two older daughters at the French school in The Hague for the sake of continuity. Twenty years later, the result is clear. The young man is an independent and balanced adult, who speaks to adults as an equal and only knows how to manage conflicts through discussion, until a solution to the problem is found. Vincent would be incapable of evolving in French society, riddled with problems, endless confrontations and conflictual relationships at work. As a young man, he himself had been confronted with a problem of integration in a school. His case had been taken seriously and resolved.

The village of Wassenaar, in the region of The Hague, brings together two communities separated by money. To the south are the beautiful districts ("Wassenaar Zuid") and its wealthy inhabitants; to the north is the middle-class population. His new school was located precisely between the two, so that a certain segregation took place at the exit of the establishment, depending on whether one went left towards the beautiful residences or right towards the ordinary neighbourhoods of the village. Young people, as is often the case, can be quite sensitive to these social differences and do not give each other any favours by denigrating each other. This, our young boy took badly when, as a new arrival from the northern neighbourhoods, he was the target of mockery. He rebelled against the ambient snobbery of which he was a victim.

Immediately, the problem was detected, the teachers alerted and he was summoned, without his parents, to clear things up before they got worse. He had an interview with the director, during which they decided to change his school. When he arrived at the other establishment, he was greeted by the director, who was aware of the situation, knew that Vincent had had problems, and told him that he had to report if he encountered any others, because he was not known, but that he had to make an effort in return. The integration went like a charm.

Sassy children, independent adults

Society educates its children to be adults as much as possible, in an environment without hierarchy and without marked distance between teachers and students, the latter do not experience any particular fear of authority, any more than they do not feel obliged to show polite respect to adults. Here, we speak to each other as equals, and the adults look with an amused look at these little adults in the making, who are doing their best to live up to the challenge, despite the difference in age and build. Of course, children feel smaller and less experienced than adults, but they have to take the plunge and hold their place, while receiving the consideration due to them, like everyone else regardless. their age. So, with the enthusiasm and clumsiness of youth helping, and insolence too, it is not uncommon to see this youth bordering on impertinence towards adults, which will shock French parents accustomed to discipline and to a certain respect which is synonymous with politeness for them.

Adolescents speak to adults in a way that, in France, could be taken for insolence, for a lack of respect or education.

Through a curious reversal of the situation, these impertinent children will then become calm adults, easy to approach, respectful to others, and above all, autonomous.

Studies and part-time work

Validation of entry to university is subject to obtaining a certain number of credits which must be obtained in one year, the "Propedeuse", otherwise the student will have to change establishment if he or she wants to continue in the same discipline, or subject if he or she wants to stay in the same establishment. Then, everyone is free, depending on their time and financial resources, to extend the duration of their university studies to be able to work at the same time as study.

It is common to see these young people, already having a small foothold in working life while remaining at university, spending long years in a state of alternation which gives them time to enjoy this intermezzo between high school and professional working life. Prime Minister Mark Rutte completed his higher education in 8 years, almost a decade. This perhaps comes from the Dutch's affinity for part-time work, which prevents them from being monopolised by a career, while allowing them to preserve free time. The notion of balance between professional and private life is seen as essential to the healthy development of individuals in their working lives, even after their school education..

No philosophy

Theoretical knowledge will be taught after the orientation test at the age of 11. However, it remains no less practical and pragmatic. We do not learn cursive writing, "Seyes" notebooks with their straight lines of writing do not exist in schools in the Netherlands. Even less fountain pens and ink cartridges.

Teaching at primary, secondary or high school will be done without philosophy as a subject, with the main consequence being a lack of interest and practice for the debate of ideas and the conceptualisation of things.

> *In literature, the Dutch rarely discuss schools of thought or cultural trends. In politics, they are not fans of ideologies which they distrust. The debate will mainly concern the economy and will remain pragmatic and consensual. They are less inclined towards conceptual discussion and ask fewer questions in their daily lives.*

There are few, if any, cultural centres. They ignore deep and confusing thoughts like "I think therefore I am", or "Hell is other people", which will not make them less happy, quite the contrary. They remain less sensitive and emotional, but more direct than the French.

From there also comes a certain admiration for French culture, its thinkers, its intellectuals and its politicians possessing a great general culture allowing them to endlessly debate purely conceptual questions. These French political figures impress with their speeches constructed and argued like literary essays, peppered with philosophical quotations and historical references.

> *« But admiration does not erase the other side of the coin which quickly becomes apparent; a tendency*

towards pompous eloquence and verbosity, combined
with a notable lack of self-deprecation »[16].

Motivation, encouragement and self-confidence

Classes at school place great emphasis on autonomy and responsibility, research work and presentation in front of an audience, from the age of 6. Compared to French classes, there are fewer lectures, the students being less placed in a situation of passive listening and submission to teaching authority. The emphasis is on cooperation and mutual aid, we do not seek to punish if we copy or steal the answers.

We practice encouragement and maintenance of motivation for self-confidence, and not denigration through systematic criticism of what is wrong..

By denigrating students, this reduces their self-confidence and their autonomy. This will make them less entrepreneurial in their lives, whether to help shape society or become self-employed.

We will not push an average student who works little, even if he has study skills. It will be up to him to find his motivation, which is a much better driving force than the race for grades.

This search for motivation justifies all paths, all avenues to explore. The child knows that he will be recognised for his work, even if it is outside the traditional curriculum. This positive way of considering the individual means that there is no "royal" academic path, no dropout or academic failure.

Everyone will find their motivation and their way, and will do what they want and what they can with their life. Recognition will come first through work rather than through diplomas.

---

[16] *Volkskrant « Peter Giesen is na vijf jaar terug uit Parijs en weet een ding zeker: 'Ik ben geen Fransman' », 8 juin 2018*

Improvement through the positive spiral

The principle adopted here, which is also found in many other Nordic countries, is based on recognising positive points rather than mistakes. To learn and improve, optimism, combined with self-confidence, has a greater power of contagion and training than pessimism. Whether during a school assessment or feedback from a company, the Dutch will prefer to focus on the successful aspects, even if it means hiding the mistakes to be corrected, while the French will first seek to recognise their mistakes, at the risk, demonstrated many times, of engaging in a negative spiral and a culture of failure. The "French bashing" that the French exercise on themselves, by openly and constantly criticising themselves in public, remains incomprehensible to the Dutch who have been educated to capitalise on the good practices resulting from their successes..

Positive education in a positive school

The debate that rages today in France on "positive education", or on "positive parenting", has no place here since the principles which govern the education of children in Dutch society are the very definition.

> *From the beginning, the school here emphasises a caring, respectful and non-punitive approach to educating children. It focuses on strengthening relationships between parents and children without pronounced authority, relationships between teachers and children without pronounced hierarchy, on the promotion of autonomy, esteem and self-confidence, as well as on the development healthy social and emotional skills.*

This entire society is based on the principle that children need to feel loved, supported and respected to grow and develop optimally. It encourages parents to adopt a proactive rather than reactive approach, emphasising prevention through civic education rather than punishment.

When we have been confronted with Dutch society and its schools, we can only remain doubtful when hearing the speeches aimed at introducing the concepts of "positive education" in France, in a system which we do not question the masterful spirit of classes, discipline, hierarchy, elitism, the program, the search for excellence before the social development of individuals, their autonomy and their responsibility towards their community. Education cannot be positive if society and school are not.

A "Canon" for a national identity

As in France, history teaching before the 1970s was made up of chronological stories, emphasising events and major historical figures, without taking into account the new social, cultural and economic dimensions which were beginning to emerge and appear in society at that time. It was only from the 1970s that education became more interdisciplinary, to offer a better understanding of historical contexts, human motivations, and social and cultural dynamics. The aim was to make history not only a subject that reported facts, but also a discipline that encouraged critical thinking, understanding nuances and reflecting on the implications of history in today's society. This development has also contributed to broadening the notion of citizenship by including social and cultural elements. Civic education made its appearance.

The approach led in 2006 to the establishment of a "Canon" - in the sense of a set of rules and principles organised - around 50 main stages, whether characters, events or social themes, which ran throughout a long historical timeline like a great game of goose, the ultimate square of which would be national identity and culture as they can be defined today. A well-illustrated and educational website[17], mainly for teachers, but also for students and citizens, has been created. It is available in Dutch of course, but also in French, Spanish, German and English, but also in Arabic, Turkish, Polish, Indonesian and Serbian.

---

[17] *https://www.canonvannederland.nl/*

As times change quickly, and the Dutch are quick to assimilate the times, updates are made regularly, the latest having been published in June 2020.

> *Among the recent additions to the canon, we should note the Srebrenica massacre[18] in 1998 which is still experienced today as a national trauma, the European construction of which the Netherlands is one of the pillars, but also, something both remarkable and revealing, this famous colour and "orange sensation" which is displayed everywhere during sporting events and national holidays, and which unites the population in a folkloric identity which galvanises the Dutch.*

The "Canon" also lives through an active partnership and network[19] between all museums and heritage institutions that work together to showcase the history of the Netherlands.

Back to school is not a national event

While in France the start of the school year is announced on television news throughout the country as a big affair on a national scale, which cannot fail to expose children to a certain anxiety, it goes unnoticed in the Netherlands, if it only marks the end of the holidays. Young Dutch people do not know the chore and ritual of purchasing school supplies detailing notebooks with lines, pockets, perforated pages, binders, fountain pens and ink cartridges... All they will have to do will be to choose a binder and a diary that they will personalise so as not to have the same model as the others. Everyone will ensure that they maintain some distinctive marks within the community.

---

[18] *See section « Srebrenica, national trauma » in chapter « Life in society»*
[19] *https://www.canonvannederland.nl/nl/canonnetwerk*

A healthy mind in a healthy body

The school releases the children around 3 or 4 p.m., to give them time to go to their sports or music club. Dutch culture places an important place on physical and manual activities, which provide balance and dynamism.

Daily travel by bicycle contributes to balance and personal development by clearing the mind and keeping the body moving, without which wise and lucid minds cannot flourish.

The school is not intended to occupy the children until the parents can come and collect them from the offices. It is another organisation, the "BSO" (Buiten Schoolse Opvang) which fulfils this role.

Not too many intellectuals

The education system is not there to push students, to raise the level of knowledge of the population, to pull average students towards excellence. The system of guidance and limitation of access to university studies ensures that the most suitable are selected who will not be held back by those who do not have the abilities or the motivation. This system also ensures that excess students are not directed towards intellectual professions that society does not need. We must first train students for the jobs society needs.

The helicopter flies at ground level

The intellectual profile of the Dutch and the way in which they approach problems are the opposite of those of the French. There is a verb in their vocabulary to designate this attitude of quickly seizing a situation to try to resolve it pragmatically, without procrastinating: "aanpakken" which can be translated into French as "tackle". They are opportunistic players in perpetual motion, who react to requests and who stumble upon situations to tackle them and restore order as quickly as possible.

We could compare this state of mind, or rather this state of action, to a helicopter which comes across a problem close to the ground, and which will circle around until it is contained and resolved. Eventually, their helicopter will gain a little height to consider the situation as a whole, in the light of a few intellectual principles and concepts, but not too complicated.

The French helicopter, for its part, will follow an opposite flight plan. The French will approach the situation with their intellectual concepts and their vision which will be as universalist as possible, to apprehend it from above, if possible with plans from a governmental authority which will dissuade any personal initiative.

Eventually, the French helicopter will agree to come back down to earth to follow a Dutch-style flight plan, abandoning the ideal solution which does not exist, in favour of the less bad solution, intellectually less satisfying, but practically effective.

The French have built an educational system that favours scientific disciplines and mass-produces Cartesian minds. These will naturally seek to study and demonstrate scientifically before committing themselves. The Dutch, for the sake of efficiency, will not hesitate to promote their ideas before even being sure that they can succeed. Their argument will be commercial before being scientific.

Pharmacists and plumbers are not failures

In France, pharmacists and physiotherapists are those who failed in medicine, plumbers and craftsmen are those who were unable to go to university. In the Netherlands, the consideration given to these professions is radically different. In the same family, a child studying medicine or law will be able to rub shoulders with his brother learning the trade of boilermaker or grocer without this creating a difference in consideration, or a feeling of success for one and the other. failure for the other.

In Dutch society, the denigration and social class snobbery which pit intellectual professions against manual professions almost does not exist. There is no sub-job.

The victory of the "Mouvement Paysans Citoyens" ("Boeren Burgers Beweging BBB") party in the last provincial elections in March 2023, mainly representing the popular social classes having followed a short school curriculum, which we often refer to in everyday language as the "low studies" ("Lager onderwijs"), put discussions against discrimination back on the agenda. There is talk of renaming "lower studies" with less denigrating terms, as well as so-called "higher" studies ("Hogeschool", BTS equivalent) to remove any tinge of superiority from them.

The school must reflect society without parental taboos

When the Dutch adopted same-sex marriage in 2000, which they called without taboo at the time "homosexual marriage", schools immediately included in their curriculum and in the list of themes to be covered, these relationships of a new genre. Without parental approval, the school began to expose to young people what society had decided to accept in its morals, namely that two people of the same sex could perfectly live as a couple, have relationships and get married.

From the moment a practice is chosen and accepted in the "living together"[20] of Dutch society, the school will have the duty to instil it in children without any taboo, following the principle that they are autonomous people who do not have to be subject to the opinions of their parents.

Van Gogh will remain French

Although the Dutch artist Van Gogh only spent the last 4 years of his life in France, where he arrived at the age of 33 (apart

---

[20] *See chapter « Life in society »*

from a short stay in Paris at the age of 22), his name was symbolically chosen for the French high school in The Hague. This provides teaching following the French school program, usually synonymous with "excellence" among students abroad.

Having educated our 4 children there from the 2000s, my wife and I can attest to the seriousness of the establishment, as well as its compliance with the principles of "French" school education. Lectures and conceptual courses, discipline and rigor, hierarchy between teachers and students, discussions with parental authority and low accountability of students, strict and busy school program, no or few external speakers, constant concern to achieve the excellence and good results in the baccalaureate, everything that makes French education, and what distinguishes it from Dutch education, is there.

French & international!

In April 2023, for the first state visit by a French president to the Netherlands in 23 years, French President Emmanuel Macron announced the creation of the "International French School, IFS" in Amsterdam. Under this acronym with discordant terms, which combines two completely opposite approaches to education, lies a clear shift in the French approach towards Nordic-inspired design. From the outset, the educational project aims to be "innovative", a complete break with the classic French approach.

"The International French School in Amsterdam has built an innovative educational project that allows its students to develop all the skills necessary to face the world of tomorrow. This project is divided into three pillars :

- A strong language policy
- The development of creativity and entrepreneurial spirit
- Kindness and differentiated support » [21]

---

[21] https://www.internationalfrenchschool.com/tablissement/propos

Then we discover with interest the vision of the establishment, which is, with the exception of the reference to academic excellence, the exact transcription of Dutch educational principles:

> « *Education can no longer only prioritise academic performance to the detriment of personal development and position obtaining a diploma as the sole objective. Education must also prepare our children for the complexity of a constantly changing world. A world in which our children will have to learn to solve complex problems, demonstrate critical thinking, discernment, know how to work with others and collaborate. A world in which our children will probably work in a profession that does not yet exist today.* »

« For this, at the International French School of Amsterdam, we believe in the notion of balance: the balance between academic excellence and personal development, between rational intelligence and emotional intelligence, between scientific rigour and creativity. This is why our educational project makes no compromise on academic excellence while encouraging personal development and takes the best of traditional education by merging it with the skills of tomorrow in order to offer our students that perfect balance which will allow them to flourish and reach their full potential to face the world of tomorrow. »[22]

> *"French-style" education is in tune with the Dutch school, of Protestant and Nordic inspiration, from which comes another conception of life in society. This approach could spread to other French establishments abroad, like so-called "international" schools.*

As for schools on French territory, it is doubtful whether they will be able to modernise their curriculum and their way of doing

---

[22] *https://www.internationalfrenchschool.com/tablissement/vision*

things in the short term, because this would amount to considering the entire society differently. Which is currently impossible.

Drugs banned in schools

The Netherlands is known worldwide for its accommodating drug policy. The sale of soft drugs, for moderate personal consumption, is permitted and tolerated. Any adult can thus freely purchase reasonable quantities of hashish or weed in the famous "Coffee shops" which are a tourist attraction in Amsterdam.

However, drug policy remains ambivalent. The market is not organised and supervised like that of alcohol or cigarettes, the profits of which are subject to a tax. The sale of drugs is not legalised and controlled as is the case in California. In the Netherlands, this trade in soft drugs, which is tolerated but not legalised, therefore operates largely covertly, and moreover causes increasing inconvenience and problems for the inhabitants of Amsterdam or residents of border areas with neighbouring Belgium where this sale remains illegal. The trend today is towards stricter control of trade and its excesses.

Furthermore, drug consumption in schools and educational establishments is prohibited. Schools are showing firmness and being intractable on the issue. They go so far as to organise police interventions who bring dogs trained to sniff out traces of drugs. Any student caught with drugs inside the establishment may be excluded immediately, without any consultation with parents and without any recourse.

14 years old, my son is in jail!

At a decidedly very stupid age, my son had found nothing better than to fill the locks of car doors parked in the neighbourhood, with a silicone gun that he had found on a construction site.

The police, alerted by neighbours who were old enough to watch the neighbourhood while going about their business, quickly arrived at the scene of the crime. She got hold of the culprits, my son and his friend, and threw them in a cell without trial for a few hours. Then, without even using a stern look to admonish them, but rather with the manner of handling a routine and procedural matter, the police officer calmly but firmly led them to negotiate their sentence; either open a criminal record and pay a fine, or carry out 3 days of community service. So they set off one morning, like municipal service employees going to work, to clean the tags on the walls and wash the dishes in a hospice for the elderly..

It is forbidden to drink in the street

In order not to encourage drinking in public, it is forbidden to drink even a simple can of beer in the street. The police regularly catch young people walking around without paying attention, with an uncorked bottle in their hand.

Very quickly, the rule and discipline

In the Netherlands, young people learn very quickly the principles of community life. They learn rules and discipline very quickly, they learn that we don't procrastinate. We first pay the fines and serve the sentences, then we can eventually contest, without much result in any case. The law is the law.

> *Once adults, the Dutch will not see rules and discipline as attacks on their individual freedoms, but rather as a guarantee of their tranquility and security in a society respectful of all.*

My son, smoker and drinker, then teetotaller and vegan

My son, who spent his entire childhood in the Netherlands, followed a path that fitted perfectly into the framework of Dutch society, which gave him individual freedom, responsibility, autonomy, and ultimately control of his own existence. This story did not go without causing cold sweats and many worries to his two French parents, accustomed to a completely different framework for the education of their children. In short, the situation had completely escaped our control for his benefit, first for the worse during his adolescence, then finally for the better.

From the age of 12, our son immersed himself entirely in the world of video games[23] that he played online at night to get around our prohibitions. By living in a parallel universe of inexhaustible richness, he completely escaped us, without ever coming into conflict with us openly, without argument or crisis. A seemingly happy and smiling teenager, pleasant and sociable, who had chosen his way of living without confronting himself, without rebelling, without marginalising himself. A comfortable teenager who lied, skipped classes, hung out at night, and barely worked at school, just enough to pass his end-of-year exams without distinction. As is the case in the Netherlands, the teachers and principals were of no help in disciplining our son, who had to understand for himself where his motivation lay and what future he wanted to give himself. The situation took an even more worrying turn when he indulged in beer and cannabis, led by a group of teenagers, each more stupid and drunk than the last.

From one day to the next, the situation literally turned around. At the end of a drunken and smokey evening, he experienced a "bad trip". The combination of alcohol and cannabis can actually intensify the effects of each substance, which can cause a disastrous experience for the body and mind. Alcohol being a depressant of the central nervous system, cannabis having psychoaffective effects which alter perception, the cocktail can become explosive and severely disrupt the balance of the brain, leading to anxiety attacks, disorientation, hallucinations, nausea and vomiting. Enough to upset my son who became frightened and who banned all consumption of alcohol and cannabis overnight.

---

[23] *Harry Potter, Halo, World of Warcraft, Guild wars, Call of Duty, Battlefield, Runescape, Dofus, Assassins Creed, Skyrim, Red dead redemption, GTA..*

Dutch society had also given him a sense of responsibility towards himself. He became abstinent, vegan and joined the animal rights cause. He took control of himself in a way that left us speechless, both relieved and stunned by this metamorphosis which was only the other side of the autonomy and responsibility that individuals in the Netherlands are endowed with. Today, he is the most independent of our children, the one who is not afraid of anything and who undertakes. He started his own business and gets up every morning with a happy motivation, with the conviction of making the right choices for his life, which he directs himself. In short, a real "Nederlander".

Totally uninhibited

Apparently, no subject of discussion is taboo, everything can be discussed publicly without anyone being offended. The Dutch are completely uninhibited, whether it's choosing a bicycle saddle that relieves the prostate, or the faecal samples you take to the doctor's office, or the age you celebrate on your birthday, everything will be discussed publicly out loud in society and without shame, without modesty and without any embarrassment.

Afraid of nothing to take a chance

The Dutch seem to be afraid of nothing, certainly not of undertaking. They do not reject risks, on the contrary they like to try their luck. It will work or it won't, it doesn't matter, it's in their nature to give it a try, as long as the motivation is there.

In the event of failure, there will remain the satisfaction of having tried and of having learned lessons for future attempts. If successful, they will be recognized for their entrepreneurial spirit and dynamism. This is reflected in their expression "He who does not shoot, will always miss his target" ("Niet geschoten is altijd mis") or "He who does not try anything, gets nothing".

No rearview mirror

For the French, the general impression is that the Dutch look ahead in life and move forward without looking back, without being burdened with regrets or hesitations. They like to take personal initiatives, set themselves more or less ambitious goals, and get started.

> *Dutch culture emphasises inspiration and personal motivation. They say that the Dutch love solutions while the French love problems, that some move forward while others regret.*

The "it was better before", which focuses France on its past glories in an attempt to escape the imperfections of the present, does not exist here. Withdrawal into oneself is not popular, any more than a return to the Florin, leaving the EU, or closing borders. Rather than regret and inaction, the Dutch character certainly prefers to take matters into one's own hands and move forward without looking back.

> « *France is not in love with its present, it is anxious about its future, and takes refuge in its past.* »[24], *quite the opposite of the Dutch.*

Pugnacity is a quality

At work and in business, the Dutch character is pugnacious. He does not shy away from effort, and when engaged in a negotiation, the Dutchman will know how to hold his positions, will know how to manoeuvre without tiring and without giving up anything. Their pugnacity, which borders on obstinacy, is indeed a quality, whether for their personal projects to have the strength to carry them out, at work to accomplish tasks, or in business where we go for the knife between our teeth . The Calvinist mentality considers that we earn our living by the sweat of our brow. And indeed, stubbornness ends up paying off.

---

[24] *Philippe Bloch, « Tout va mal... Je vais bien ! », éditions Ventana*

Never stressed, always happy

Although subject to the same vagaries of modern life as the French, the Dutch seem to be of a less nervous nature and not very sensitive to stress, as if they did not feel it[25].

> *The Dutch seem to have a stable underlying character, not very emotional, almost impervious to panic or loss of calm. All enhanced with an unwavering touch of good humour, combined with a natural propensity to take things on the positive side.*

Like a joy of living that sticks to them, unlike the French who remain perpetually unhappy and complaining.

Moderation as a point of balance

Moderation, which in France could denote a lack of character, sincerity or opinion, is seen here as a quality of balance, of middle ground, of weighting which will be able to ensure the contentment of the greatest number. What would be perceived in France as a lack of panache or brilliance, will on the contrary be recognised here as a mark of living in good intelligence. Life in society and relationships between individuals are in constant balance around a point of moderation of which we must be aware in order not to fall. The individual cannot adopt behaviour that is excessive, emotional, impulsive, even less radical, without this being perceived as being harmful to others and to society.

In politics, moderation naturally leans toward a centrist or pragmatic approach that seeks to find compromise while avoiding radical positions. Dutch politicians will avoid extreme, even revolutionary, approaches to favour the stability and security of citizens and their communities, around a point of balance that must constantly be sought through government coalitions.

---

[25] *See chapter IV Life in society, One has to manage stress*

No violence!

Violence is not accepted, the Dutch immediately intervene to calm the ardor of a virulent individual looking for a fight.

In a bar, when an individual shows aggression or loses his temper, it will not be uncommon to see other customers come spontaneously to overpower him in groups, without hitting, while waiting for the police without getting angry. When she arrives on the scene, she will then take the time to assess the situation and discuss calmly, without authoritarianism or verbal aggression.

After two years of pandemic and successive confinements, there were some excesses and urban violence in some villages against travel restrictions. The population, surprised by these excesses which are not accepted in Dutch society, became indignant. The next day, members of the local football club patrolled the streets to keep the agitated people at bay and avoid further excesses which would disturb the peace and tarnish the reputation of the village.

Violence is not only physical and material, it is also verbal and psychological. The consequences of an aggressive attitude, with its threatening or mean words, are not to be neglected in the community or at the national level when they are held by political figures. Beyond the bad example, they will be harmful in social relations, and therefore damaging to the "living together" which remains fragile.

« Compared to France, the level of verbal and social violence is much lower in Dutch society. »[26]

While the Dutch do not hesitate to negotiate, to make remarks and give lessons in civics, to say openly what they think to anyone, whether it is their neighbour or the King, they will always do it

---

[26] Tanguy Lebreton, Association Les Français des Pays-Bas

without violence and without animosity, as if to do you a favour, and without ever compromising their attitude within their society.

Travellers and polyglots

The Dutch are by nature great travellers, curious about the great outdoors and other cultures.

> « Holland represents less than one percent of the Earth's surface. KLM (national airline) will take care of the rest. »[27]

They are easily multilingual, their language being a natural foundation towards English or German which they can master without great effort. Growing up in Dutch society, children will be naturally exposed to the English language which they will master as a regional variant of their native language. Being a small country, foreign films are not dubbed but only subtitled. Cinemas are thus the best language classes for young people who will listen to a soundtrack, often in English, while reading the Dutch translation. The German will not pose any more difficulty. French is still used by older generations, but its practice is being lost today.

Generally speaking, it seems that the Dutch, like other northern peoples, are more willing to learn foreign languages than the Latins, and more inclined to use them without fear. Language teaching, which begins in primary school, then rapidly intensifies from middle school to high school, seems effective in ensuring that young students learn quickly, and are inclined to use their acquired knowledge, even if it is brief, in contact with foreigners, even years later.

---

[27] Advertisement of the national airline KLM, 1993

Interest in other cultures and in oneself

When I was writing this book, my French interlocutors, to whom I shared it, did not show a marked interest in the subject. Holland was certainly picturesque as far as they knew, but not so picturesque as to seek comparison. The French, being happy and proud of their culture and way of doing things, are self-sufficient and do not seek to know how they are perceived by their foreign neighbours and what sets them apart.

Conversely, my Dutch friends and acquaintances whom I informed about the writing of this book, wanted to know what these differences were that characterised them. Above all, they wanted to read how I had perceived them, what my personal experience had been in contact with them, in their own country.

The Dutch are thus sincerely curious to know how they are perceived by a foreigner who has chosen to be interested in them, without interpreting what I describe as reproaches or personal comments without feeling judged.

Rotterdam, departure for the new world

In the heart of the port city of Rotterdam, above the Meuse, stands the Erasmus suspension bridge with its elegant white structure, which locals nicknamed "The Swan" because of its single asymmetrical pylon which rises to 140 meters high at one end, and from which the flight of stays juts out over the deck which support the plateau in the elegant movement of the flight feathers of a large outstretched wing. "The Swan" is not the only architectural symbol of the city. It serves the large rehabilitated docks where another symbolic building is located: the "New York" Hotel, located at the end of the pier facing the sea. It was built in 1917 in the purest massive and conquering Art Deco style, on the major cruise terminal. It is the former administrative building of the "Holland-America Line (HAL)" which transported passengers between Europe and America during the Belle Epoque. This pier, which bears the name of Queen Wilhelmina

(1890-1948), has seen many emigrants leave for New York, since the Pilgrim Fathers, English dissidents exiled in the United Provinces, embarked from Rotterdam in 1622 to Southampton in England, from where they sailed to America on a merchant galleon named the "Mayflower."

Many of these migrants were Dutch. They all set sail for the "New World" in hopes of a better life. While for the French, the European emigration which would populate the British colonies then the United States of America, remains an abstract lesson in human geography in school textbooks, in the Netherlands it is felt as a cultural and emotional strong link.

> *The French contribution to American immigration, following the revocation of the Edict of Nantes of 1685, was relatively weak compared to the Irish, the British, the Germans and the Dutch. His memory was quickly erased from the French national novel, while he is still present in the collective Dutch memory today, between connivance and pride in what the elders achieved by establishing the first world power.*

We always remember that, before being called "New York", the emblematic and cosmopolitan city of the new world, the most European of American cities, was created by the Dutch and was called "New Amsterdam".

Birth register, thank you Napoléon

A few hours after the birth of my last daughter in Delft in 1999, I went to the municipality to register her. I am greeted by an agent at the counter who congratulates me and who visibly shares my satisfaction at being a father again, which has always been a magical and so gratifying moment in my eyes. We smile and proceed together to what would seem like a drink of bureaucratic friendship without alcohol, cordial and affectionate. The agent, visibly proud of the keeping of his register, then explains to the Frenchman that I am, that he inherited this system from Napoleon himself, then passing through conquests, and who had taken the time to put in place order in local administrative affairs.

The agent explained to me that, in fact, Napoleon transformed the Dutch civil status by giving it the framework of the French Civil Code, also known as the Napoleonic Code. It was at this time that many regions of the Netherlands saw the introduction of civil registration systems with the systematic and uniform assignment of surnames. Civil registers were created to record births, marriages and deaths, and the assignment of surnames was regulated. Some 200 years later, my municipal agent closed the loop with dignity with a young French dad whom he assisted with the best will in the world.

An integrating living language

Far from seeing it as a threat to their culture, the Dutch like to integrate words of foreign origin into their vocabulary by transforming them. In doing so, they integrate foreign expressions into their linguistic corpus which will assimilate them deeply.

The "Van Dale" dictionary organises each year a call for new words to designate new concepts that have appeared in our modern societies. The Dutch (and the Flemish) began to assemble new idioms which they composed with fragments of existing words or which they created from scratch. Some will then be chosen to appear in the updated dictionary, such as:

"Prikspijt" or "shot regret", the regret of having had to be vaccinated reluctantly

"Tegelwippen" or "slab change", the frequency with which the municipality replaces and readjusts road paving stones which quickly become loose on soft ground

"Knaldrank", "want to pop the cork", irrepressible desire to party

The Dutch like to bring their language to life, which thus assimilates new concepts, without fear of losing its authenticity. They are concerned with making it live more than defending it, without seeking to protect it from developments in the world.

Poverty, ancestral fear

At the end of the Second World War, the Dutch people displayed animosity and total dislike towards the Germans, whose bombers had razed the city of Rotterdam, and whose army had organised the blockade and starved the population during "the winter of hunger" in 1944 to punish her for her reluctance to support the Nazi war effort. Several tens of thousands of people died of cold and hunger.

For decades, the families maintained a visceral hatred towards the German aggressors. Despite peace and reconciliation, the Dutch continued for a long time to maintain a feeling of rejection and mockery which was openly expressed against German tourists on vacation on their coasts.

Then a generation succeeded the old one, the European Union succeeded the European Economic Community and the Euro replaced the Gulden and the Deutschmark. A new area was opening for the country which would return to sustainable economic growth. Antipathy towards the Germans gave way to another ancestral fear which had been hidden until then, without ever disappearing from popular memory, and which bore witness to an era not so long ago. That of poverty and hunger, of the hardness to earn one's bread and the harshness of life.

In 1885, well after the rich and opulent golden age of the 17th century, the painter Van Gogh painted his painting "The Potato Eaters" in dark and gloomy tones. "I feel this painting so well that I can literally see it in my dreams.» testified the painter, who had carefully observed the peasants of the time living in harsh and miserable living conditions. The memory of the major economic crisis of the 1930s is still very present, that of the war as well as the years of reconstruction which were far from opulence, then that of the new economic and energy crises of the 70s. This was not that from the 1980s and 2000s, the country was able to return to relatively stable and beneficial growth.

Since the 1970s, the Dutch have known what they owe to the European Union and the single currency, from which they have been able to derive great economic benefit.

The displays in the stores or the attendance at Schiphol airport, today the busiest airport in Europe in terms of the number of planes stopping there, no longer resemble what they were in the 1970s. There remains in popular culture, in discussions between grandparents and grandchildren, this fear of economic crisis and poverty, which can occur at any moment.

The satisfaction of spending less

There is no denying that the Dutch are thrifty by nature. They like to manage their budget and put limits on their spending.

Spending less gives the Dutch satisfaction. The money earned with effort through their work will also be spent with reason and parsimony..

As much as the French in general like to receive bonuses and allowances to be able to spend them, the Dutch like to track down good deals, commercial offers at reduced prices. Among friends, it will be common to discuss offers and discounts obtained for recent purchases.

It is certain that money and the price of things are not taboo in the Netherlands, it is even a safe bet.

Eat cold on the go

The Dutch do not have a pronounced culinary culture, quite unlike the French who are able to continue talking about recipes and cooking while eating something else.

To avoid being bothered by the digestion of a hot meal, they prefer to send out a cold lunch in a quarter of an hour so that they can get back to work, and above all, leave the office earlier having finished what they had to do. In the Netherlands, one definitely doesn't live to eat.

Foreign visitors in a work meeting at the Ministry of Foreign Affairs where my neighbour works may be given a box for lunch containing 2 sandwiches, a cup of milk and an apple, which could cause a diplomatic incident with the emissaries French people accustomed to offering a good restaurant and good wines in honour of foreign delegations.

A popular song to stand out with humour

In 1996, the song "15 Million People"[28], originally written for an advertisement for the Dutch postal bank Postbank, broke the ratings, and, by becoming number 1 in the top 40, acquired national fame.

Beyond its musical qualities, the text[29] of the song lists the character traits in which the Dutch people like to recognise themselves, without taking themselves seriously in this benevolent derision to which they are accustomed. They have since adopted this popular song as a national anthem which they sing at full voice in the stands at football or speed skating victories.

---

[28] *There are 17,8 millions inhabitants in the Netherlands in 2023*

[29] *See annexes*

Words	Meaning
Land of a thousand opinions	The plurality
The land of sobriety	Thrifty sense
All together on the beach	Often in groups
Rusk for breakfast	Typical rusk, like the baguette for the French
The country where no one lets go	We don't lose our means, we don't get excited
Unless we win	Except in the event of a football victory!
Then the passion is suddenly unleashed	An outburst of popular joy! but without violence or degradation.
So no one will stay inside	Often be out celebrating together
The country resistant to condescension	No condescension, we take charge
No uniform is sacred	The authority does not prohibit questioning
A son who calls his father Piet	Young people are also adults who speak to adults on familiar terms
A bicycle is not safe anywhere	The bicycle, instrument of their life, which is stolen
15 million people	A little people
On this tiny piece of land	A small, vulnerable country
Who does not dictate the laws to you	The people do not accept dictates
Who leave you in their value	Individual value is recognized
15 million people	A little people
On this tiny piece of land	A small, vulnerable country

They don't have to go through the straitjacket	We do not enslave the people
They leave you in their value	Individual value is recognized
The country full of protest groups	Plurality, organized in associations
No boss who is really the boss	Little hierarchy
The curtains are always open	We have nothing to hide from the eyes of the neighbours (in fact, we can see into people's homes through the windows)
Lunch is a cheese sandwich	Food habit and summary culinary culture
The land of tolerance	Tolerance
Not for the neighbour	We remind the neighbour how to behave well in community
The big question that always remains	What is important
How does he pay his rent now?	it's the money
The country that takes care of everyone	The goal of society is the well-being and safety of all
No dog is in the gutter	No one will be left on the street
With nassi balls in the wall	"Nassi" is a ball of meat for eating on the go
And no one eats dry bread	The fear of poverty and misery

IV. The bicycle, the "great queen"[30]

★ *The royal family on bicycles, like everyone else.*

★ *The population revolts against the massacre of children on the roads.*

★ *More than a picturesque means of transportation, the bicycle allows an art of living in certain happiness.*

---

[30] *In French, the expression « The little Queen » refers to the bicycle. See Chapter Epilogue.*

Open air

The sky is immense, it is everywhere. Wherever you turn, as far as you look, there is only the immense sky in this country. It is larger than in a mountain country where the relief divides the air into volumes that can be seen. In mountainous regions, we can see the hollows of the valleys and we barely notice the sky which stands out between the peaks.

Conversely, in this flat country lower than the others, without the slightest hill or valley undulating in the distance, in this country which is only an immense field open to all the offshore winds, the sky invades space from all sides. The flatness of the Netherlands, which could also be called the "Flat Countries", inevitably stands out from the rest of Europe, making it the ideal country for cycling.

Other countries, such as Belgium, or other regions in France along the Loire, in Pas-de-Calais, or even in the moors in Gironde, offer the flatness suitable for cycling. However, we are far from the importance of bicycle use that Dutch society practices on a daily basis. Certainly, something unprecedented happened in the history of this country. We have to go back to the 1880s, when the craze for bicycles was widespread throughout Europe, in France and England, but also in the United States.

It was in the 1970s that the Netherlands took a proactive and original turn so as not to suffer from the exclusive development of the automobile, unlike other countries which then saw the bicycle go off the road. Certainly, something unprecedented happened in the history of this country.

The craze of the 1880s

Just like the United States, Great Britain and France, the Dutch experienced this worldwide craze for cycling from the 1880s. In 1883 the famous "General Dutch Cyclists Association"

ANWB[31] was created, the aim of which was to support the practice of cycling, and above all to develop the necessary infrastructure, which was done in 1890 with the construction of the first cycle paths. This craze spread to all social strata of the population, even to the royal family themselves, who easily showed up on bicycles.

> *We must see already at the time, the lack of pronounced hierarchy and the proximity of royalty to the people which prevailed in this little piece of Europe. Wilhelmina, who was Queen from 1890 to 1948, traveled by bicycle in her kingdom.*

The blockade of the First World War

Despite its neutrality, the country was subjected during the First World War to the English blockade against the German Empire. Deprived of gasoline and resources, the population could only ride bicycles. The cessation of imports made it necessary to start domestic production, and it was at this time that the manufacturer Bavaria designed the bicycle model that was to become emblematic, the famous "Omafiets" ("grandmother's bicycle"), as well as its male model "Opafiets" ("grandfather's bike"). It is still this popular model of bicycle, urban and robust, suitable for all ages, which appears on the country's picturesque postcards.

Faced with war shortages, the ANWB cycling association was authorised to create more cycle paths, which motorists' associations in the 1920s viewed favourably, since it moved cyclists off the roads. In 1924, a 5% tax on bicycle sales was introduced to finance the construction of cycle paths, which became compulsory for any new road built[32].

---

[31] « Algemene Nederlandse WielrijdersBond » ANWB

[32] Frédéric Héran, The return of the bicycle, A history of urban travel in Europe, from 1817 to 2050.

True to its reputation, the Dutch people did not stay with both feet in the same wooden shoe. It faced adversity by taking concrete and practical measures for the entire community.

By 1928, there were twice as many bicycles per capita as in France (around 300 compared to 170). On the eve of the Second World War in 1938, the country had almost 2,700 km of cycle paths when Germany had about half as many and France almost ten times less.

Sudden end to the improvement

Throughout Europe after the Second World War, the rapid development of the automobile in the Western world meant a sudden end to the improvement in the bicycle industry. In all Western countries, cycling fell in favour of the reconstruction and modernisation of the country. It was the all-out car traffic that almost completely obscured the use of the bicycle, although less in the Netherlands than in other countries. Everywhere else, the widespread use of the bicycle in daily life would almost completely disappear, never to be recovered from it again. In the 1970s, cycling in the Netherlands was reduced to a third of what it had been in the 1950s. In France, or in the United Kingdom, it decreased by more than 7 to 10 times, which meant an almost total disappearance.

The turning point in the energy crisis

In a population traditionally keen on practical solutions, the global energy crisis that broke out in 1973 quickly put cycling development back on the agenda. Once again pioneers in this area, the Dutch proposed in 1977 to reduce automobile traffic in the city center by leaving cars in locations on the outskirts, and then to take bicycles or public transport, which foreshadowed parking lots, "P&R" these days.

Road mortality

But it was above all the catastrophe of road deaths and the human tragedies that it caused throughout society, which was at the origin of a reaction which the Dutch people are accustomed to in the face of ordeals[33]. In 1971, motor vehicles killed 3,300 cyclists on the roads[34], including 500 children, in a macabre number never before seen. Relative to the population, this represented a mortality rate twice that of the United Kingdom, but unfortunately equivalent to that of France which also experienced a peak in road mortality in 1972 with more than 18,000 deaths. In all Western countries, significant efforts were then undertaken to reverse this deadly curve; seat belt, blood alcohol control, speed limits, points on licenses, speed cameras...

In the Netherlands, the movement against road deaths took a unique turn under the banner of a national movement aimed at protecting the lives of children.

« Stop the killing of children!! »

It was at this time that the son of editor-in-chief Vic Langenhoff of the newspaper "De Tijd" was mowed down and killed on the road. Desperate, his father wrote a series of articles under the title: "Stop the massacre of children!! » ("Stop Kindermoord!!!"). He revolted against this inhumane killing and demanded that children, in danger of death along the roads, be protected when they went to school. In a society that attaches great importance to the well-being and security of its inhabitants, this cry of despair aroused an unprecedented outpouring of popular support.

The activists of the 1970s hippie movement "Flower Power", who were already campaigning against automobile traffic and

---

[33] *See paragraph "Delta Plan" in chapter VII "The centuries-old fight against nature"*

[34] *https://mag.hollandbikes.com/la-place-du-velo-aux-pays-bas/*

pollution in city centers, and against the destruction of heritage which resulted from it, took up the cause on their own.

> *Unlike France, associations of individuals and residents are better considered in the Netherlands, their demands are better taken into account and less denigrated by conservative political parties.*

Coming from feminist and progressive circles, a 23-year-old young mother from Amsterdam, Maartje van Putten, took up the title of the article "Stop Kindermoord" for her own activist association. The organisation grew rapidly with the support of parents and children themselves, who took part in events organised to attract the attention of the media and early television.

The renaissance of the bicycle

Over time, the first association created in 1883, originally for cyclists, gradually transformed into a club for motorists and tourism, following the evolution of a modernising society. The popular acronym ANWB, which originally designated bicycle users, had been retained but without any real meaning. It was therefore necessary to create a new union for cyclists under a new acronym. This was the ENWB[35], an acronym which was immediately sued by the previous national automobile organisation ANWB for usurpation of the name. The new cyclists' union lost its case, but gained immense popularity and 30,000 members nationwide in a short time. The acronym for cyclists was eventually transformed into ENFB[36].

This new cyclists' union quickly achieved the expected success and was able to undertake major achievements thanks to a typically Dutch policy, combining pragmatism and compromise, without directly opposing the power of the automobile which had become omnipresent.

---

[35] *Eerste Enige Echte Nederlandse Wielrijdersbond (ENWB)*

[36] *Echte Nederlandse Fietsersbond (ENFB).*

In a spirit of discussion and compromise, rather than directly opposing the ever-increasing power of the automobile, the associations and the population proposed alternative and complementary solutions to support and facilitate the development of traffic, both car and cyclist, especially in town.

It was the renaissance of cycling throughout the country.

National cycling plans [37]

In 1990, the Netherlands launched its first "national bicycle plan" to develop cycling facilities and enable residents and their children to cycle safely along the roads. The success was such that a second plan followed in 2009, with the government investing 25 million euros for the rapid construction of cycle paths.

It was therefore thanks to a proactive public development policy that cycling increased by 35% between 1978 and 2005.

This successful experience, unique in Europe, clearly demonstrates that the development of bicycle use necessarily involves the establishment of dedicated trails and infrastructure to enable riding in complete safety.

Tracks per kilometer !

The results of these proactive policies are laudatory and can easily be measured in kilometres of track. For once, the figures speak for themselves and quickly make you dizzy: 19 million working bicycles for 17 million inhabitants, 37,000 km of track compared to 18,500 km in France. This country, which represents barely 7% of the surface area of France, has twice as many kilometres of cycle paths! This gives 2 meters per inhabitant compared to 30 cm in France. The Dutch travel on average almost 1000 km per year, compared to 90 km for the French. The bicycle represents 30% of means of transport (compared to 3% in

---

[37] https://detours.canal.fr/pourquoi-le-velo-est-il-aussi-populaire-aux-pays-bas/

France), ahead of walking (18%) and the car (15%) but still behind public transport (45%)! [38]

The share of electric bikes in the fleet has increased explosively over the past 10 years. They make riding much easier, especially for adults and the elderly. By extending the distance traveled by 30 to 50%, they easily replace a second car.

Highways without traffic interruptions

The Netherlands has exclusive motorways reserved exclusively for cyclists, to the exclusion of all motorized vehicles. The advantage of these paths compared to other cycle paths is that there are no more intersections with motorized traffic, nor traffic lights, which means a shorter journey time. It is easy to travel longer distances while avoiding traffic jams.

Just like the road network, these motorways have a number, preceded by a letter, the letter F for "Fiets", which means bicycle, "Fietssnelweg" meaning bicycle highway.

To try it is to adopt it

Cycling is here not only a mode of transport, but also and above all a way of life.

The use of a bicycle in daily life contributes greatly to the reduction of stress, the improvement of health, the positive attitude of people thanks to the practice of regular physical activity, and the comfort provided by autonomy. and freedom of movement, especially for children and students.

This also contributes to the reduction of pollution, the beautification of urban areas and routes, cycle paths being able to take more attractive routes than ring roads. Being suitable for short journeys, the bicycle encourages regular use of urban

---

[38] *https://mag.hollandbikes.com/la-place-du-velo-aux-pays-bas/*

centers in small towns, which facilitates extra shopping during the week. We prefer to go by bike to small local shops rather than to the large stores in the shopping areas on the outskirts.

Men and women equally on a bike

Denigrating remarks like "women driving" no longer have their place behind handlebars. Social status, affirmation of masculinity and misogyny disappear instantly. Men can go shopping by bike just as much as women, or pick up their young children from school.

Give us paths for our bikes

It's not just about providing bicycles for rental or free access. The bicycle remains the property of the user who will choose it according to its uses, sports or tourism, for the countryside or for the city.

It is essential to provide users with the necessary and safe infrastructure, dedicated cycle paths, signage and shelters, in order to protect the cyclist and their equipment.

Free access bicycles are just an extension of public transport. They play little part in the generalisation of cycling as a way of life, to go from home to go shopping in the village, to go to school, to the cinema, to the sports club or to dance classes, or to go on a sporting or cultural outing. It is important to have your own bike that you can use on multiple occasions. The personal bicycle does not replace public transport for distances greater than 10 or 15 km, but it opens up a field of mobility and additional freedom in daily life, which the car cannot provide. This makes everyday life more natural, more intelligent, more balanced and more social. Traveling by bike, alone or in a group, on cycle paths is infinitely more rewarding and satisfying than being locked alone in your car on difficult and congested main roads, the use of which quickly becomes tiring.

We could also argue that cycling is suitable for a flat country like the Netherlands. It should nevertheless be noted that the wind blows very often and strongly in this flat country, which does not discourage its inhabitants. In addition, the rise of electric bicycles has radically changed the situation to the point of replacing the car for distances of less than 15 km. More than half of new bicycle sales in the Netherlands are electric bicycles, which unfortunately tends to cause more dangerous situations on cycle paths, to which we must now adapt.

Death at the turn

The adoption of the bicycle on an entire country's scale as a means of daily transport does not come without risks. Unlike road deaths, which are only fleetingly noticed along the roadway, and which are erased as quickly as possible in order to no longer hinder traffic, bicycle accidents are all the more noticeable as they occur amongst other cyclists to whom this could have happened a few moments earlier on the same route. Many come to help immediately, the others watch the police and emergency services. Everyone can feel sympathy.

In a quarter of a century of presence in the Netherlands, I was able to witness 3 serious accident scenes, including two fatalities. The first time, I saw a man lying inert on the road in front of a stopped truck, which must have run him over in the opposite direction. Even if the cyclist's speed may have been moderate, the inertia of the truck coming in the other direction must have been fatal on impact.

The second scene, years later, was the most terrible. I was coming home from work along the track along the sea via the coastal dunes. Coming back inland to return to the village, I started by seeing a small car with all four wheels in the small canal that ran alongside the road, with water up to the bottom of the doors. On board, a driver haggard and paralysed by what she had done. Outside next to her, a cyclist was trying to open her door stuck in the mud with his feet in the water. We could clearly see the tracks dug by the wheels of the car in the grass all the way to the canal. As I followed the tracks back to the road, I saw the horrifying scene. The inert body of a young woman lay in the middle of the intersection, her head crushed to the ground in the middle of a puddle of black blood. She was surrounded by several people who were helplessly trying to help her. Her face, undoubtedly damaged, had been covered with a scarf. Someone raised her lifeless arm to attempt a gesture. Another young girl, perhaps a friend of the victim, in a state of shock and shaken by spasms of tears, was kept aside by another group to calm her down. The cars, whose drivers had come to help, were parked in disorder along the canal. We could hear the sirens of ambulances arriving quickly.

I learned in the newspaper the next day that the young student had died while being transported to the hospital. This scene took place on a country road near my home. Since then, every time I pass by this place, I can see, with a tight throat, a basket of flowers and a wreath left there, summer and winter.

No one here can ignore the danger of bicycle traffic sharing with cars. The Dutch know well why traffic rules exist. And they have good reasons to respect them.

Closed protection

Everyone keeps in mind that a cyclist puts himself in a vulnerable position in relation to the cars around him. Cycling is, in essence, an activity that involves a significant physical risk, something that any cyclist who travels in the city among cars feels, unconsciously or not, constantly. They must therefore be protected by providing tracks that are distinct from the roads, and which are not just marked by a simple strip of paint on the ground that motorists can happily cross without worrying about the lives of others. It is necessary, as much as possible, to establish a physical separation, and to assign a distinct color, here red ocher, to distinguish the cycle path from the black asphalt of the road.

Wherever they may ride, cyclists should feel not only safe away from cars, but also within their rights.

Motorists must understand that, when the road is shared with the track, they are among the cyclists to whom they must pay special attention, and not the other way around.

Protection also comes through the law

The order of priority of responsibilities is first the bicycle, then the pedestrian, and finally the car. In the event of an accident with a cyclist, a motorist will systematically be held responsible with regard to insurance, whatever the circumstances.

Cyclists are too physically vulnerable to cars not to be advantaged and legally protected from motorists. Whatever the circumstances, a driver will systematically be at fault regarding insurance in the event of an accident. This does not exempt cyclists from respecting the highway and traffic laws. They will have to pay fines like everyone else if, for example, they do not obey a stop sign, or if they do not have a light on at night. They will be fined for any infraction, like any driver.

As of 8 years old on a bicycle

Parents do not hesitate to let their children go to school by bike, from around the age of 8.

Half of primary school students go to school by bicycle.

We can thus see these groups of students on bicycles parading in long processions in the morning, in one direction in the morning, then in the other direction in the afternoon. They punctuate the day with their regular and somewhat nonchalant comings and goings. If the grandparents live in the same village, which is not uncommon in this country whose small size allows families to stay close to each other, the children will not fail to stop by to greet them in front of the windows in a very friendly atmosphere.

> *It is proven that daily morning exercise on a bicycle before classes or before work increases the concentration abilities of students and the efficiency of employees. This constitutes a beneficial muscular and cerebral awakening for the entire student and active population.*

Circulation by bicycle is learned according to the rules

At the age of 10, children must take an official traffic test[39], which tests their riding on a bike, as well as their knowledge of the highway code. This develops their awareness of traffic with other cyclists, while working alongside car traffic. This awareness of cycling traffic will then always be present in their minds when they themselves are behind the wheel of their car, sharing the road with bicycles.

Learning a car driving license, which takes into account the presence of bicycles on traffic lanes, is more demanding than in France. Respecting traffic rules, particularly speed, whether by car, motorbike or moped, is not taken lightly.

Batavian style by bike

Just as the Dutch have invented a way of living in society that is unlike any other in Europe, they have also developed a particular style that inevitably sets them apart when they cycle. You can be sure to recognise a Dutch cyclist if, and only if, he responds to one of these three characteristic behaviours:

- He, or she, holds his or her umbrella open over his or her head while riding when it rains
- He or she walks their dog on a leash next to you on the slopes

---

[39] « Verkeer examen »

- They ride side by side and chat as if nothing had happened, driving at a pace that allows them to have a peaceful discussion without worrying about anyone behind them.

Anthills by bike

Today, the country has 23 million bicycles, that is to say much more than inhabitants (17.5 million) which is not surprising since it is not uncommon to have 2 frames per person. In the stations of the main large cities, often in the basement, there are large sheds which house bicycles by the hundreds, lined up, often piled up, in rows or in clusters which seem inextricable to the untrained eye. It is better to remember the precise place where you left your bicycle so that you can find it quickly in the evening.

There are numerous bicycle shelters, especially in the city center, where you can drop off, lock up and pick up your bike in complete safety and convenience. Be careful with impoundment, especially around train stations, if the bikes are not parked where they should be.

V. Life in society

★ *The "living together" of an entire community erected as the pinnacle of harmonious life in society.*

★ *We talk frankly about everything, without taboos, and without malice.*

★ *First of all, responsible and autonomous citizens, who have the right and the duty to decide for themselves and take responsibility.*

★ *To govern oneself, one rule for all and all for the rule.*

★ *The people are entitled to 2 hours of madness per year, no more!*

The sacrosanct "living together"

At all ages, the Dutch cultivate the sacrosanct "Samenleving"[40], "living together" in community which must be permanently preserved and cultivated.

> *The Dutch attach the highest importance to a harmonious life in the community, following the principle of good "living together" in society, established as a quasi-constitutional rule. Good human relationships in the community, made of tolerance, assistance, respect and pacifism, are established as the cardinal law of life in society.*

This golden rule could be summed up as "living together in harmony". Visitors fresh from France are often struck by the good-natured, stress-free atmosphere that reigns in Dutch society. It is common to hear journalists tackle a social problem, such as the reception of asylum seekers, the influx of tourists into the city center, excesses during football matches, the aging of the population, by considering 'first and foremost the problems that these situations could cause for the famous "living together", which must be preserved at all times.

The "together" comes in multiple forms, such as the "aging together" program to help the elderly, which puts them in contact with younger people to support them, or the "good health together" concerning all aspects of daily health and a healthy lifestyle. This sense of community life concerns all Dutch people at all ages, from primary school onwards and throughout society, among all. It is not specifically associated with the coexistence of communities of immigrant origin, as the concept of "living together" often is in France.

---

[40] *See Chapter IV "Life in Society, Samenleving"*

Racism and anti-Semitism are intolerable

Racism or anti-Semitism are intolerable for this society that cherishes harmony and good relations between individuals. On December 24, 2024, for his Christmas speech, the King launched an appeal to protect the bond between religious communities, put to the test since the war in Gaza that broke out in October 2023, and especially since the violent attacks in Amsterdam in November 2024 against supporters of the Israeli football team[41], attacks described as anti-Semitic by many Western governments. Despite the powerlessness of the Netherlands to be able to weigh in on a conflict that was foreign to it, the King himself then had a clear and direct message to a society determined to preserve its threatened "living together".

> « *What we can do is make sure that we do not bring bitterness and hatred into our streets.* »[42]

Man left dead at home for 5 days

In 1966 a tragedy occurred which provoked the indignation of the population at the time and which remained in the collective memory under the expression «The man left dead for 5 days at his home" ("Dode in de woning"[43]). What in France would have been a banal news items, provoked the first major information and indignation campaign on a national scale on this subject.

Cees Heuvelman died in January 1996 in his apartment in Rotterdam without his body being discovered for five days, despite the signs of his death being visible to the neighbourhood. The case caused great excitement and was widely publicised, highlighting communication failures between the authorities and neighbours. This reinforced in the minds of the population the importance of community vigilance.

---

[41] *Europa League football match between Ajax Amsterdam and Maccabi Tel Aviv, November 2024*

[42] *The King's Christmas Speech, 24 December 2024*

[43] *affair « Heuvelman »*

SIRE, "the society is you"

In 1967 the independent association SIRE[44] was founded, with the help of the media and advertisers, based on the model of the "American Advertising Council"[45] association in the United States, whose aim was to attract the attention of the public, opinion leaders and decision-makers on social issues deemed essential for harmonious life in society. The first national information campaign treated this case as "The man left dead at home for 5 days".

Since then, more than a hundred campaigns have been carried out on subjects such as road safety, the environment, public health, or education.

> « *SIRE wants to wake people up, make people think, make difficult things negotiable, stimulate debate and get people moving. Make them understand that some issues that receive little or no attention deserve it. With its campaigns, SIRE wants to make society a little more beautiful.* »[46]

The founders of SIRE, Frits Baylé and Paul Mertz, were named Knights of the Order of Orange Nassau[47] in 2019.

Compared to France, this state of mind is distinguished by its objective of refusing to classify tragedies under the heading of "news stories" without taking action. There are also humanitarian and benevolent associations in France which fight against poverty, social exclusion, racism, discrimination and inequalities, attacks on fundamental rights and individual freedoms. These associations tackle problems that unfortunately develop and take hold in a very conflictual society. The SIRE association, for its part, wants to be a "call for more humanity" and wants to ensure

---

[44] *Stichting Ideële Reclame,by Frits Baylé, Louk van Haastrecht, Henny Janssen, Jos Kluiters, Paul Mertz et Joop Roomer*

[45] *Created in 1942*

[46] *Sire.nl*

[47] *The Royal family*

the preservation of "living together" and good human relationships between individuals, considered essential in the eyes of the Dutch.

Polarisation Alert [48]

Recently, in order to preserve the essential "living together", the SIRE association launched a campaign to defend a fragile balance threatened by the rise of polarisation in public debate. In May 2023, a campaign against the harmful effects of polarisation and the aggressiveness that it can induce in human relationships was launched:

"Don't drift apart when polarisation draws near.".

It is about warning of the sneaky signs of bad relationships and above all giving practical advice to be implemented by everyone to preserve good relationships between everyone.

The morale of the population under permanent survey

There is an independent Bureau of Investigation and Statistics in the Netherlands, the SCP[49], which permanently surveys, in a transparent and public manner, the subjective feelings of the population regarding all political, but also social issues. cultural. Apart from qualitative and statistical data, the SCP mainly focuses on the subjective dimension and the morale of public opinion.

It plays an important role in understanding perceived social trends and challenges in the Netherlands. In return, his work is widely used to fuel public debate and influence policies.

Conversely in France, we could say that public debate and public policies influence the subjects of the polls which are carried out

---

[48] *See Annexes*

[49] *Sociaal en Cultureel Planbureau*

according to current affairs issues of the moment, and that the data collected is more quantitative and statistical, than subjective. Sensitivity and listening to the population are approached differently in France. More than the morale of the population, it is the political decisions and actions of the government which are evaluated through elections, demonstrations, public debates, citizen consultations, deliberations, more than by polls.

In the Netherlands, the questionnaires intended to survey the morale of the population are surprising to say the least. The content of the questions, their wide openness on subjects of all kinds, as well as the familiar tone focused on the feelings of individuals, will be both instructive and amusing for French people. Anthology of some declarations submitted for public appreciation, resulting from a survey carried out in April 2023 published in the newspaper Volkskrant. Check the boxes you approve of:

☐ The country is going in the wrong direction.
☐ I am still satisfied with my own life.
☐ The problems in the Netherlands are piling up because nothing is really resolved.
☐ The government should not force policy on the issue of nitrogen pollution.
☐ The government should invest a lot more in the things I agree with instead of wasting money on nonsense.
☐ The series on my Streaming subscription are quite numerous which does not encourage me to watch television.
☐ I always laugh a lot at "Today Inside," a show that's mostly about all things shit.
☐ I completely trust Johan Derksen when he says daily that there is no nitrogen problem.
☐ I am for fewer asylum seekers but against more money for development aid.
☐ The Netherlands should take an example from countries where things are improving.
☐ The minimum wage should not be increased, because it will continue to be reflected in the price which serves no one.
☐ The sentences in the Netherlands are too low.

- [ ] Traffic fines in the Netherlands are too high.
- [ ] The Netherlands' fifth place in the World Happiness Report 2023 on the happiest countries in the world, published last week, is far too low.
- [ ] The government should do more to support the middle class.
- [ ] I think it's crazy that my online groceries are delivered within three hours.
- [ ] The government must do more to tackle the problem of traffic congestion on the roads.
- [ ] I don't let people on the ramp pass because I was on the highway before them.
- [ ] Catering staff in Amsterdam, asparagus fields in Brabant and/or slaughterhouses should be required to speak Dutch.
- [ ] I'm afraid that if little is built, I soon won't have a vacation home, let alone be able to buy a place for my middle school child.
- [ ] I refuse to admit that our two greatest sporting heroes are Belgian.
- [ ] I'm considering emigrating to Portugal and continuing to tweet all day about how shitty everything is in the Netherlands.
- [ ] According to the AIVD, conspiracy theories about "an evil elite" holding power in the Netherlands pose a serious long-term threat to security in the Netherlands.
- [ ] Europe must mind its own business.
- [ ] At the end of April there should have been at least a few nice days
- [ ] I'm driven crazy by all the tourists in my area.
- [ ] If there are still extreme crowds at Schiphol Airport, I will consider traveling through another airport next time.
- [ ] I really need the sun because of the bad weather, otherwise I would almost consider not taking the plane.
- [ ] It would be nice if we finally had a beautiful spring on King's Day, but that won't be the case.

Intendance will not follow!

The famous phrase "Intendance will follow", attributed to de Gaulle, sums up well the state of mind of French politicians who consider the economy and organisation to be negligible in the face of major political designs. It is exactly the opposite in the Netherlands. Any project will be confronted with the material realities of its realisation, in particular that of financing, before having a chance of being implemented.

An impeccable organisation

The organisation of the society and its proper functioning come first. Coming from the south of Italy, the contrast is striking: you have the impression of arriving in Switzerland or Japan. The trains and buses are punctual, the administration is direct and efficient, and so are the services. One wonders if the oiled operation of the cogs of this great watchmaking industry is not the reason for the existence of the inhabitants who like to go about their business in good order.

This smooth operation, combined with respect for traffic rules and that of people, provides peace of mind at all times. Everything becomes simpler, without unnecessary tension and without fatigue. My cousin, who visited me, was surprised by this apparent calm and this tight organisation. As a good Frenchman, he wondered if "it didn't get boring after a while?..". No, the Dutch do not know the boredom of an efficient organisation and a well-ordered life.

Straight talking

The Dutch are fans of straight-talking that goes straight to the facts, without malice and without ulterior motives.

They will not hesitate to say openly what they think out loud, without preambles or polite expressions, without fear of offending the interlocutor who will not see any personal offense in it. They speak without embellishment and without restraint about things as they are, as they present themselves in life, without ever falling into aggression or vulgarity.

Stop painting, start taking photos!

During an evening with friends, Wilco, like the good Dutchman that he is, confided to me, unexpectedly but sincerely, what he thought of my photographs, which he found well framed with an eye that others don't have. He liked to see the world through my personal vision. There he found a rendering of the film which meant a lot to him. He liked to consult the albums at his ease because he found there an enrichment and a reassurance that the beautiful, well-made and sensitive images gave him. He told me he was looking for, he admitted, my sensitivity and my outlook which he did not have. I was touched by the compliment, which quickly turned out to be a simple observation on his part, followed by another, less complimentary observation.

In an equally direct and sincere way, he found that I was spreading myself too thin by the practice of painting, through which I was trying to convince myself of a non-innate talent. I sought through work and effort to produce an art without facility which would have more credit in my eyes. It was an attitude, he told me, that he had already noticed among young students, when choosing a course or discipline. They abandoned natural talent for which there was little effort required, to turn to studious studies which benefitted from the reassuring aura of work. The embarrassment of ease and talent has difficulty resisting the seriousness of effort and study. As a good sincere Dutchman who seeks to be of service by saying what he thinks without ulterior motives, he therefore encouraged me to abandon painting, which required too much laborious effort, to produce photo albums on paper in order to reveal and share my own innate sensitivity. He preferred the ease of talent to laborious and dull effort. Naturally, if you have an innate ability, you might as well use it. And above all, you might as well admit it without false shame.

No "soft mobility"

This frank speaking contrasts with the French practice of using phrases, definitions and syntax elements fabricated from scratch to make a subject that is nevertheless simple and practical conceptual or politically correct. In the land of bicycles and plain speaking, you will have no chance of hearing about "soft mobility". Unlike the French, the Dutch do not know the need to conceptualise and give definitions to everything to make themselves serious or credible. The definition[50] by a French public prosecutor of "soft mobility" will seem convoluted and superfluous to them, even funny. "The definition of soft mobility in terms of transport is broad: it includes so-called "active" modes of mobility, which only use human energy (walking, cycling, scootering, etc.) but also any means of mobility, collective or individual, contributing to a reduction in CO_2 emissions.» . Rather than talking, they will get on their bicycle, the usefulness and advantages of which for life in society are as obvious as they are natural to them.

Defending yourself in the midst of chaos

Having practiced Krav Maga in France and the Netherlands, a combat technique used for self-defence, it is striking to note that this practice, which should a priori be the same everywhere, is practiced very differently in the two countries. Sport also reveals cultural differences, and in a glaring way in this combat sport.

In the Netherlands, where people are not used to embracing principles, especially if they fly too far from reality, and where people like to take action for the sake of action, they do not procrastinate, except by feint. Under the threat of a weapon from an aggressor who wants to dispossess you, they will pretend to go and search their pocket to give them their money while appeasing them with words of submission: "Okay, calm down, I'll give you everything! .. ", to brutally push the weapon aside and strike to hurt. We mainly train in techniques for releasing chokeholds, disarming and neutralising knives and firearms. It is about removing the threat to escape as soon as possible, while getting your loved ones out of danger. We will use sidewalks and parked cars to trip the opponent. We will use walls and the ground to

[50] Web site « La vie publique » du Ministère https://www.vie-publique.fr/eclairage/279082-transports-le-defi-ecologique-des-nouvelles-mobilites#:~:text=La définition de la mobilité,baisse des émissions de CO2

bang his head against, so we work on ground fighting and its techniques, which are just as vicious as the others.

One does not remain motionless, with both feet in the same shoe; we act with maximum efficiency, as quickly as possible, with the least possible effort, so as not to weaken ourselves.

In France, one prefers to invoke the principle of prudence and not take any risks, on the laudable grounds that we are not going to risk our lives or injury for a cell phone, our money and our car keys. One gives everything away, only to flee later.

But above all, one trains for chaos. An attack, as in life, is made up of unforeseen events that only follow one another. We train to continue to react without freezing, depending on the disorders that arise and change the situation, which opens up new possibilities. Warm-ups are done in a restricted space that squeezes the participants into a small crowd. It is impossible to develop a broad gesture without colliding, impossible to know where the attack is coming from, impossible to develop a sequence of movements in an academic way. There reigns a joyful chaos where it is impossible to say who wins or who loses, everyone does their best without thinking too much to save their skin. Techniques and sequences are not practiced according to the rules of the art, because this is not possible in real life. You have to know how to change in full motion, whether the technique works or not, depending on the interruptions and changes that occur and to which you have to adapt, opportunistically. In France, we prefer the clarity of a well-oiled academic sequence, the conformism of a fight according to the rules of the art, we like the gesture that aims for perfection more than efficiency.

As for respecting the framework of self-defence, it is a very French concern to ensure that we act in complete legality, so as not to risk legal consequences in the event that the aggressor pretends to be the attacked in front of the judge. We will curb the attacks and ensure that they are proportional, which is a utopian thing in the heat of the moment. In the Netherlands, there is no such scruples, and people even practice shouting out loud that they are the victim, "stop attacking me, stop hitting me", when they are clearly on the offensive, hammering the opponent's head and genitals.

Discussion around a table on television

Unlike France where it is important for politicians to shine with their oratorical talents and their aura, it is rather frowned upon in the Netherlands to show off verve and charisma, which could hide a lack of competence or a certain duplicity. Added to this is the lack of hierarchy in relationships at work and in society because this would promote an artificial and unwelcome distance between individuals.

Television shows resemble discussions between friends at the corner of a table, everyone rubbing shoulders in a friendly manner, where it would be frowned upon to display one's knowledge. The most banal testimonies of individuals without rank will be considered with as much attention, if not more, than those of experts, whom the study of books will have kept away from practical life.

The media is factual

The difference with France is all the more obvious as it is shown every evening on the television news. We strive to provide factual information, certainly accompanied by certain testimonies and positions, but which strive to remain biased. The tone used is dispassionate and factual. Under no circumstances will we indulge in sensationalism to hook the viewer with their emotions, or worse, with their anxiety. While the Covid pandemic raged on French television, which then gave the full measure of its anxiety-inducing power to the spectators it terrorised, it was relaxing to watch the evening news in the Netherlands, which, as usual, treated a serious subject with calm and distance, without devoting all the coverage to it.

Furthermore, political discussions do not give free rein to personal attacks which are considered both impolite and inappropriate, because they are hurtful to people, and above all, because they do not address the substance of the subject being discussed. Mocking, harsh or insulting criticism is not allowed here. In the midst of negotiations to form a new government coalition with the far-right party, one of the protagonists, Pieter Omtzigt, abruptly left the negotiating table in February 2024, leaving the discussions and his interlocutors in limbo. At no time did Pieter Omtzigt say inappropriate words towards the man who nevertheless surpassed him. At no time did his colleagues attack him personally, although they complained bitterly about the situation. At the same time in France, the opposition media and political parties fueled the fire with their harsh and hurtful criticism, a protest against the appointment of a new Minister of National Education. Compared to the Dutch media, certain comments made in France by certain extreme commentators became nauseating.

Frank politeness, way of life

The Dutch have developed a politeness of familiarity that is never haughty or overly familiar. It's one of the rare places where people who don't know each other will greet each other and say hello as they pass each other in the street. They speak to each other in a polite and respectful manner. They will politely wait for their interlocutor to first finish a discussion with another person, without interrupting them, before speaking to them. They undoubtedly take these respectful manners from their education received in nursery classes when they took turns addressing the whole class each morning.

In everyday language, the Dutch use a number of small words without any particular meaning, whose only purpose is to smooth out corners and maintain a cordial tone. They pepper their sentences with "well", "eh", "so" or "well". This softens the frank and direct speaking that they are adept at, giving it forms so as not to cause personal harm.

The guts of laughter

The Batavian, despite a Calvinist culture, have a jovial background inclined to frank laughter which is expressed in the slightest social activity in groups, in particular within the clubs and associations of which they are assiduous members.

I was able to note, with astonishment, this propensity to often laugh at everything, during lessons in self-defense and military close combat, which are not strictly speaking relaxing practices to be taken lightly. And yet, in the middle of training, my colleagues couldn't help but go crazy, while listening to the coach's teachings with attention and seriousness. One did not prevent the other, obviously. For example, during these lessons, we refer to an arm hook to the opponent's face as "a 360" (perhaps because the arm forms an arc to deliver the blow). Systematically, my colleagues played with words by pronouncing incorrect numbers to deceive their opponent or designate a missed shot ("370!" or "342! damn, missed.."). Their humour was all the more curious to me as they set about the task and typing without pretending, with a lot of energy and commitment, especially since the Dutch generally have a physique more imposing than that of the French. Or were their jokes a diversion to create the opening for the attack?

During friendly sports races, it is not uncommon to see the runners' friends and supporters showing up along the route in a demonstrative manner, wearing exuberant and crazy outfits, and providing encouragement by shouting and singing. If these are nautical events in lakes or canals, you will be entitled to inflatable mattresses and large circular buoys with swan or duck necks, riveted around full bellies which have visibly abandoned any sporting pretensions. In short, even in effort and competition, the Batavian likes derision.

Porous privacy

The Dutch can report behaviour that they consider inappropriate, and say so without hesitation to the person they are speaking to. They do it directly, always calmly and without malice, without intending to harm. For a French person, it will be difficult not to feel judged in this way. The French person will inevitably tend to think that his interlocutor is meddling in what does not concern him, because everyone, in French culture, can do what they want in their private life without anyone coming to make comments.

The two cultures differ in the appreciation of the boundaries which delimit the private sphere, more or less porous, and to what extent each person can penetrate it to interfere in the affairs of others, who concern him, or not.

It is clear that the Dutch openly meddle in the affairs of their immediate neighbourhood, which they observe and comment on without false shame, which for a French person amounts to meddling in what does not concern them.

Open windows days

Any visitor who goes to the Netherlands for the first time is struck by the absence of curtains on the windows and windows, which discreetly exposes the interiors and the occupations of the inhabitants to the gaze of all passers-by. These windows can be as wide as the room like a knocked down wall revealing an interior that fully overlooks the exterior. It is a window through which we greet each other and smile at each other, a surface of welcome and exchange much more than of exclusion and intimate protection. This openness could be seen as a form of intrusion into France, or even as a means of generalised surveillance, with everyone exposing themselves to the gaze and judgment of others. But since we lead an impeccable life in society, we have nothing to hide that could be suspicious. Transparency is synonymous with and guarantor of honesty.

Surveillance cameras, as well as neighbourhood associations ensuring neighbourhood vigilance, are common. They constitute the extension of a generalised protective social gaze.

The inventors of the reality show

Social control through the gaze makes the Dutch observant and curious about everything, without false shame. Combined with their active and enterprising character, this results in individuals who are on the lookout for anything to create. You had to be Dutch to observe what was happening in the world at the beginning of the 2000s, and to invent a new form of television program which would become the "reality show" with the success that we know.

In the late 1990s, an experiment was carried out in the desert by scientists in the United States who enclosed themselves in a biosphere to simulate living conditions on another planet. In order to study the effects of their isolation on their behavior, they were filmed throughout the duration of the experiment. What was not the aim of the scientists, but what they could have anticipated, were the love stories that appeared between these human beings endowed with emotions and feelings.

Then it was the turn of a young American woman who decided in 1996, something as new as it was absurd at the time, but which has now become common practice, to film her daily life as a student every day with a webcam, and to post one image per day on the internet. At the time, it was a revolutionary idea that reached the height of uselessness combined with a total lack of interest: observing the intimacy of an unknown woman...

It didn't take much for a Dutch television producer[51] to come up with the idea of a concept for a new formula: permanently filming a group of men and women locked in an enclosed space. It was the beginning of a cult series called "Big Brother" which

---

[51] Paul Römer, Néerlandais, Lignes de vie d'une peuple, Ateliers Henry Dougier

experienced phenomenal popularity from the moment the love stories between the protagonists began.

The show sold internationally to 70 countries. It made the Netherlands the third unsuspected country exporting television series, behind the United States and Great Britain. These reality shows being culturally neutral, they can indeed suit any country and the tastes of all viewers. Many programmes were invented in the Netherlands and exported to France: *Loft Story, Secret Story, Star Academy, L'Amour est dans le pré, Les Marseillais, Les Cht'is, Adam recherche Eve, L'Ile de la tentation.*

Celebreties on a canvas

The Dutch love shows that feature "Mr. or Mrs. Average" who are filmed live doing something that is quite ordinary, but which has been staged to become exceptional for the duration of a shoot, and which will be experienced live by many viewers. Emotions count as much, if not more, than the achievements.

The programme is called "Stars on a canvas" ("Sterren op een doek"). It consists of bringing together individuals who practice painting, without necessarily claiming to be artists, around a national celebrity of whom they will have to paint a portrait in a few weeks. The programme will film them as they progress, while having the celebrity talk about his or her life. The latter will only see the work once it is finished, during a carefully orchestrated staging, in the presence of the artists who will reveal their work. One of them will then be chosen, by elimination to increase the suspense, by the celebrity who will take the canvas home.

I suddenly became interested in this TV show when my painting teacher, who works in the small, remote rural village of Voorhout, was chosen to take part in it in October 2019. She won the competition by painting a portrait of a film actress.

Personal service

This behaviour, considered intrusive by a French person, nevertheless proves useful and considerate in life in society. A passerby seeing a car parked with its headlights on will ask in the neighbourhood who it belongs to and will personally go and notify its owner. The same will go for an identity card or a phone found on the ground. The individual who finds them will spontaneously make an effort to find the owner and return their lost item in person. This is possible in a neighbourhood where everyone knows everyone, everyone talks to each other and observes each other. Paying attention to neighbours is normal, without being a particularly good deed. This is how an illustrious stranger rang our doorbell one day to bring us the identity card that my wife had lost at the store.

Ordinary denunciation

By monitoring your neighbourhood, you will not hesitate to call the police if bicycles have been left in an unauthorised location, or the animal protection services if a dog has been left alone in a garden for too long. Owners will then have to pay for the pound or shelter services upon their return to recover their bike or pet.

> *The Dutch do not consider calling the police or administration as a cowardly and anonymous act of denunciation, but as an honest and sincere participation in the life of their community to be of service to everyone.*

And also to put neighbours in their place by telling them what to do and what not to do, a little social morality in this society of Protestant and Calvinist inspiration does no harm...

The hierarchy without height

Generally speaking, the distance between authority, whether the administration, the police, the army, the gendarmerie, teachers, doctors, and citizens is much smaller than in France. Some are at the service of others who in return respect them without fearing them. We speak as equals.

This mentality makes it possible to build a society that is open and not very hierarchical in its functioning, unlike French society which appears closed and hierarchical. It is inconceivable for a Dutch citizen not to be able to find a telephone number on the websites of government authorities, political parties or even action groups. In France, contact will only be possible through an e-mail form, to which of course, in perfect bureaucratic logic, no one will respond. The French will have to obtain the right contacts through their personal relationships, if they have any. If you have no connections in France, you count less, or little.

The counter-power in your hands

Like the organisation of the Protestant church, authority is not exclusively held by the leaders or the administration, in whose hands citizens are not subjected, but rather served. A mayor will not speak of his "administered" as an abbot of his "flock". The right to oversee civil affairs is anchored in all individuals, who have the duty to remain vigilant. Each one individually carries his counter-power vis-à-vis the local authority, or even national.

Anyone, personally, or within an association, will be able to request accounts, with detailed figures, of the management of civil affairs that concern him directly or indirectly, whatever the administration, whether it is a town hall, or a ministry. And he will obtain them quickly and transparently, something completely inconceivable in France.

Accessible and popular royalty

Royalty itself wants to be accessible to its people. We can thus approach King Willem Alexander who is walking around town at his home in Wassenaar, where I lived for more than 25 years. This isn't common, but it happens and doesn't shock anyone. What would shock would be quite the opposite, that is to say a haughty and condescending distance on the part of royalty or the authorities towards those administered.

> *King Willem-Alexander said this himself in 2013 during his enthronement. "I'm not a protocol fetishist, people can address me however they want as long as it makes them feel comfortable.»*[52]

"Little house, little tree, little animal."[53]

The expression "Subway, work, sleep" (typical French expression « Metro, boulot, dodo ») translates into the Dutch language by the combination: "House, shrub, pet" to translate a routine and unoriginal life. The traffic jams on the roads in the morning to go to work, the congestion of public transport, the work which loses its interest becoming a task of eating, the lack of time for leisure and the fatigue which accumulates, the monotony of life daily, crystallise in a reference to their cozy little interior in their little house, with a small garden which offers them a little piece of nature to prune and hoe, and a domestic animal which sleeps quietly inside. It is true that their habitat is very standardised, that all the houses in a neighbourhood are built on the same model which is reproduced endlessly in monotonous rows, like absolutely similar dolls' houses. Rather than the heavy task and fatigue, the Dutch prefer to refer to a small, absolutely standardised home, which has a strong emotional value to comfort them. They like this expression to represent not the idyllic life which does not exist, but a quiet and pleasant domestic life. The house, the shrub in the garden and the pet symbolise stability and family happiness, the aspiration for a calm and comfortable life.

The expression was also used as the title for a weekly school television program "Huisje Boompje Beestje" in which children are encouraged to reflect on the monotonous and regulated life that awaits them, and on themselves. We address social issues,

---

[52] *Roi Willem-Alexander 2013*

[53] *« Huisje, boomtje, beestje »*

nature and technology, life at work. The programme, which was produced from 1988 to 2014, is still on the air.

We throw everything away and make everything new

Regularly, whether during a new installation or not, residents clean and reorganise their interior from top to bottom. In the neighbourhood in front of houses, we often see these construction containers which fill up with rubble, doors and bathtubs, furniture and sofas which we get rid of without hesitation. The Dutch have a heavy hand when it comes to renovating their interiors. They undertake the task regularly, like a big spring cleaning every ten years.

Responsible and autonomous citizens

Respect for others is guaranteed by equal relationships at all levels in society, with the function giving little or no privileges or consideration to those who must submit and obey it.

Hierarchical relationships are not very marked in business or in society in general. In return, individuals, who are given great autonomy by trusting them, feel empowered and will do their best to prove themselves worthy of the esteem granted. It will be more natural for them to take charge.

Just as students decide for themselves their behaviour and their future without having to refer to parental authority, citizens have the right to speak, and can decide without having to systematically submit to the judgment and approval of the 'authority. Their opinion will be respected.

"It's not Rousseau's fault."

It's all about trust. Empowering people means trusting them. In exchange for the trust and responsibilities given to them, people feel valued and will be inclined to do well.

As Rousseau thought, we consider from the outset that "most people are good"[54] by nature, but unlike Rousseau, we want to believe that a harmonious society guaranteeing the trust and responsibility of individuals will not corrupt this state of good natural disposition, but on the contrary preserve it. There is no need in principle to control people.

There is no need for a social contract by which the individual abandons in the hands of government and education the responsibility of making him good in spite of himself by "educating" him, no need to abandon his individual freedom to substitute social freedom. Dutch culture does not take a pessimistic view of history in general and civilisation in particular, on the contrary it maintains a reasoned optimism about human nature which a priori is trustworthy and can be held responsible. This will be done without excessive recourse to laws or regulations.

Freedom of religion in the choice of schools

Just like France, the Netherlands has become a secularised country in which religious practice and church attendance have melted like snow in the sun in the 20th century. It is no longer possible to judge freedom of worship, which remains a founding and existential principle of the country, except in the variety of schools, denominational or neutral, that exist everywhere. Parents, and especially students, will have the choice between so-called "special" schools ("bijzondere scholen") which can be Protestant, Catholic, Islamic, Muslim, or associated with specific educational trends such as Montessori, Dalton or Freinet, and so-called "neutral" public schools, open to all. No less than 70% of students attend "special" schools in the Netherlands, the exact opposite of the distribution in France where they are only 20% in so-called "private" establishments.

---

[54] *« De meeste mensen deugen »*

However, the religious orientation of the establishments and the rather weak influence of religion in Catholic or Protestant education must be put into perspective.[55] Le catéchisme reste une matière optionnelle, à laquelle personne ne sera obligé d'assister. Et on ne demande rien à personne concernant sa pratique religieuse, n'importe qui, quelle que soit sa religion, pouvant intégrer ces établissements.

> *The Dutch education system is based on the Basic Law of 1917, which reflects their tradition of pluralism and religious tolerance in education. It aims to promote freedom of choice and practice through equal public funding for all types of schools, denominational or neutral, as long as they meet academic standards.*

France prefers secularism, enshrined in the 1905 law on the separation of Church and State. It transcribes a principle of equality aimed at offering the same education to all, regardless of religious beliefs. Public schools are secular, so as not to favour or teach a particular religion. Ostentatious religious symbols have also been banned in public schools since the 2004 law. Freedom of choice is therefore more limited compared to the Netherlands. Even if in France parents can still choose private religious schools, these establishments only receive partial public subsidies and are therefore fee-paying. Egalitarianism leads to standardisation and less choice, which would be perceived in the Netherlands as a limitation of everyone's freedom and contrary to religious tolerance.

You are sick ? Heal yourself! [56]

> *Patients are held accountable to their doctors. They a priori hold a certain share of responsibility in the illness that affects them, in any case certainly in the treatment that should be given to it.*

---

[55] *Je ne suis pas en mesure de porter un jugement sur les établissements judaïques ou musulmans.*

[56] *See also Health chapter*

It is up to patients to call the medical office that received their test results themselves. However, in the case of abnormally serious results, the doctor will then contact the patient himself. It is up to everyone to take care of their healthy lifestyle and psychological balance with the help of loved ones, family and society, which offers numerous home and personal assistance services. Particular attention is paid to ensuring that everyone can remain independent at home. There is no shame, but rather dignity, in assuming one's autonomy, and in using walkers, tricycles or wheelchairs in the city. It is customary to treat nervous breakdowns or overwork with personalised fitness programs, available at any local sports club or gym, in addition to therapy with a psychologist.

As soon as medically possible, patients are removed from the hospital environment and sent home to complete their recovery.

Returning home immediately after giving birth

On the very day of delivery, mothers, who are not considered sick but rather tired people in need of rest, are sent home, where a handy assistant awaits them who will take care of everything, the logistics and organisation of the home for 10 days, so that the mother has nothing more to do. Shopping, cooking, cleaning, dishes, laundry, ironing, as well as the diary and visiting times, everything will be governed by this childminder with full powers, which the husband must respect. As a nurse, she will also monitor the infant's general condition, his diet and his weight; she will advise the young mother on breastfeeding. Every day, the mother will receive a visit from her family doctor at her home. All medical and domestic care will thus be provided, without hospitalisation.

You have to manage your stress

The Dutch are certainly subject to the same vagaries of hectic modern life, its risks and the uncertainties of a world in perpetual movement. Like all French people, they are subject to the servitudes of working life, separations and divorces, family tragedies, illnesses, economic ups and downs and financial problems, economic crises and history always in motion which continues its course. chaotic course and which does not spare them any more than others.

However, the Dutch are distinguished from the French by an apparent lack of stress and by much less nervousness.

There is of course this more stable, less emotional and less nervous temperament which characterises this people. There is also this desire to take things in hand to try not to be overwhelmed by stress. They are fans of yoga, relaxation and meditation, but also consultations with the psychologist. These practices, far from being reserved for people in poor mental health who must "take care of themselves", are considered healthy mental and bodily hygiene practices in order to prevent illness.

Oral hygiene

The Dutch value oral hygiene, so much so that being able to brush their teeth will reassure them in stressful circumstances. The Ministry of Foreign Affairs thus provides returnees returning from disaster situations or war zones with toothbrushes and toothpaste, as a first measure to calm and reassure, and initiate a return to normal. The drugstores and "ETOS" stores, which are unmarked pharmacies selling all types of generic first and second necessity medications, such as painkillers, paracetamol, anti-inflammatories and other vitamins, offer an unrivalled assortment of products for oral hygiene, as one would find shelves filled with various pastes in stores in Italy.

Say it with flowers

The Dutch are not the champions of tulip and flower cultivation for nothing. They like to decorate their homes with flowers as the mark of an interior that is both well-kept and warm, where life is good and welcome friends to spend a relaxing time together. Here, flowers are bought in armloads at prices that seem ridiculous to the French. And here, the flowers last 4 to 6 days, instead of withering overnight. When the French bring a bottle of wine to a dinner with friends, the Dutch will bring flowers.

Minorities protected

Minorities are not only defended, welcomed and protected, but completely assimilated so as to be integrated as best as possible within society. Homosexuals, gays or lesbians, are recognised as having the same rights as any other individual. They are accepted and integrated into society, to the point of becoming trivial. Far from being a particularism that stands out, or a posture of protest, homosexuality is part of normality and can no longer be used today to distinguish oneself, homosexual marriage having been very common for many years.

Limits of tolerance

This acceptance, if pushed to its limits, can lead to indifference and detachment. In a society where everyone takes their responsibilities and can go about their business in good conscience, the minority, by becoming normal and trivialised, can find themselves alone, left to their own devices, or even pushed aside, literally "apartheid". in Dutch, whose invisible walls are indifference. The spirit of the community combined with the permanent attention paid to good living together are there to prevent the development of hermetic islands in which we would be free to practice a way of life going against the rules of life in society.

The acceptance of differences and the protection of minorities cannot be pretexts for excessive and unbridled communitarianism, or for refusing to assimilate the rules of living together in society for those who wish to settle down in the Netherlands. It is at this price that differences are respected and minorities accepted.

Ambulances for animals

If there is a weak minority which does not have the means to defend itself, and which the Dutch have ardently defended for a long time, it is that of animals, mainly domestic animals, but also those on the farm. Anyone seeing an animal in distress, whether dog, cat, rabbit or pigeon, can call an ambulance specially designed to provide emergency first aid to animals. The vehicle is even equipped with an oxygen mask for canines. The collected animals will then be transported to specialised animal shelters. Police barriers will be erected around the nests of swans hatching their eggs along canals, roads and cycle paths.

Spaces and patience for children

Society provides a proper place for children.

There are areas in banks, post offices and public administrations offering construction games or puzzles to keep the little ones waiting when their parents are busy at the counter. Playgrounds with swings, slides and playhouses can be found in all neighbourhoods right in the middle of homes and buildings. There are enclosures for sheep, chickens and rabbits in all the villages, when they are not real small farms, the "kinderboerderij", to allow children to come and see and feed the animals.

At the supermarket, no one will be impatient when a young child helps his mother unload items onto the checkout belt at a snail's pace, trying not to drop anything, especially fresh eggs. The cashier, and the other adults, waiting patiently behind in the line, will show no signs of impatience. They will even go so far as to congratulate the little one for having managed to help mom until the end.

As a general rule, it is inconceivable that parents would lose their means with wayward or disobedient children. You never see Dutch parents get angry or scold. Slaps or spankings are simply inconceivable.

It would be unacceptable to spank or punish a child. The whims and the tears seem to pass over the parents like drops of water on the wings of a duck...

Saint Nicholas, a national affair for children

The anniversary of the arrival of Saint Nicholas ("Sinterklaas") is celebrated in the Netherlands more than Christmas. Three weeks before December 5 of each year, the Holy Man, adorned like a pope with his red and white miter and his episcopal crosier, arrives in all the villages and towns of the country at the same time, aboard a small steamboat, and surrounded by a flock of scoundrels, their faces blackened by the soot from the chimneys through which they had previously deposited their gifts for the children in the homes. Saint-Nicolas will travel throughout the day through the city in contact with families and children who are fervently waiting to see him pass by. During the following days, he will visit nurseries and nursery schools, triggering cheers and ovations with cries of ecstasy and childish joy.

Previously, during the 3 weeks preceding his arrival, the children had been able to count down the days using an Advent calendar. But above all, they were able to follow all his adventures on television, because, just like adults, children have their own television news program entirely devoted to them, the "Youth Journal" ("NOS jeugdjournaal").

The feast of Saint Nicholas is a national event organised and celebrated especially for young children, and broadcast on news channels in the same way as affairs for adults. Children find their place in national news and are considered a stakeholder in what is happening there.

The exception that confirms the rule of calm in society

In a well-organised, calm, respectful and polite society, adolescents and students enjoy a special exemption. They will be allowed practically anything. They can party late at night, drink and shout until late in the morning, in these "fraternities" (student associations) whose aim is to organise meetings, pretexts for drinking and other exuberance, to celebrate loudly and dirty national holidays, throwing their cans and trash everywhere. Every year, the city of Leiden celebrates the liberation of the city in 1574 from the Spanish yoke, and every year, it suffers from student excesses.

The lack of accommodation in university residences leads students to crowd into townhouses. They then cheerfully disrupt the life of the neighbourhood in the evening, which clashes with the orderly social life everywhere else. We could see it as the exception which confirms the rule of good "living together". We must see this as the right for young people to be adolescents and students once in their lives, before entering adulthood.

Feminine flirting

Young single French women who have just arrived in the flat country will be able to admire the stature and athletic build of the boys. They will nevertheless be surprised that one does not speak to them at any time, and that one does not approach them spontaneously to give them a little flirt. Pushy flirting is certainly not typical male behaviour in this society. On the contrary, it is considered inappropriate. Young French women will have to take the initiative if they wish.

The young girls will be in peace here. They will not suffer from eyes staring at them or following them behind their backs in the street, nor from sexist remarks which are considered totally inappropriate and disrespectful.

Cafes, cafes everywhere, to chat

Local democracy is practiced a lot in cafes and places of conviviality. The Dutch are the champions of bar chat, accompanied by a coffee or a beer. These places for discussion and conviviality are present in large numbers in towns and villages, wherever possible, whether at the sports club, the municipal ice rink or at the university. "Living together" is a shared responsibility, which the Dutch maintain with a certain fervour, when they meet at home or in a café, to chat, to talk about these little nothings that make up their daily life and the passing of time.

> *The Dutch have a consummate art of palaver in society and in the family.*

They use the word "chillen" or "gezellig" to describe these moments of friendly relaxation, specific to their life in society and difficult to translate into French.

> *This word "chillen" is a clever and tasty cocktail mixing the natural ingredients of informal discussions to talk about everything and nothing; procrastination, relaxation, letting go, relaxation, carefreeness, comfortable boredom..*

A minister's diary

The life of the Dutch is so full of discussions in cafés, professional and private meetings over drinks with family or friends, that you have to make an appointment to hang out. The practice of time management with your diary, which only applies to work in France, is perfectly generalised to private life in the Netherlands, to seriously manage all these moments of relaxation and casual discussions , nonsensical.

Welcome at home

Whatever the time of day, a visitor will be offered a coffee as a welcome sign, whereas in France, drinks are consumed at specific times. The French wait until snack time for children or aperitif time before bringing out the glasses, which will make a Dutch visitor uncomfortable, to the point of feeling unwelcome.

As in England or Germany, we also dine earlier in the Netherlands, around 6 p.m. By 7 p.m. everything is finished and put away so you can watch the news on television or go to evening classes and activities. Which can give rise to funny situations. Novice French people invited at 7 p.m. to visit Dutch people will not know that the latter have already had dinner. Visitors will be treated to coffee as a welcome sign, then leave disappointed with perhaps a few chips and peanuts in their bellies. Novice Dutch people, having already eaten light at home as usual, invited at 7 p.m. to a French home, will be offered an aperitif and peanuts to start. Then will come the starter that they will have for the coffee snack after dinner and which they will consume frankly. The main course then the cheese will therefore be major surprises that will have to be overcome. The final blow will come with dessert.

What matters in the Netherlands is being together and having a good time informally. It is easy to go to other people's homes at any time without fear of inconvenience, as long as you have made an appointment in a busy schedule, and it is easy to entertain in a relaxed manner, without a meal or dinner. The French spend more time preparing the meal which must be up to standard, the table being an important affair in France, but not in the Netherlands.

Birthday, the most important day of the year

If there is one day of importance in the year, it is the day of a birthday, the famous "Verjaardag". We remember that the induction of a child into nursery class takes place on his or her birthday. Annual national holidays are occasionally celebrated, which are mostly enjoyed as extra vacation days. But we will never fail to celebrate, with friends and family, everyone's birthday, a meeting elevated to the rank of family tradition of the highest national importance. The birthday is celebrated with friends, but also with the whole family gathered for the occasion, from grandparents to grandchildren, the small size of the country making travel easier. We will congratulate, orally or by mail, the person who has just passed another year, but also all their loved ones who will also be rewarded with personal congratulations "Gefeliciteerd! ", as if it was their birthday too. This is how we present our heartfelt compliments to all members of the close family, to personally reward them with a "Sincere congratulations on (the birthday of) your daughter! your wife ! your grandfather ! etc.», "Hartelijk gefeliciteerd met je dochter! met je vrouw! met je opa! ..".

At school, the children will bring a box filled with sweets which they will pass around to their little friends in an entire classroom decorated for the occasion as it should be, with flags and big letters C.O.N.G.R.A.T.U.L.A.T.I.O.N.S, huge and inflated with helium. For a day, they will be the center of the world and the attention of their little friends who will sing for her or for him.

The birthday calendar

> The birthday calendar of family and friends is a document of the greatest importance in the social life of individuals.

Its updating is discussed with the family. It traditionally sits on the wall in the toilet, a strategic place where all members of the family, as well as people passing by, must necessarily stop. Everyone will be able to see their name there, or not. There is a birthday calendar for the family at home, but also one for office colleagues, members of a sports club, and even pets registered in veterinarians' offices who will also receive their congratulatory card on their anniversary date. They are often richly decorated with folkloric images which represent an essential element of traditional Dutch culture. These calendars are often referred to by the name of the Dutch artist "Anton Pieck" (1895-1987) renowned in the Netherlands for his illustrations and prints of fairy tales, scenes from traditional and popular Dutch life. We therefore speak of "Anton Pieck" calendars to indicate these birthday calendars to celebrate.

Buying and sending birthday greeting cards, decorated in the most traditional or folkloric, eccentric or wacky way, is an enduring practice throughout the country even today.

The Queen's/King's Birthday

There are two very popular annual festivals in the Netherlands where the inhabitants like to get together in a festive and good-natured atmosphere, in sometimes burlesque and heavily orange-tinted outfits. The first is "King's Day" in April.

Once a year, the Dutch celebrate the birthday of their Queen or their King, in a friendly and festive atmosphere which knows no formality, as if everyone were part of the royal family and were celebrating the birthday of one of the theirs.

For 30 years, it was Queen's Day ("Koninginnedag"), in honour of their sovereign Beatrix, from 1980 to 2013. Being born on January 31 in the middle of winter, which was not an auspicious season in the Netherlands to bring her subjects out into the street in the rain, she decided, with a very Dutch pragmatism, but also with the concern to take care of them, to change her anniversary date and to establish it at the end of April, in the sweetness of spring and the flowering of the tulip fields. She had to abdicate in favour of her son on April 30, 2013, and this birthday has since become that of the King ("Koningsdag"), always at the end of April, Willem-Alexander having been born on April 27 by a serendipity.

This day, which celebrates the monarch's birthday, has remained in the spirit of a popular festival during which a people appropriates their royalty, without formalism and without distinction of social classes. The celebration is fun, with music, street parties, flea markets and fairs. All under the flags of the nation, but especially under the orange banners, symbol of the Orange-Nassau royal family. The royal family, which appears, as usual, accessible and benevolent, enjoys real popularity. Each year, the sovereign goes to a different city on this anniversary to meet the inhabitants, far from his royal residence, unlike the celebrations in England, where the people are invited to gather around the royal palace of Buckingham. It is in a way a tribute to all the Dutch, who will go out everywhere else in all the towns and villages of the country, wearing the colour orange on their clothes, hats and banners, in a huge joyful and popular celebration..

In the Netherlands, national holidays and celebrations are above all intended for these people with a naturally festive spirit who like to find themselves behind the symbol of the royal and popular crown: the colour orange.

The landing of Saint Nicholas

The second annual festival celebrated with joy, takes place on the occasion of the landing of this good Saint-Nicolas who has the good idea to disembark simultaneously in all the villages of the flat country, to the great amazement of the young children who come in crowds, with parents and grandparents, attend the event. The festival has been organised for a long time on a national scale for young children still in their early childhood, but it is naturally shared with adults who come to be touched by the innocence and enchantment of these young people's souls. It is a family festival celebrated in crowds in the streets of the village as if the country itself was a big family. It takes place at the end of November, 3 weeks before the feast of Saint-Nicolas which will be celebrated in the privacy of homes. And the atmosphere is worth the detour, even for those like me whose children have now all left home. Last party, this Saturday, November 19, 2023, I was not the only one who came without a child.

Families leave their homes at the beginning of the afternoon and come in procession, strollers in front and little ones clinging to the hands of parents and on the shoulders of dads, to reach on foot the canal which will serve as the port of arrival for His Holiness. , decked out with her entire troop of merry burlesque performers. Everyone gathers on both sides of the canal, and begins to tap their heels rhythmically to the songs of the entertainers and carnival music which warms up the atmosphere with loud decibel blasts from the speakers. In the Netherlands, the wait does not last long, everyone arrives on time, even Saint Nicholas who comes from Spain. He is preceded by the boat of his costumed and colourful troop of kids who move in all directions and begin to distribute treats to the little ones. Then there he is, certainly a grandfather from the village, fully disguised in a Santa Claus coat, with a long white beard, a red and white miter on his head, and leaning on his episcopal crosier so as not to slip down. water when disembarking. There he is on the ground, he walks towards the children gathered, they greet them at length by walking along the crowd and raising his hand as if to bless them, the little ones exult, the traditional songs spread and are taken up in chorus. Then the Holy Man tries to mount his mount, a brave, absolutely placid white horse, but his leg lacks flexibility and he collapses on the animal's back with his head forward! Acolytes come to his aid, stand him up, readjust his tiara and tighten his long red cape to cover the animal's rump, under the amused gaze of the parents. The procession, led by the orchestra in parade costume, moves through the streets along which residents have gathered to see it pass. Police mounted on bicycles close the procession. Behind them, municipal agents in yellow security vests are already busy dismantling the platform and the lanterns at the port. In 20 minutes, everything will be tidied up and cleaned around the port. The holy man will continue to a podium in the village square, to sing and greet the crowd. Then he will disappear, and the children will return home expecting to return to class as soon as possible, because Saint Nicholas will visit all the schools in the village throughout the following week. Each appearance will trigger cries of joy that will echo in the surrounding streets. The spirit of the party will take several days before dying out.

« Black Pieter » is racist!

In 1850, a certain Jan Schenkman published a book "Saint Nicholas and his servant", in which said servant was a black character of African origin. The book was so successful at the time that since then, Saint-Nicolas has been adorned in all his travels with a band of merry burlesque people with blackened skin, who make jokes and mischief, distributing sweets from their burlap sacks at arm's length.

In 2014, Verene Shephard, of Jamaican origin and advisor to the United Nations, denounced this tradition which she considered racist and degrading. She launched a denunciation movement in the Netherlands which would cause some stir among the population. Some argued that all children dreamed of being "Black Peters" ("Zwarte Piet") to whom anything was permitted. The big brothers and big sisters, who had stopped believing in the existence of the Holy Man, insisted on blackening their faces, whatever the colour of their skin, in order to be part of the joyful group on the day of the festival without being recognised by their little brothers and sisters, which therefore proved that this tradition was in no way offensive. Others preferred to highlight the tradition, as in the east of France, of chimney sweeps who passed through chimneys at night to distribute gifts at the foot of slippers. The controversy nevertheless grew, there was a movement "Black Peter for all!"[57] which aimed purely and simply to ban them, without knowing the extent of a "Black lives matter" movement like in the United States. The important thing remained the satisfaction of the children for whom the party was intended, politics should not ruin everything.

---

[57] « Zwarte Piet voor iedereen »

Black Peter with colours!

In 2023, a pragmatic and consensual approach, which preserved the pleasure of young and old, was already in place. The faces of the perpetrators were still blackened, but more lightly, to make them look like chimney sweeps. They all wore black page outfits, but with highlights, edging, muffs, belts, capes and feathers on the hat of a specific colour, whether blue, green, fuchsia, violet. or yellow. In this way, all the imps had blackened faces, which was necessary so that the little ones did not recognise the big brothers and sisters, but they were all distinguished by a specific colour. We then heard their new name: a "blue Pierrot-le-noir" or a "yellow Black Peter". In a pragmatic and consensual manner, the matter was resolved within a few years. And the "Black Peter for All" movement, which aimed to banish them, has now completely disappeared.

Celebrating sport for the party

With a festive temperament, looking for every opportunity to celebrate loudly but always amicably and peacefully, the Dutch have found in sport, football in particular, the ideal alibi to get together with friends or to party with orange hats in the streets, decked out and decorated with orange pennants and flags. The fervour of the inhabitants for their teams is stronger than in France, where the fever only starts to rise if the national team reaches the semi-finals and the final. In the Netherlands, we will not have waited to party.

Small personalised gifts

The Dutch prefer small, inexpensive but personalised gifts to standardised and expensive items from luxury brands. Spending time finding what will best suit a person is a sign of care and affection for them.

Adults also celebrate Saint Nicholas Day, on the evening of December 5, by getting together with friends. Everyone will bring a small, inexpensive gift for the person they have drawn, and about whom they will have written a little poem that is both humorous, gently teasing but affectionate.

Small, dense and dynamic country

The Netherlands is also and above all the "Small Country". We can see the extent to which the small size of the country, which should not exceed a few French departments, conditions and facilitates life in society. It is entirely possible for the family to get together for birthdays, to look after the grandchildren if necessary, or to lend a hand to young couples who live nearby or in the same area as the grandparents.

Urbanisation quickly reaches a sufficient density to allow access to services and infrastructure for the greatest number of people. Everything becomes more easily accessible by car or train, or by bike, when the roads are too congested.

A country at the campsite

The country is dense, the houses are cramped, so that the inhabitants aspire to live in the open air as soon as possible. As soon as the holidays arrive, the entire country goes to live at the campsite in rather rustic conditions which satisfy their need to be in nature. Campsites and holiday residences, offering bungalows nestled in the woods, with restaurants and places of activity, a small farm where to feed the kids and rabbits, a swimming pool and its slides, the inevitable bars for chatting around a beer or a coffee, all covered by countless cycle paths giving access to all the surrounding areas, all these small villages recreated in the heart of nature crisscross the country from north to south.

Hence the natural propensity of the Dutch to go camping abroad to find more sunshine. We can certainly see their inclination to watch their expenses when they bring with them the provisions purchased before leaving. But we hardly suspect this attraction to outdoor life and contact with the green nature that they love wherever they are, especially in their own country.

Omnipresent grandparents

Grandparents are heavily involved in the organisation of family life, apparently for the happiness of all generations.

Whether at the school's end-of-year performances, the sports or music club, or the swimming graduation ceremony, grandparents are always present in large numbers to applaud their grandchildren. They fill half of the rooms and stands.

Nowhere else do grandparents do as much babysitting as in the Netherlands. The high price of daycare, as well as reduced child benefits, means that 60% of Dutch children up to the age of 3 have a grandfather or grandmother as a babysitter. In France, as in Denmark or Sweden, most young children attend daycare for more than 30 hours per week. This rarely happens in the Netherlands where grandparents look after their grandchildren 2 days a week on average. In holiday villages, it is customary to see families bringing together 3 generations in nearby bungalows, spending their entire vacation.

And of course, they will never miss the birthdays which will be more numerous the bigger the family is.

This proximity of generations, combined with the natural friendliness of the Dutch, gives the country the air of a large family village where everyone can live together.

At the heart of the European spine

In the southern half of the country, a metropolis has been formed, bounded by the large cities of Amsterdam, Rotterdam, The Hague and Utrecht. This space forms what is called the "Randstad", literally "town(s) on the edge", which concentrates a third of the country's population in one of the highest density in Europe.

Located on the axis that connects London to Milan in Europe, the Randstad constitutes the backbone of the great European megalopolis, also called the European backbone, a densely populated and highly urbanised area, centered on Rhineland Europe and connected to global trade, within which the production of wealth and the most important flows in Europe are concentrated[58].

On Dutch territory, the Randstad brings together 7 million inhabitants, or around a third of the population of the Netherlands, in one of the largest urban areas in Europe. Life is active there, work and exchanges are dynamic, the universities attractive and flourishing.

> *Without being frenetic, the society there is energetic and busy. The state of mind in the Randstad is certainly not one of pessimism, nor of depression, but of development.*

Volunteering, a real job

Volunteering, is an almost "professional" activity in the Netherlands. It affects absolutely all sectors of activity of the working population. The only difference with professional activities is that this voluntary work is not paid in money, but in kind. Volunteers are officially recognised as such by an individual card, which entitles them to price reductions, in exchange for which they undertake to provide a certain number of hours in the service of the company. They are held to a rigorous schedule, and must take their vacation in advance like any active employee..

---

[58] Roger Brunet « Structures et dynamiques du territoire français » 1973

Open days

The Dutch like to visit places and buildings, usually inaccessible to the general public, during open days, such as the fire station, the old village windmill, the Second World War blockhouse, the local military base, the gendarmerie, or the technical premises and test rooms of the European Space Agency located in the town. They are interested and like to see what their taxes fund, what they consider to be theirs in some way. Above all, they like transparency in the concrete use of public funds.

Compared to the day dedicated to historical monuments in France, the buildings and places visited in the Netherlands are not restricted to a historical and cultural framework, but touch all areas of the functioning of their society.

The three army corps, Land, Air and Navy, independently organise open days each year, or gatherings with demonstrations of forces, for the general public. These events take place in the municipalities where military bases and airports are located.

Civilians love their veterans

There is a "Veterans day" ("Veteranendag"), a day of commemoration and celebration dedicated to soldiers who participated in conflicts, even recent ones such as the war in Yugoslavia or Afghanistan, in which the Netherlands was engaged. These "veterans" are therefore not only veterans of the last world war, almost all of whom have disappeared today, but also soldiers of the Dutch army in service, or having recently been in service..

These days are the time to demonstrate the recognition and support that civil society has for its committed soldiers. There is a certain fervour and popular sympathy expressed there, and which testify as much as they strengthen the link between civil society and its military.

Even if the events are not comparable, we can note striking differences between the July 14 parade in France, and that of Veterans Day in June in The Hague in the Netherlands. The first is formal, disciplined, precise and distant. It must illustrate the greatness and military power of France. The second is informal, friendly, friendly and accessible to everyone. The marches are not straight-lined, the uniforms are not all adjusted, and the bodies of the volunteers parade in jeans under their military jackets.

Bikers and motorcycle clans, many of whom are veterans, parade in slow motion on their whirring machines. They display on their jackets the badges of the military operations in which they participated. Unlike Belgium or the United States, these biker "gangs" are not criminalized. Beneath their appearance as tough backpackers, they demonstrate unfailing loyalty and fidelity to the army and the service of the nation.

Finally, the Dutch veterans' parade ends with a gathering of the parade and spectators in a large park in The Hague. The public comes to meet veterans and military personnel, retired or still active, and can admire their equipment and vehicles, and have their photos taken with them. Everyone will attend, beer in hand, the rock concert which takes place on a platform in a festive, gently unbridled and good-natured atmosphere..

> *We are far from the solemnity of the French military parade, the distance displayed by the military, and the respectful admiration of civilians kept at a distance.*

2 minutes of silence for the victims

Every year on May 4, whatever the day of the week, working day or public holiday, in all public places, restaurants or transport, the Dutch observe 2 minutes of silence between 8:00 p.m. and 8:02 p.m., in memory of the victims, civilians or soldiers, who were killed or murdered in the Kingdom of the Netherlands, or elsewhere in the world, both during the Second

World War and the colonial war in Indonesia, as well as during war situations and peace operations which follow up.

> *This commemoration concerns all residents, in the midst of their usual activities. Wherever they are, alone, in groups or with family, without ceremony, in a way as simple as spontaneous, they stand up and remain respectfully still and silent for 2 minutes. It is not an official commemoration carried out by representatives of public authority with flags, but rather simple citizens who celebrate the day of remembrance in unison in the middle of their occupations.*

The police are friendly and active

From nursery class, and throughout their schooling, young Dutch people will receive regular visits from police officers who will warn them against bad practices and the behaviour of dangerous individuals. Do not accept candy from a stranger for the little ones, do not get into the car of someone you do not know, do not believe fraudulent messages about scamming bank details on the networks.

> *In all schools and at all ages, the police regularly come to give advice and lessons so that everyone can better protect themselves. In doing so, it continually presents itself to its population in a protective and reassuring light.*

In the Netherlands, the level of safety in urban areas is high. Young men and women can travel in groups peacefully late at night in a big city like The Hague.

> *The police are present in large numbers and can be seen everywhere. Wherever we go, we come across police cars that are constantly driving and patrolling.*

The police are always in action, monitoring the streets, carrying out alcohol tests, stopping to speak to young girls walking alone in the evening, calming the ardor of tipsy individuals, repressing any socially prohibited behaviour such as walking in the street with a bottle of alcohol in his hand, even if uncorked.

This is a striking difference with France where we are more used to seeing police officers standing still and disapproving along the roads, scrutinising the offending motorist. The French police seek to enforce the rules through fear of the gendarme.

> *The police communicate a lot with their population, in which they are perfectly integrated and accepted as guarantors of their security. It is certainly not seen as a coercive foreign body which would seek to control and deprive the population of its freedoms, despite the severity of the fines and sentences handed down for the slightest infraction.*

The police regularly organise information campaigns against thefts and home break-ins. They speak directly with the population to advise them, for example to adopt automatic practices when leaving home in the evening: "Close the windows, leave lamps on, lock the door." The police do not wait for break-ins and breaches of rules to advise residents. They are in constant contact with the population and work with them to ensure the safety of the community.

The police host their own television show searching for missing children, chasing suspects or fleeing criminals, and appealing for information, often with a reward. The population does not see this as denunciation, but rather as active protection.

Police officers take selfies

On my way back from work by bike as usual, I pass by the sea dike in the village of Katwijk. The place offers a beautiful view of the sea, and many walkers frequent it. I then notice a parked police car, accompanied by two motorcyclists from the national gendarmerie. The car and the motorcyclists display the characteristic fluorescent blue and yellow decoration and stripes, reminiscent of the abstract and geometric paintings of the painter Mondrian, which are also visible from afar. Fearing an accident, I approach cautiously when I see the police officers, laughing, taking selfies against the backdrop of the scarlet sea. They explain to me that they are preparing the farewell ceremony for one of their own who is retiring. Amused, and almost their friend, I take a photo of them in the general good mood.

One rule for all, all for the rule

Before accepting the rule in itself, the Dutch want it to apply to everyone. They submit to it individually under this condition, to be like everyone else, and so that others are subject to it like them.

Unlike the French who accept the rule if it meets principles or a doctrine, such as equality of opportunity, or free healthcare for all, the Dutch see it first and foremost as a practical method of allowing better organisation of the life in society. When a French person judges and criticises the rule or the law in the name of his famous critical spirit, the Dutch ask fewer questions.

It doesn't matter if a rule is logical, it doesn't matter if it conforms to a political principle, as long as it is effective for life in society, and above all that it is the same for everyone.

Controlled traffic

Road traffic is regulated and controlled. It provides a soothing ride, sometimes considered soft and boring by the French. Drivers know how to regulate it themselves when there is a narrowing, by giving way to every other car, without forcing passage in a thoughtless and impolite manner.

There are speed cameras to control speed everywhere and on all roads. Controls are strict and fines are scrupulously applied. Fines are triggered at the first km/h above the limit, and must be paid before any dispute.

What passes here for a good organisation and application of road safety, could be considered as a rather coercive police state in France.

Big Brother is watching you

All systems are connected, the population is recorded and controlled much more than in France, whether by the health system, technical inspection of cars or customs. An individual who has not paid his fines may be recognized by the computers at Schiphol International Airport. He will then have to pay his fine if he wants to be able to take the plane.

Of course, like all citizens of the European Union, the Dutch benefit from the same guarantees for the protection of their personal data, none of this is illegal.

Hot spots to control them all

The "Coffee shops" where the distribution of hashish is tolerated for moderate personal consumption, as well as the studios with prostitutes, who are registered workers, project an image of permissive tolerance that is misinterpreted by visitors. There is a clear contradiction between this erroneous image and the social pressure exerted in Dutch society, which is much more civilized than it seems. These illegal but tolerated activities, as well as the practice of prostitution, take place in broad daylight in well-defined places, precisely in order to be able to better control and contain them, and protect society from criminal excesses. These are hot spots under control, exhaust valves under continuous monitoring. Everywhere else, drugs are strictly prohibited, particularly in schools which are subject to regular police raids, with sniffer dogs inspecting the bags of students lined up in a row along the wall in the corridor.

Drug couriers

It was the end of the 1990s, we were driving back to the Netherlands after our holiday in France. As we were driving through Belgium nearing the Dutch border, we were systematically approached at full speed by small sports cars, typically Volkswagen GTIs, whose passengers invited us to pull over at the next rest area, with gestures reminiscent of smoking big joints. They were "drug runners", sellers of cannabis and other harder drugs, who were selling illegally at 150 km/h on the motorway.

And then suddenly, they disappeared from circulation overnight. In the middle of the Franco-Dutch diplomatic war, the Hazeldonk operations had just begun.

The Franco-Dutch diplomatic war

On May 17, 1995, Jacques Chirac became President of the French Republic, while the Schengen Agreement, which meant the gradual end of borders and the free movement of goods and people, had just come into force on March 26. The Dutch permissive policy immediately attracted foreign tourists to the coffee shops of Amsterdam, some of whose streets filled with a haze of hashish smoked in abundance by the new consumers. This was the beginning of disorder and inconvenience for the neighbourhood, in Amsterdam, Rotterdam but also in Belgium. France, for whom the Netherlands thus favoured drug trafficking to France, opened hostilities by calling it a "narco-state" and by maintaining controls at the Belgian and Luxembourg borders. On the other hand, the Netherlands suffered this brutal smear campaign from French politicians, including President Chirac himself who called for a boycott. They were hurt by this, which rekindled resentment against the French, who were accused of not knowing Dutch society. The two were, and still are, irreconcilable.

"Two irreconcilable philosophies were opposed:
French repression on the one hand, Dutch

pragmatism on the other, the Netherlands being convinced that drug consumption was inevitable, and that it was better to bring drug trafficking out of the shadows to avoid abuse and nuisances. In France, drugs were, and still are, sold on the streets by traffickers, without the police systematically intervening, which generates delinquency and suffering for the populations living in these so-called lawless areas."[59]

Sensitive to the populations who were suffering locally from this new drug tourism, the Dutch authorities set up operations to curb this trafficking. In Rotterdam, thousands of Dutch and foreign clients and dealers were arrested during the so-called "Victor" operations. In the vicinity of the village of Hazeldonk, on the Belgian border, the operations of the same name were carried out in 2006, which put an end to the tempestuous actions of the "drug runners". This cross-border cooperation between the Netherlands, Belgium and Luxembourg, and which still bears the same name of "Hazeldonk", is still operational and active. Recently, in 2022, it made it possible to seize 48 kilos of marijuana, 70 kilos of hashish, 73 kilos of cocaine, 79,000 ecstasy pills and almost 264,000 euros in cash. Upstream investigations also led to the dismantling of a drug production laboratory and a cocaine "laundry" located in Belgium. The so-called "drug runner" operations, which take place several times a month and focus on smugglers and networks using the motorways, resulted in the seizure of a total of 60 kilos of cocaine, 35 kilos of heroin, 45 kilos of marijuana, 20 kilos of speed, 360,000 ecstasy pills, 3 litres of GHB and 700,000 euros in cash in 2022..[60]

Also to limit the nuisance and associated damage, the Dutch government reduced the number of coffee shops, particularly targeting the illegal establishments that caused the most problems. Their number fell from over 2,000 in 1995 to around 1,200 in

[59] *« Histoire des Pays-Bas, de l'antiquité à nos jours », Thomas Beaufils, Ed. Tallandier*

[60] *Journal belge « La Libre », janvier 2023. https://www.lalibre.be/belgique/judiciaire/2023/01/25/la-cooperation-internationale-hazeldonk-permet-la-saisie-de-stupefiants-et-le-dementellement-dun-laboratoire-de-production-MX2KTJT5TJARZL2LNDXQ5HJETI/*

1997. By 2014, there were only 600 coffee shops left in the entire country. In addition, the prison sentence for industrial cannabis cultivation was increased from two to four years, and the penalties for traffickers of hard drugs were significantly toughened.

> *The Franco-Dutch diplomatic war ended with Jacques Chirac's state visit in February 2000, each side having reinforced its own point of view. The French were satisfied with their policy of repression, the Dutch were satisfied to have effectively corrected the excesses and nuisances caused to the inhabitants, without denying their policy of tolerance. In short, an excellent compromise.*

Delirium for 2 hours, but no more!

Dutch society operates in a very organised way, with rules and standards that citizens respect scrupulously, with calm and restraint. The whole is polite, orderly, cordial and peaceful. And this every day of the year. Except for one day a year, for two short hours, a very short time during which the Dutch will let go of everything, outside the rules, and let off steam by setting off firecrackers and fireworks at all costs!

> *On January 1 of each year, from midnight to 2 a.m., the Dutch treat themselves to an interval of delirium and unbridled madness in their usually very regulated social life. Two hours of pure delirium, but not beyond!*

At midnight, at the first second of the first day of each New Year, the Dutch go into a trance and go wild with fireworks that they start setting off in front of their homes like crazy. For two hours, they will be allowed to go wild in a deluge of rockets, firecrackers, smoke and explosions that tear the night apart and light up the night everywhere at the same time throughout the country. Everyone went out in front of their homes to burn as much gunpowder as possible and make as much noise as possible, in an irrational outburst that squandered hundreds of euros in smoke in a few minutes. It's a real bombing scene in the middle of the city that tears apart the night, the ears and the eyes. At the crossroads artillery pieces are installed which spit out their fountains of lights and fireworks. The rockets scream from all sides as they rise into the sky, then explode in showers of light as they fall on the roofs. On the beaches of The Hague, stacks of wooden pallets are burned which burn up to the sky like gigantic pyres at the end of the world. The whole sky is lit up like broad daylight. The slag and burnt red paper from the firecrackers fall everywhere, littering the ground in indescribable chaos.

At two in the morning, it's all over. As suddenly as the crash had begun, it stopped in the breathless silence of the last firecrackers which crackled here and there for a few more moments. Soon night falls on everyone. Dawn will reveal the smoking remains of a night of rampage, the streets everywhere littered with burned rubbish like a city waking up in the rubble of a nighttime bombardment.

In the following days, everything will be erased as if nothing had happened. The Dutch will have regained their usual restraint and cleanliness. Two hours of wildness per year. But not more.

The unleashing is not without risk

Naturally, these nocturnal delusions give rise to outbursts which are more and more frequent. The current trend is to prohibit fireworks lit by individuals in large cities due to the risk of fire. It must be said that they are drawn after everyone has already had a good start to the new year.

In December 2018, the huge bonfires of towers of burning pallets on the beach in The Hague showered the adjoining neighbourhoods with a shower of flames. In the din of the firecrackers and the blow of the wind coming from the sea which spread the incandescent coals on the roofs in a red glow of a war sky, the fire sirens howled in the night along the avenues. Several fires broke out, and the next day the carcasses of the charred bicycles were found under their burnt shelters.

Every year, the government carries out information and warning campaigns against explosives banned but smuggled from China and Belgium, and the risks of amputation of fingers and hands which unfortunately occur every year.

The shower radar

The inhabitants have become accustomed to adapting to the northern and oceanic climate of their country. They are helped in this by a radar which detects upcoming precipitation with good precision. As soon as they can, between the showers announced locally very precisely by this "Shower Radar" ("Buienradar") on their mobile phone, they immediately go out to run, go cycling, walk the dog or go shopping.

In typical and somewhat laughable fashion, the Dutch rush outside to the benches and café terraces as soon as a ray of sunlight breaks through the cloud layer, without coats to convince themselves of the welcome warmth. In sunny weather, they never seem to be cold, even in winter.

Srebrenica, national trauma

In July 1995 during the war in former Yugoslavia (1992-1995), more than 8,000 Bosnian men and teenagers were executed in the Srebrenica region of Bosnia-Herzegovina by the Serbian army. This massacre was the first since the end of the Second World War, perpetrated on European soil, which had not seen a genocide for 50 years. This massacre was made possible, or was not prevented, by the irresponsible attitude of the 400 Dutch peacekeepers who constituted the UN interposition force, supposed to protect the civilian populations in this area. The Dutch command had refused NATO air support due to the risks to their own troops, and ended up allowing the Serbian army to enter the area without opposition. Worse, he organised the division between men and women, before the latter were shot and the women expelled. Astonishment and incomprehension struck public opinion, which suddenly realised what horror their naivety, their tolerance and their carelessness had led to.

> *"The Dutch no longer know how to deal with violence (until 1958, for example, we were very violent in Indonesia) because of the risk that Muslims, Christians and atheists would come into conflict with each other, which would destroy everything we have tried to build since the 1970s."*[61]

This massacre was described as genocide by the International Criminal Tribunal for the Former Yugoslavia (ICTY) and the International Court of Justice, both sitting in the country's administrative capital in The Hague. This trauma, from which the Dutch have not recovered and which will haunt their collective memory for many decades to come, now appears in their history books, in particular in the "Canon of the Netherlands", which is a historical frieze comprising 50 themes, characters or events, having contributed to the emergence of what they consider to have become their national identity.

A Veterans Day to Remember and Support

The Dutch Veterans Day ("Nederlandse Veteranendag"), which we mentioned in this chapter, is an annual event that has been held in The Hague since 2005. The first edition took place on 29 June 2005, a date chosen to honour the birthday of the late Prince Bernhard, who was highly regarded among veterans because of his role during the Second World War.

Although officially the creation of this day was not directly linked to the Srebrenica massacre, it was intended to heal wounds that were still deep and painful. It was about rebuilding the bonds between military personnel whose honour was tarnished and civil society whose self-esteem was also suffering. Civilians recognise that their military personnel are faced with dangerous and

---

[61] René Prins, 2004

complex situations. These veteran days promote better mutual understanding between them and Dutch society.

MH17 national mourning

On July 17, 2014, the Boeing 777 of Malaysia Airlines flight MH17 from Amsterdam to Kuala Lumpur was shot down over Ukraine, leaving no survivors among the 283 passengers and 15 crew members. That day, 193 Dutch people died, causing immense emotion throughout the country and national mourning. The poignant image of the endless procession of hearses transporting the bodies of the victims on the A4 motorway from Schiphol airport, which was published on the cover page of all the press, will remain engraved in the collective memory for a long time. I felt this tragedy personally at the time, so much so that the sight of this heartbreaking photo still brings tears to my eyes, 10 years after the tragedy. July 17 has since often been marked by commemorations and moments of contemplation in memory of the victims.

«Farewell, beautiful and anxious country »[62]

These are the words with which journalist Peter Giesen ended his extended stay in France (2013-2018) as correspondent for the newspaper Volkskrant in Paris. Through a mirror effect, he paints a portrait of Dutch life, which is so different.

> « The French have a rich culture and a great love of history. But while their joie de vivre is contagious, they are far more unhappy than we holidaymakers often think. »

The Dutch saying goes that one can "be happy as God in France" ("Gelukkig als God in Frankrijk"). France has been their favorite holiday destination for decades. The journalist observed a country "that is constantly trying to connect with modern times, constantly refreshing itself with this colorful past."

---

[62] Peter Giesen, « Retour de France » Editeur Thomas Rap

« France is a fascinating and irritating country. Sometimes closed, sour and conservative, sometimes impressive, elegant and full of love for the good life. Where else could you sit in a restaurant during your two-hour lunch break complaining about the world, while glasses of red wine are filled? I will miss France, this beautiful and anxious country. »[63]

[63] Peter Giesen, « Retour de France » Editeur Thomas Rap

VI. Work and politics

★ *Traditionally, Dutch society has the ability to adapt to the constantly changing world. Traditionally, royalty provides constancy and stability.*

★ *Without contesting everything in principle, we discuss everything and about everything, for professional or private matters, constantly.*

★ *In a real world, neither politicised nor fantasied, the Dutch know full well that the ideal solution does not exist. Compromise is settling for the least bad solution.*

★ *Citizens meddle in state affairs, that is to say, in their own affairs.*

Society moves, the Monarchy remains

> *« Traditionally, the power of the Netherlands lies in our ability to adapt to a changing environment. The world is changing more and more quickly. One constant remains: the Dutch Royal House of this small country by the sea. »*[64]

This is how Princess Beatrix herself defined the temperament of her people in her Speech from the Throne in 2005. The Dutch have the innate faculty, developed over the centuries for their survival and their identity, and which the Queen does not do not hesitate to call "strength", being able to constantly adapt to the world that changes around them and to the hostile nature that surrounds this small country stuck somewhere by the sea. Indeed, the least we can say, is that the Dutch do not stay with both feet in the same shoe.

It is also a way of defining the role of the royal family, which is popular in the Netherlands, as a pole of stability and tradition, a receptacle of traditions and ancestral history. Royalty is not seen here as a system of subjugation or organisation of a class society.

« Polderen » or permanent consultation

> *The Dutch cultivate the practice of excessive consultation, consultations on all subjects and with everyone, no one should be left out, especially not minorities. Whether in private or public companies, committees and meetings are legion.*

The origin of this practice dates back to the struggle of the Dutch people against the waters, and to the patient and tenacious conquest of dry lands and polders, hence the name "polderen" to designate the practice of river discussions. Indeed, the establishment of dikes and ramparts against rising waters involved constant monitoring of the state of the installations, in an endless battle, without ever being able to let down our guard. To do this, it

---

[64] *Princesse Beatrix, discours du trône, 2005*

was necessary to involve the entire population in monitoring and maintaining the dikes, a small negligence could prove fatal and cause thousands of victims. It was necessary to involve and empower as many people as possible to ensure the safety of the community.

This is how in the 18th century in the province of Friesland, it was necessary to consult the 11 towns and 30 villages of the province to be able to make a decision relating to the management of water and infrastructure. Since then the expression "doing something at 11 and up to 30" ("iets op zijn 11 en 30tigst doen") has stuck to refer to the large number of parties involved and the endless discussions that result. Today, the spirit of consultation and accountability of all remains.

The spirit of compromise or the least bad solution

Consultations are also credited with having the beneficial effect of resolving problems before they fester and erupt into social conflicts, as is often the case in France. It must be recognised that strikes and harsh confrontations are not common in the Netherlands, although they tend to occur a little more in recent years. What is specific to the Dutch mentality is not only the fact of taking into account the demands, so that the plaintiffs obtain, in part, their case, but also, and above all, that they accept the compromise and its consequences.

Consultations and negotiations go hand in hand with a spirit of compromise shared by all parties in discussion, which implies the acceptance of a half-hearted solution, which is never the best, often the least worst. Pragmatic by nature, the Dutch do not believe in too strong opinions. In their real, little politicised world, far from any dogmatism or ideology, there is no definitive yes or definitive no.

This can only happen in a society which empowers individuals from their childhood, and which also, and above all, empowers political parties by including them in government coalitions whose responsibility it is to make things possible and governable.

Any party in negotiation, any political party in coalition, bears a certain responsibility to move things forward and must find an agreement to resolve the situation. It will take as long as it takes, but ultimately a solution will have to be found so that society can function again.

Compromise to involve everyone

Recently in 2019, consultation was not enough to avoid a blockade of the city of The Hague by farmers on whom the government imposed the reduction of their activities to reduce greenhouse gas emissions. Farmers were protesting the closures of farms and animal breeding facilities. On which they could not win their case. They also contested the fact of being held solely responsible for gas emissions, when the concrete and construction industry, as well as automobile transport, also contributed massively. On which they won their case. Overnight, all motorists saw the speed limit throughout the country increase to 100 km/h during the day on expressways! Everyone was involved. The compromise resulted in a solution that everyone could support.

Then in 2022, while farmers restarted their blockades, Schiphol airport in turn had to reduce its air traffic by more than 10% to also participate in the effort to reduce emissions.

Coalitions to make and redo

We must get used to this idea which is so strange for the French, accustomed to the majority political party, and who love a strong and charismatic man: there has never been (except for one exception) a majority political party in the Netherlands. since the end of the Second World War. All governments will have been governmental coalitions, sharing responsibilities and necessarily practicing dialogue and consensus. The Dutch do not speak of government but of "Cabinet" to designate these governmental and parliamentary coalitions. The Netherlands are thus equipped with a real parliamentary system and a proportional electoral system, without limitation of access, which allows categorical parties such as the party of animals, the elderly, retirees or people of foreign origin, to be elected to the assembly.

The Dutch do not expect everything from one person, they have learned to find solutions together. This total proportionality prohibits a party from imposing its views on other parties, and thus arousing frontal, systematic and blocking opposition in public opinion.

Since the Second World War, the lifespan of coalitions in the Netherlands has tended to shorten.

Between 1950 and the late 1970s, government coalitions generally tended to last several years. The "Drees-Van Schaik" coalition formed in 1959 lasted almost four years, the "de Jong" coalition of 1967 lasted more than five years.

Starting in the 1980s, the lifespan of coalitions began to shorten. The "Van Agt-Wiegel" coalition of 1977 lasted about four years, while the "Van Agt II" coalition of 1982 lasted less than a year.

Since the 2000s, coalitions have tended to be more unstable and their lifespans increasingly short. The "Rutte I" coalition of 2010 lasted about two years, while the "Rutte III" coalition of 2017 (coalition) lasted about four years.

Following the provincial elections of March 2023, won by the populist "Farmers and Citizens" (BBB) party, a final coalition was urgently formed within the "Rutte IV" cabinet (in office since 2021), which should nevertheless cause it to fall 3 months later, in June 2023.

In this case, when disagreements paralyse a coalition, or when a new one must be formed following elections that reshuffle the cards, the current government coalition ends and new negotiations for a new viable coalition begin again. These can even last for months[65], more than 7 months for the last Rutte IV coalition (2021-2023)!

> *During these long periods of negotiations to form coalitions, it is democracy and parliamentary negotiation on all programs that stumble, which is operating at full capacity.*

Civilising extremes

On 6 May 2002, after making a thunderous entrance into Dutch politics by shattering the codes of political correctness against the establishment, the populist Pim Fortuyn was assassinated a few days before the legislative elections that he was about to upset in a populist tornado. It was a real political earthquake that propelled the populist extreme right to the doors of government. Pim Fortuyn's funeral was the subject of spectacular processions throughout the country. In 2004, the Dutch ranked him among the most important figures in their history, ahead of icons such as the painters Rembrandt and Van Gogh, the philosophers Spinoza and Erasmus, as well as Queens Juliana and Beatrix. Despite – or perhaps thanks to – the tragic loss of its charismatic leader, the radical populist LPF list won 17% of the votes cast and won 26 seats in the Chamber of Deputies. In the space of two years, an extremist populist party emerged from nowhere and became the second political force in the country in a single election.[66]

The Dutch did not deviate an inch. They followed their logic through to the end by opening negotiations for the formation of the government coalition. Such a situation would have triggered the outcry in France of a "cordon sanitaire" in order to exclude the rising extreme right from the government. The winner of the

---

[65] *See Appendix "Duration of government coalition negotiations"*
[66] *« Histoire des Pays-Bas, de l'antiquité à nos jours », Thomas Beaufils, Ed. Tallandier*

elections, the Christian Democratic Party CDA (28% of the vote), was tasked with forming a coalition with the extreme right of the LPF and the liberal party VVD. The result was not long in coming. The coalition fell apart in less than 90 days, during which time the four LPF ministers, insufficiently prepared to exercise power, lost all credibility. Internal divisions, both within the government and the LPF, accelerated the fall of the first Balkenende cabinet.

The Dutch know the corrosive power of the coalition and the compromises it demands, of the categorical statements and outrageous political posturing that can only exist in the opposition freed from all responsibility. The government coalition has the power to "civilise the extremes".

Minority cohabitation

Practicing coalition government with dexterity, Dutch politics reveals astonishing creativity. Having emerged victorious from the 2010 elections, the liberal (VVD) Mark Rutte, known as "the chameleon" for his ability to take on the new colours of coalitions, had the difficult task of forming a coalition government with the CDA. Unable to convince a third partner to form a majority in parliament, Mark Rutte proposed an unprecedented solution: a minority cabinet (minderheidskabinet), supported, or rather tolerated (gedoogsteun), by the 24 deputies of the PVV, the controversial far-right party led by Geert Wilders. In exchange, the government agreed to integrate part of the proposals of Wilders' populist programme, particularly in terms of immigration, integration, security, assistance for the elderly and reduction of public deficits. When the PVV's support was lacking, this unlikely alliance was maintained by the occasional support of other parties, such as the Labour Party (PvdA), which supported the government's positions during the Greek debt crisis and during the negotiations on the Dutch pension system.

However, the radical right of the PVV eventually abandoned its partners, forcing the Rutte I government to resign in April 2012.

New elections were held in September 2012, won by Mark Rutte's liberals (VVD) and Labour (PvdA). Punishment by its voters after the experience of the minority cabinet, Geert Wilders' radical right (PVV) lost seats.

> *Mark Rutte forma alors un gouvernement relativement plus stable, en coalition avec les socialistes du PvdA. Ce nouveau cabinet, union incertaine entre la droite libérale et la gauche modérée, alla pourtant jusqu'au bout de son mandat en mars 2017. Cette alliance, considérée comme une union des centres face à la montée des populismes, dura cinq ans, soit un quinquennat complet.*

The scout, the informant and the trainer

A coalition must bring together at the negotiating table political parties that have just campaigned in direct opposition to each other, denigrating opposing proposals, and openly taking a position against other candidates who were declared adversaries. An electoral campaign therefore in no way predisposes to compromise; on the contrary, it dangerously undermines the ground for future negotiations. Forming a coalition with yesterday's enemies is a risky operation that will be doomed to failure if special measures are not put in place.

The method, which has proven itself in the fire, is similar to diplomatic negotiations between former belligerents, all losers because all are minorities, but forced to find a peace agreement that will bind them all and make them work together on reconstruction. It has three distinct stages and functions: the scout, the informant, and the trainer.

As in any military operation in a minefield, reconnaissance must first be carried out. The Second Chamber, the equivalent of the French National Assembly, appoints a "scout" or "explorer" ("verkenner"), who will talk to all the parties to find possible alliances that would obtain an absolute majority. Some parties will refuse to ally with others, others will be more open. The scout is not affiliated with any party, so he does not represent any. He comes to inquire about political affinities or incompatibilities, without seeking to convince. He draws up an inventory of the situation after the electoral battle.

Then, he submits his report to this same Second Chamber that had mandated him and which will be able to thank him, to then appoint another person who is an expert in political diplomacy, an "informant". This time, he is a negotiator who will lead the discussions on the substance between the parties of the future coalition. In other words, we will get to the heart of the discussions, not to mention disputes and open crises that frequently lead to deadlocks. In this case, each party will have to give ground by alleviating some of the demands that are stumbling. We will also sacrifice the informant on the negotiation hotel by replacing him with another, which will erase the bad memories of the altercations with a new start. It is also possible that we will change alliances with other parties for another majority. Finally, at the end of long nights of discussions, an agreement will be concluded in a written document of a hundred pages, bringing together in detail the entire programme, point by point. This is an in-depth and long-term parliamentary work, to provide the country with a very precise road map. When this coalition agreement is finalised, it is presented by the informateur to the Second Chamber, which will thank him, and will appoint a third person, a "formateur", who will often be the future Prime Minister. The latter generally comes from the party that won the most seats in the elections. But this may not be the case if the candidate has a personality that is too discredited to be able to represent his country, as was the case with Geert Wilders, leader of the radical right who came out on top in the November 2023 elections, when forming his cabinet in March 2024. During this final phase, the formateur interviews the candidates for ministerial positions and proceeds to form the government team. He can then be officially appointed and presented to the King.

It is this long process, scouting, informing and then formatting, which lasts at least six months, which leads to the formation of a coalition government, a "cabinet", which can include up to five different political parties.

Politics without a President

You have understood: with parliamentary elections with proportional representation, which produce government coalitions, the Netherlands does not have a President of the Republic who takes center stage, to the detriment of Parliament where oppositions and political manoeuvres are unleashed. Government coalitions, which must bring together different parties from the political spectrum, are condemned to merge into consensus. As a result, extremist speeches, scandals and the damage that this causes in public debate and life in society - and which are the lucrative business of an entire political-media system in France - are necessarily contained and limited.

Politics here, being more efficient and pragmatic, is necessarily more boring. We talk politics to settle the affairs of life in society, then we move on to something else, like after a medical consultation or an appointment with the heating engineer. There is not only politics in life and, above all, not everything is overly politicised. School, the baccalaureate, health, wind turbines, public transport... are not the battlegrounds for political dogmas.

The world is economic

The Dutch see the world from an economic, not a political, point of view. Far from the French conception which wants to believe that the economy must be at the service of politics, and not the other way around, the world is seen in the Netherlands as a game of impersonal forces in which individuals can only have a marginal influence. The global economy resembles the ocean in the middle of which we can navigate if we adapt to its constraints, to take advantage of the changing weather and the opportunities offered. The Dutch are navigators at heart who know how to adapt the sail to maintain or change course depending on the circumstances.

> *Rather inclined to accept reforms which promote the free movement of goods and services, the Dutch do not seek to protect themselves from a liberal hegemony which they do not perceive as a threat but as a means of development. They adopt a resolutely enterprising and flexible attitude allowing them to adapt, without closing themselves in a defensive attitude which would rely on the State to protect them from the vagaries of the economy.*

Comforted by unemployment figures that are half as high in the liberal countries of northern Europe as in France, the Dutch have a much more open attitude on the economy and their future than many French people.

We must save the soldier Euro

In 2007, the subprime financial crisis broke out in the United States. It was going to bring the global banking system to the brink of collapse, and put the Greek state, which was too heavily indebted, into default on payments. The Greek crisis threatened to implode the entire euro zone which had no other choice than to financially support this bankrupt member country, under penalty of seeing other countries, such as Italy, also heavily in debt, be undermined, and to provoke the withdrawal of other States which could no longer pay to replenish such large budgets. The breakup of the Monetary Union would have meant the end of its single currency.

The Dutch, although attached to economic dogma and the good management of public budgets, reluctant to pay the debts of poorly managed States, felt the wind of the bullet. The Dutch know well what they owe to the euro. Its importance is crucial for their economy. Without blinking an eye, and as usual, the country adopted a pragmatic and constructive attitude in developing the instruments necessary to combat the economic crisis.

> *«The creative genius of the Dutch treasury experts was crucial in controlling the unprecedented events which then struck the European Union.»* [67]

Brexit ?!? No Nexit !

In 2016, Brexit sounded like a bolt from the blue in a country very attached to the European Economic and Monetary Union. Incomprehension and surprise quickly gave way to rejection, despite the traditional support and cultural proximity that the two countries have maintained for a long time. The reaction to what was felt to be a betrayal by a member and ally of the Union in which members should stick together was one of open disappointment. " Good riddance !» exclaimed my neighbour, a former diplomat. We must remember that the Dutch population feels concerned by economic issues and the budgetary choices of their government coalition, to which they have entrusted the management of their wallets without ever signing a blank check. What the English had just done was an attack on their economy, their jobs and their savings. Brexit was felt by the population as a betrayal and a personal matter.

> *Overnight, talk of a possible withdrawal of the Netherlands from the Union, the "Nederland Exit" or "Nexit", spontaneously disappeared.*

By playing with fire as the English had done, by letting the idea of Brexit develop without being taken seriously, and therefore without contradiction in the public debate, the Dutch risked losing everything and dragging down the euro zone. in turbulence harmful to all.

---

[67] *Tom de Bruijn, preparatory text at the Dutch Embassy in Paris on March 23, 2023 as part of a series of meetings on the Franco-Dutch relationship carried out in the run-up to Emmanuel Macron's state visit to the Netherlands on April 11 and 12.*

A Nation of "Shopkeepers"

Napoleon Bonaparte considered the Dutch a nation of "shopkeepers," in which he was right.

Short studies and learning a manual profession being well accepted, even favored by the education system which filters access to long and university studies very early, manual and craft professions are well regarded in the Netherlands.

Society needs plumbers, craftsmen, and tradesmen. It organises education and professional training accordingly. This further satisfies the need for autonomy of Dutch individuals, who like to run their own affairs and be independent.

The survival of small businesses in town

Small businesses of all kinds, varied boutiques and especially cafes, popular places for conviviality, are legion in Dutch villages and towns, whereas they have been eliminated from village centers in France, under the devastating influence of the gigantic shopping center on the outskirts.

The lack of space in this small country makes the establishment of the large parking lots necessary for large areas particularly expensive. In addition, the cramped conditions of two-story housing, which generally do not have an entrance, pantry or cellar, do not make it easy to store food supplies for a week. Unable to store large shopping carts by car, the Dutch therefore opt for more frequent small shopping trips in the city center and by bike.

Authorisation for the establishment of large stores falls under the authority of the regions, and not the municipalities. Trade unions and craftsmen, very well organised in "guilds" or corporations for centuries, are careful to restrict the establishment of large stores so as not to kill small businesses and life in the city.

The contrast is striking with France in which mass distribution has become a predominant industry, which today enjoys economic and political power greater than that of the manufacturing industry.

Inventiveness in genes

Understandably, the French judge the Dutch through the prism of their own culture, which does not look kindly on money and business. This pushes them to consider the Dutch as individuals motivated by the pursuit of business and money at all opportunities to make a profit from it. Seen from France, we easily qualify this people as individualists and traders, without a noble political vision and without a universalist ideal. The caricature has truth, but you have to experience it from the inside to approach the analysis through the other end of the lens, and discover with astonishment the creativity and inventiveness that these people demonstrate, often in the trials and hazards of life and history.

> *Entrepreneurship, in the sense of doing something of groping and tinkering to find a practical solution without procrastinating, could rather be compared to an ability for economic tinkering, an inclination to constantly have personal initiative.*

We even have the impression that the Dutch are only waiting for this, and that they are only waiting for the problems which inevitably arise on both sides, and which they immediately come into contact with to contain and plug them. This they will do at their individual level, without waiting for directives from above.

Inventors and pioneers

For more than a millennium, the Dutch have owed its territorial survival and economic prosperity, which lifted it out of poverty, to technical innovations that benefit society as a whole. They are naturally inclined towards the diligent search for a technical breakthrough that will help them collectively overcome the problems they face. Without technology, combined with openness to the world and unwavering group confidence, the country would no longer have existed for a long time.

In the 15th century, they transformed the mills to drain the marshes and create polders. Then in the 18th century, they developed the first steam pump for polder drainage, known as the "Dikkepomp". It was first installed in Groenlo in 1787, then permanently in 1802 at the Cruquius drainage plant near Haarlem by the engineer Jan Blanken. This pump is still considered an engineering marvel of the era. Also in the 18th century, they perfected cartography techniques and navigation instruments to find the best maritime routes to the Indies.

Today, the Dutch are at the forefront of research and development, applied to well-identified and concrete sectors, with the aim of solving the problems of rising waters which constantly threaten them, to obtain a competitive advantage in the global economy, and to benefit community life. They are masters in the art of combining civil works, dikes, cycle paths, urban constructions, green and recreational spaces, such as the "green heart" ("Groene hart") developed and preserved in beautiful middle of the "Randstad", this most densely populated conurbation in the Netherlands, which brings together the cities of Amsterdam, The Hague, Utrecht and Rotterdam.

> *« This nation has always had a remarkable capacity to regenerate itself, thanks to unparalleled strength and creativity that has never faltered. »*[68]

The precursors in Bordeaux

Freshly arrived in the Bordeaux region where we have just established our residence in France, while continuing to live in the Netherlands, we follow a guided tour to discover the history of the city. What was our astonishment when we heard the guide begin

---

[68] *« Histoire des Pays-Bas, de l'antiquité à nos jours »*, Thomas Beaufils, Ed. Tallandier

by first thanking the Dutch for their unique contribution! It is a story which illustrates this spirit of initiative, but which the people of Bordeaux tend to forget, as it makes them indebted to the Dutch of the 17th century for having created the Médoc, white wines and spirits, as well as the technique conservation of wine in barrels. Nothing less for a vineyard known throughout the world as the standard bearer of French wine production.

In 1579, the Dutch had obtained political independence, which gave them great freedom of manoeuvre and trade in Europe and around the world. In the following century, their navy was superior in number and in navigational quality to all European navies combined. That is to say, it crushed both the French and English navy combined, in terms of numbers but also in terms of efficiency. Their commercial boats were both more numerous, but above all more profitable. Before docking in Bordeaux, which was just another destination for them, they were already doing business with Germany and Hungary.

Before the arrival of the Dutch, Bordeaux did not produce sweet white wines, and for good reason. Their only major clientele at the time, the English, preferred red wine, which was however rather clear and which was called "Claret" for this reason. The Dutch changed the situation by changing the technique of vinifying red wine, which made it darker, and by introducing white and sweet wines, the production of which quickly equaled that of red wine.

Furthermore, it was the Dutch who drained and dried up the entire Médoc region, which was then very marshy and unusable. They transformed the marshes into exceptional vineyards, which became Pauillac, Saint-Estèphe, Margaux, Saint-Julien, and took part in the operation of some large châteaux, such as that of Lafitte Rothschild.

To complete it all, it was they who invented the sulfurisation of barrels, in order to allow the conservation of the wine. They explained to the people of Bordeaux how to burn a wick in sulfur before filling the barrels to disinfect them. This innovative technique marked the break with medieval viticulture, the first steps towards modern viticulture and the aging of quality wines. Finally, the Dutch also had a great influence on the production of brandy, which went from non-existent to the creation of two very famous productions today: Armagnac and Cognac.

Covid triggers initiatives

Beginning in March 2020, it became clear that the world was experiencing a serious viral pandemic that was spreading through aerosols. It had to be contained by closing non-essential stores to reduce contact between humans. Restaurants in the Netherlands immediately began preparing take-out meals and home delivery, as did florists. Everyone tried to adapt their local business by practicing it without physical contact, everyone tried to make their business viable as much as possible, without waiting for government directives explaining how to react in such circumstances. Personal initiative was in full swing.

Sport, cancer, courage and commerce

With my Dutch friend Jan, in the 2010s I practiced the combat sport Krav Maga, which is a personal defence technique against attacks, but also hand-to-hand combat used by the military and intervention groups such as the police. We were both moving briskly towards our fifties, which made us the two elders of the group among young, energetic people who were approaching their thirties. But the atmosphere was good, welcoming, with everyone leveling up to each other. A few years later, Jan was struck by a most dangerous cancer, Hodgkin's lymphoma, which statistically left him with only a reduced chance of survival. After trying, and courageously enduring, heavy chemotherapy treatments, Jan temporarily went into remission, but received distressing news a few months later about the resumption of the disease. He only had one last chance left, that of immunotherapy. When he told me, he simply said goodbye, as the Dutch do who are familiar with death and are going to leave this world without any apparent fear.[69]

Jan underwent immunotherapy and was saved. He is still alive and in good health as I write these lines in 2024. But the illness will have exhausted him, robbing him of his energy and drastically reducing his ability to concentrate. He can no longer work more than 20% of his time. Chase away the natural, it comes back at a gallop, especially among the active and enterprising Dutch. Subject to a natural desire not to remain with both feet in the same shoe, Jan tackled the situation. He began trading online, buying raincoats and warm clothing which he piled up in his garage to ship back. Jan was a nuclear physicist by training. He began by working in a particle laboratory with CERN where he manipulated the mathematical statistical tools of quantum mechanics. He then went to work for banks to model financial markets with these same mathematical tools. The financial crisis of 2007-2009 caused a wave of layoffs. Jan had to leave the bank and open his risk analysis firm to advise his former clients. This work, as a statistical mathematician and financial markets banker, had obviously not dulled his commercial sense. This meaning was to find suppliers of quality products, avoid bad merchandise, and ensure the real performance of the product. By buying from him, you could be sure that the rain would not get through the seams of the raincoat, and that the supposedly warm garment would effectively protect against the cold. He tested the clothes himself to make sure.

Russia's invasion of Ukraine in February 2022 caused a sudden influx of orders for Ukrainian soldiers sent to the front in the cold of winter. Customers also began asking for helmets and body armor they could trust. Jan got to work. He chose suppliers who looked serious. Then, armed with a few samples, he rang the doorbell of a NATO ballistics research institute in The Hague, which agreed to test the helmets and vests in a real situation with live bullets. The tests were carried out with the greatest scientific

---

[69] See Chapter "Health, life then death"

rigor. The power of the bullets, the velocity, the shooting distance, the measurement of the force of the impacts (it is in fact a question of resisting a bullet impact without transmitting a devastating shock wave for the body), everything was calibrated with precision. Jan obtained certifications for his helmets and vests that could save the lives of his customers and ensure the reputation of his store. Since the outbreak of war in the Gaza Strip in October 2023, Israeli families living in the Netherlands have been ordering from Jan to equip their reservist children called to the front.

> *In my eyes, Jan is the archetype of the Dutch temperament who faces his own death, who undertakes on his own individual level without hesitating to change careers, and who has this sense of business to understand the needs of his clients and provide real help.*

Miniaturist geopolitics

Living in the Netherlands means living in a small country. Its surface area is sixteen times smaller than that of France, the largest country in Europe, for a population density four times higher. This smallness is even more noticeable when you know that a quarter of the territory is below sea level. Unconsciously, this conquered space remains in danger, as if this threatened land was at risk of sinking…

The scope that the use of language can confer in the world is also incomparable. There are fifteen times fewer Dutch speakers on the planet than French speakers. The economic and political importance completes this miniature picture. Unlike France, the Netherlands is not part of the G7 or the G20 (except through the EU headquarters).

But while France's economic power is essentially due to its size relative to the European average, the Netherlands is much richer, ranking fourth in GDP per capita, far ahead of France, which ranks eleventh in Europe. Worldwide, the Netherlands generally ranks between tenth and twelfth, while France is around twentieth to twenty-second.

Smallness and fragility, combined with prosperity that is earned through individual dynamism, permeate the minds of this small country. The diplomatic posture resulting from this is radically different.

A country without grandeur

This country has no need for grandeur in its diplomatic vision or its political speeches. I have never read or heard that the Netherlands prided itself on participating "in the concert of Nations" and that their national pride was comforted by this. The influence of the Netherlands in the world is judged by its economic performance, the wars that are brewing and its defence which the country can only ensure in cooperation with its powerful ally, the United States, and its large, close European neighbour, Germany.

> *While, like France, they emerged from the Second World War defeated, occupied, then liberated, their port city of Rotterdam was razed in 1940 by bombers, and their population was starved during the "hunger winter". in 1944-45, the Dutch did not seek the glory of the winning side and the victorious posture to save face. There is no need to erase a defeat, take revenge and assume the supposed rank of world power.*

No, none of that, the Netherlands is a small country that knows it and takes responsibility for it. Given its small size, geography and population, it would not occur to it to place itself higher than it is.

However, like France, the nation had a glorious and exceptional past, during its famous "golden century" of 1600, which no one in the country is unaware of. Lost in the gloomy swamps and cold mists of the North Sea, the emergence, literally and figuratively, of a small people who conquered a large part of their territory by pushing back the ocean by will, to become during the appearance of States in Europe at the Treaty of Westphalia in 1648, the most powerful of them, was a historical miracle. Maritime trade and colonisation propelled this small country stuck in the delta of Europe to the rank of leading European power. Today, the splendour of this glorious era still shines in Amsterdam and in the provinces in the architecture of the beautiful bourgeois residences which line the canals with prestigious names, as well as in the world-famous paintings of great masters such as Rembrandt or Vermeer.

> *However, there is no nostalgia for a bygone time, no desire for greatness, even less for wanting to hold a supposed rank which no longer belongs to it among the powers of today. While in France the idea of rediscovered greatness still torments people's minds, the Dutch have no motivation to be dominant or influential in the world, even if only through a strong European Union, of which they know well the power and the very limited strategic autonomy.*

The influence of the world on the country, and not the other way around

> « *The French practice geopolitics, the Dutch prefer to stick to the domestic side. The French want to perform at major international events; politicians here focus on their own country.* » [70]

The contrast could hardly be greater. Immediately after the attacks on the Twin Towers in New York in September 2001, French President Chirac was the first head of state to visit President Bush, to reinforce France's role as a major ally alongside the United States in the international anti-terrorism response that was to come. During the Arab Spring, the Dutch contributed only modestly to liberating the Libyans from Gaddafi with a meager financial contribution, but there was much discussion about the impact these upheavals would have on their

---

[70] NRC, 22 maart 2022, Thijs van Dooremalen et Jan Willem Duyvendak

relationship with Islam within their society. The election of Donald Trump as president of the United States in 2017 had the same effect. The Dutch media were primarily concerned, with some anxiety, about whether this event would not trigger a new, harmful populist breakthrough in their own country.

> « It was an evening in which the Dutch [...] said 'watch out' for the wrong kind of populism. »[71]

Although events occurring abroad can indeed provoke strong reactions in the Netherlands, these concern much more the domestic side.

> « While in France foreign events are primarily seen as opportunities to "Frenchise" the world stage, in the Netherlands they are primarily a reason for "domestication" – for thinking about all kinds of domestic issues. Because we are insignificant on the world stage, foreign countries "get into" us much more difficult. »[72]

America first, the Netherlands second..

On January 20, 2017, the inauguration ceremony of Donald Trump, who had just been elected 45th President of the United States, took place at the Capitol in Washington, to cries of "America first!". A Dutch columnist added on the occasion: "America first, the Netherlands then...". Aware of the Netherlands' dependence on the American liberator and protector, he prepared a short humorous film[73] for the new president, extolling the merits of his country, in the outrageous tone characteristic of the new president D. Trump. "Because we understand that it is better to get along, we decided to introduce him to our small country. In a way that will probably please him.". The end of the film ends on

---

[71] Prime Minister Mark Rutte, victory speech in the elections to the House of Representatives in 2017

[72] NRC, 22 maart 2022 , Thijs van Dooremalen et Jan Willem Duyvendak

[73] https://www.youtube.com/watch?v=ELD2AwFN9Nc

terms which well summarise the assumed awareness of their dependence on the USA.:

> « We have a great great great dependence on the United States. It is enormous ! If you screw up NATO, our problems will be huge again. They will be huge, they will be gigantic. It's true. Don't do it, please. We understand perfectly: It will be America first. But could we say "The Netherlands second?"» Is this ok? »

The film garnered more than 29 million views!! and inspired other countries on the theme "America first, but my country second...". Comedians, journalists, citizens from all over the world hijacked President Trump's "America first" to promote their country, in terms not always distinguished it is true, in an attempt to reach second place in the ranking! First it was small countries like Belgium (2 million views) and Switzerland (13 million views). Then came the turn of Germany (11 million views) and France (1.4 million views) which on this occasion agreed to deride itself, to recognise the defeat of 1940 and its debt to the USA. Compared to the Netherlands, which accumulated 30 million views, the French only gave 1.4 million views to this theme which was unflattering to their national honour.

Strikes, demonstrations and riots in the Netherlands

> Going on strike is not common or usual in the Netherlands. The job market there is more flexible and dynamic than in France, where people are less reluctant to change positions and companies. They see this as a natural thing that positively evolves work, experience and remuneration.

Compared to strikes in France, those in the Netherlands are less frequent, more limited in duration and number of demonstrators, while having a strong media impact in a country little accustomed to this type of event. During the COVID pandemic, strikes were limited, even anecdotal. Statistics show an average of 9 days of strikes per year, compared to 171 in France.[74]

> *Having been made responsible since their earliest childhood, the Dutch do not understand the lack of sense of responsibility of the French strikers who are sawing off the branch on which they are sitting, biting the hand that feeds them. Infantilised since their childhood, the French, for their part, see it as resistance to authority to which they have never had any other choice than to submit, at the cost of a loss of initiative and freedom.*

Like strikes, demonstrations are also less frequent in the Netherlands, and concern issues other than pensions and social security schemes. We are demonstrating in the Netherlands against global warming, animal abuse, and racism.

However, in this relative calm compared to France where certain classes of the population demonstrate regularly every year, the Dutch have also experienced repeated demonstrations since 2019 by farmers, confronted with measures to reduce greenhouse gases, nitrogen dioxide in particular, which threatens almost half of their farms. This protest movement is deep and has taken on a national scale, and propelled the BBB Farmers Party into the government coalition in 2023.

Not to mention the riots of football fans during a confrontation between the Amsterdam club "AJAX" and the Rotterdam club "Feyenoord", sworn enemies for decades, the country practically does not experience large-scale riots which spread like wildfire in the suburbs of France, and which last several days or weeks. There were some impulses in the wake of the demonstrations and the excesses of the Yellow Vests in France, which were suppressed in less than a few days. Then sporadic riots broke out

---

[74] https://www.reddit.com/r/europe/comments/34hq47/comparison_of_european_countries_average_number/?rdt=55322

against the containment measures during the pandemic, which were also quickly contained by the police.

The population does not like violence and sees no justification for it. The right to protest does not give the right to break, pillage and burn.

Unions

The relations between employers and unions are of a different type here. They take place within the Work Council (the equivalent of the « Comité d'Entreprise », CE), in a relationship of partnership and dialogue, in the form of real working meetings that involve everyone in the company's projects. The staff representatives are simply seconded there, devoting only part of their work to it, unlike their French counterparts, who are busy full-time at the task, being proven professionals in unionism.

The powers and the mode of operation are also radically different. The Dutch CE can block a management project by a vote. The latter will therefore have to carry out numerous preliminary discussions and preparatory meetings in order to reach a consensus at the time of the vote, which makes negative votes quite rare afterwards. We can say that this is the opposite of what happens in France, where the CE vote is only consultative, a vote against does not prevent the implementation of the project presented. Such a provision casts doubt on the usefulness of this fictitious consultation, which leads to posturing votes that change nothing.

The Dutch works council also has a right to review the appointments of senior managers from a certain level of hierarchy. In this case too, consultation will be necessary to reach an agreement.

Only the Court of Justice in the Netherlands can contradict a negative vote by the works council. It can also go further by overturning a strike decision, as was the case in 2016 against the

KLM ground staff union, which threatened to strike in the middle of August. To protect summer tourism and to counter the high risk of attacks in Europe at that time, the Court decided to freeze the planned strike.

No yellow vests

The sudden surge in gasoline prices in 2019 to €2.40/l caused neither outcry nor large-scale social movements, which would have been unimaginable in France then in the midst of the vest protest movement. yellows in the streets. The return of inflation following the war in Ukraine has not provoked either a debate on purchasing power or political discontent.

The economy has always fluctuated normally and regularly, without anyone, or almost no one, batting an eyelid.

The national flag upside down, what a stir!

When farmers began to demonstrate in 2019 against measures to reduce greenhouse gases, in particular the nitrogen dioxide that agriculture produces in quantity, and against the reduction of livestock and the planned closure of half of their farms, they took the initiative, considered outrageous by many, of displaying the national flag by hanging it upside down! The affront quickly became the symbol of their rebellion and a sign of rallying to their cause. We saw flag stickers stuck upside down on public lighting, or flags hoisted the wrong way in gardens or on the facades of buildings as a sign of support. It was enough to mishandle the national flag to create a stir.

National constants

There are, as in any nation, cultural constants shared by all political tendencies and which are no longer even discussed. These subjects are self-evident as being the unique character of the Dutch. The smooth running of everyone's business and the economy in general, tolerance and protection of minorities, the welfare state and social support, are usually constants shared by all political parties whatever they may be, from the right or left. The economy is not exclusively right-wing. Social protection is not exclusively left-wing. Both are the foundations of all Dutch politics.

Local democracy

Like the "bottom-up" structure of the Reformed church which gives broad autonomy to the faithful, the Dutch social fabric is full of associations, consultative bodies and representative bodies which are the hallmark of their democracy. All causes are thus defended by any authority, whether it be animal welfare, retirees, cyclists, the denunciation of the macho spirit, or the excessively high taxes paid by taxpayers.

In the Netherlands, "It is not so much the State that meddles in the affairs of citizens as the reverse" [75]

During electoral campaigns, the programmes and projects of political parties are made public and compared in detail[76]. They mention practical and local subjects, such as the installation of wind turbines on the edge of a village, or the maintenance of green spaces or small livestock farms in the heart of a town..

The subjects are treated at a local level, and are not transcribed into a debate of ideas at the national level.

It is not uncommon for elected officials belonging to the same political party to make opposing recommendations because they are applied to different municipalities and situations. For example, the same political party will oppose wind turbines in one place, but may approve of them elsewhere.

---

[75] *Ernest Zahn, sociologue allemand*
[76] *www.kiesraad.nl*

For each election, local or national, websites bring together and detail the offers and programmes of political parties. It is possible, by responding blindly to an online questionnaire, without knowing who the proposals come from, to suggest the programmes that political parties best meet the responses and expectations of each person. It is therefore offered to the voter in a factual manner without bias.

The flag out without vehemence

The Dutch openly display their opinions and preferences during elections, as in the United States. They plant the flag of their political party on the lawn or in the windows, which demonstrates an openness and tolerance to diverse political opinions, unthinkable in France.

The population likes to display the colours of the national flag, or the orange colour of royalty. Every household parades during national celebrations and displays a good-natured, tolerant and festive nationalism.

In politics as in economics, the Dutch essentially demonstrate a pragmatic, factual and dispassionate character, certainly not ideological or passionate.

One works young to take charge

From the age of 13, young Dutch people get involved in work, often in stores where they arrange the displays and take care of the cash register, or deliver newspapers to homes. It is not uncommon to find stores and bars staffed exclusively by teenagers and students, who can therefore relatively easily find extra work to finance their studies.

Young people do everything, on their own, with complete autonomy.

They look for accommodation, obtain their grants, and find extra work, alone, without their parents. They work to be able to ensure financial independence, to buy their scooter, finance their driving license, then pay for their studies, which can last a long time, depending on their income and the time they will have to devote to having to earn money. They go to the doctor alone, without their parents, and receive their medical analyses directly at home. They take charge of their health and their contraceptive choices.

> *Everything happens as if we are pushing young people to stand on their own two feet as early as possible. In other words, they learn early to be adults and take responsibility.*

No "n+1" or "n+2" in the hierarchy

The Dutch are always surprised to hear their French colleagues in business talk about their bosses by referring to their hierarchical level "n+1" or "n+2". They are amazed when these same colleagues stand up when a boss bursts into a meeting in progress. In the Netherlands, there cannot be great chefs when they are called by their first names.

No pretend work

At work, effort, honesty and efficiency prevail. We do not try to impress our superiors and colleagues by staying late in the evening, claiming a time-consuming workload and dedication to the company to which we claim to devote a lot of time. On the contrary, extended hours will be perceived as a lack of efficiency that will have to be corrected by changing the way you work in order to be able to leave your office before 5:30 p.m., or even before if the employee has to go pick up their child somewhere.

Privacy before work

As we have seen, the Dutch celebrate their birthdays, and those of others, not only when they are children, but also when they are adults, which will lead them to leave work early that day, or to take vacation days. They will do this by openly giving the real reason without shame, and this regardless of the importance of the meetings planned and which they will therefore not be able to attend. This is exactly the opposite behavior that prevails in France, where it is not possible to put a birthday before a professional reason.

This difference in mentality is also noticeable when employees have to introduce themselves to each other during a round table meeting. While the French will explain their job title, the Dutch will naturally start to explain whether they are married, whether they have children, what sports they practice and what their hobbies are. The same will apply to the announcement of family events that they will share with their colleagues and that they will not hesitate to celebrate, briefly, at the office.

> « *Private life therefore takes precedence over professional life in all circumstances in the Netherlands.* »[77]

Serious about form

The priority given to birthdays and family events does not mean that work is neglected. Quite the contrary, the Dutch always remain rigorous, especially in terms of form, while the French will be in terms of substance. Meetings are managed methodically and efficiently so as not to let them overflow; the agenda, actions taken and time consumed will remain under control. The tasks assigned and their progress status too. Emails will be answered within the hour, a question will not be left hanging for long, to the detriment of the in-depth study of the subject that the French mind prefers to support a complete and concise answer.

Power of conviction

Since their studies, the Dutch have learned to present their work, to document it and to explain its stages and progression. This is not what French students do, accustomed to working on

---

[77] *Un champs de Lys et de Tulipes, Les cultures française et néerlandaises, terreau du Groupe Air France KLM, Jérôme Picard, The BookEdition.com*

the content more than the form of files. This means that at work, the Dutch are the kings of PowerPoint presentations and formatting, to which they devote a lot of time. They will not hesitate to embellish summary or even non-existent content, when the French prefer to get to the bottom of things to get a synthetic overview. One thing is certain, the Dutch know how to present themselves and sell themselves.

Dutch companies thus breathe the flow of trends and new developments in technology, particularly in IT and digital. Employees can be convinced by a sales pitch that unfolds an impressive force of conviction. Not only are the followers sure of themselves when they talk about it, but the teams themselves seem to be waiting for just that, an ad hoc solution that fits their opportunistic, optimistic and go-getter temperament. The methods used and their speed of propagation would arouse distrust, or even rejection, among the French, who do not like to have solutions imposed on them quickly without putting them through the mill of their Cartesian mind. They would prefer to study everything in detail to understand everything before being convinced. Since the Dutch are not resistant to change, they more easily accept the uncertainty inherent in it, even if it means paying the price later, or adjusting course along the way, when the French are contained by their executive desire for security and precaution.

Short-term vision and permanent change

Basically, the objectives, principles and methods that the Dutch favour at work are not the same as in France. The Dutch like efficiency and speed of reaction to adapt to the market and the changing world. From there, they consider things in the short term, preferring small steps that take precedence over quality, to the detriment of robustness and sustainability over time. They like change that brings its dynamism, innovation and movement. They like the future, in small successive short-term steps, small steps that are repeated and make them move forward every day.

I remember a colleague, responsible for inventory logistics, a modest and fairly routine position, who started each day by repeating out loud to himself: "Today is a new chance!" He spent his days looking for improvements to his computer system, making endless updates, optimising storage spaces, doing and undoing everything without being asked. He found satisfaction in daily improvement, stimulated by change and movement. I never heard him say: "Well, we've always done it this way, I don't see why we would change…"

Frankness as proof of seriousness

As in social life, the Dutch are adept at speaking frankly and abruptly, which the French take for a lack of tact. At work, this frankness, which at first glance can be perceived as aggressiveness, is on the contrary a sign of honesty and seriousness in this country. Perceptions are reversed here compared to work in France.

While the French use turns of phrase to smooth things over in meetings, with "I'm not sure of what you're saying, we could talk about it again" or "We should study the subject more deeply before making a decision", the Dutch will say "You're wrong", or "I refuse", or even "There's no way I'm doing this". In addition, these abrupt statements will be delivered in a calm and courteous tone, almost kind, which will completely unsettle the French interlocutor.

Imagine yourself as a French person organising a meeting with your colleagues, some of whom are Dutch. They will easily be able to respond to your invitation with "No thanks, I don't feel like it" or "I'm not interested", while your French colleagues will try to justify themselves and excuse themselves with "I don't feel like it" or "I have other commitments", even if of course, this is not true, for fear of not offending you. You will move your own meetings to accommodate the Dutch colleague, thinking you are accommodating him, you will ask your French colleagues to change their commitments to find a date that suits everyone.

Imagine then having the surprise, a few minutes before the meeting, of receiving a note as terse as it is effective from your Dutch colleague, who ultimately will not attend! A French person would have been profuse in apologies, while for him it was only a matter of priority and efficiency.

> *This frank and direct behaviour is a guarantee of honesty and efficiency. Laziness and lying, even diplomatic, are not part of the work culture. An employee is considered loyal and hardworking a priori. When he acts and decides, it is for the sake of efficiency and for the interests of the company he works for. It would be wrong to interpret this behaviour as aggressive and disrespectful, when by nature, the Dutch hate conflict and prefer compromise and respect for others. It is about being professionally and openly honest.*

In such a work culture, daring to confront and oppose, even sharply, is considered a professional skill that deserves respect. One can confront a colleague head-on in the middle of a meeting, even at a higher hierarchical level, without risking being "grilled" by one's colleagues or superiors. It is understandable that the nerves of the French, in such an environment, would be put to the test.

Quick decision making

This inclination towards change and modernisation is fuelled by very short decision-making circuits. The risk of an untimely decision, which would not produce the expected effects or which would cause problems, will be hidden by this same desire to move forward to find the necessary repairs. Since we look forward without regrets and without criticising people, we will keep this same positive spirit to focus on the situation and on the improvement it requires. The Dutch do not play the stakes personally, not looking for individual responsibilities to blame. They play collectively, in the movement forward, which exempts them from months or years of prior studies.

« It will then be perfectly acceptable to reconsider a decision once it has been made, without taboos. In the Netherlands, it is customary to say that we start discussing once the decision has been made. »[78]

Such a culture works with short decision-making and thus promotes rapid implementation at all levels in the company. Many Dutch companies transformed their offices into open spaces in the 2000s. Many quickly adopted mobile phones to replace landlines. They were quick to substitute personalised avatars for their corporate identity to communicate with the press and social networks. In the 2010s, barely a decade after the explosive appearance of social networks, the European Space Agency, whose technical headquarters are in Noordwijk, the Netherlands, created a friendly little mascot in the image of its Rosetta satellite, then in the middle of a space expedition to intercept a comet in flight. This little character, with the laughing and expressive eyes of a simplified emoticon face (smiley), with solar panels as wings to fly in space, began to issue press releases in his own name, relating his moods during this adventure full of surprises and twists. The little cartoon character "Rosetta" had become the official spokesperson for the mission he embodied. The media played the game with enthusiasm. Everyone jumped with both feet on the train of personalised communication introduced by social networks.

Freedom versus control

A Dutch individual has been educated to be responsible and independent while respecting the cohesion of the group. In such an environment, the manager will be content to monitor the results at fixed deadlines, without supervising in detail the work of his collaborators, whom he trusts and whose wings he especially does not want to bridle. It will be the responsibility of the subordinate, who should not be considered as such, to report

---

[78] *Un champs de Lys et de Tulipes, Les cultures française et néerlandaises, terreau du Groupe Air France KLM*, Jérôme Picard, The BookEdition.com

the problems that he would not be able to overcome alone. In this case, he will not be afraid to mention his difficulties to his hierarchy without it being perceived as incompetence or failure. This is possible when the corporate culture is like a society and its education that does not discipline by personal judgment or by the fear of failure. The good manager here will be the one who will not hesitate to delegate, without being too present, in order to give employees the opportunity to progress and flourish, without the latter feeling neglected, quite the contrary.

This autonomy and trust given a priori, a condition for making individuals responsible and motivating them, cannot work without the possibility of sanctioning if the rules have not been respected or if this trust has been betrayed. In this case, like their police force which can be as affable as it is intransigent, the Dutch do not hesitate to punish quickly, not being hampered by barriers and administrative burdens with Unions. In France, we prefer to control before, because it is difficult to punish after.

We have long observed that upstream controls infantilise and remove the responsibility of individuals, who only ask to give the best of themselves if we trusted them a priori. The French system, because of its difficulty in sanctioning and managing exceptions, leads to adding constraints for 98% of employees, for want of being able to quickly sanction the 2% of those who want to cheat. The Dutch prefer ex post controls, which are much less costly than upstream controls and validations. Especially in terms of trust.

The manager is not an expert

The Dutch manager bases his credibility on his personal leadership and managerial skills. He will not need to demonstrate technical or scientific expertise in the field of activity of his colleagues, the latter taking care of it themselves. He will not have to answer all the questions personally, which will not cause them any inconvenience. The important thing for him will be to be able to rely on the experts in his teams and to consult them before making a decision. His managerial competence lies in his ability to decide between several different opinions that will then be submitted to him.

Such a system therefore forces the manager to consult and involve his teams, whose accountability will be reinforced. Openly lacking technical knowledge, he will not risk deciding alone, by staying far from the teams and the reality on the ground, in a centralised system that would hold all the controls and all the decision-making power. It is always good to confront different opinions and to give the teams the opportunity to make decisions for themselves.

Systematic consultation

From this mentality and corporate culture, which are found throughout society, right down to the political organisation of the country, comes the Dutch atavism to systematically seek consensus and consultation. A leader does not decide alone for everyone, a decision must be collegial.

From this also comes a reinforced autonomy of individuals, who grant themselves the freedom, even the duty, to openly contest a decision that has not been submitted for their approval. In France, we like to proceed by small committees of delegates mandated to represent their colleagues. Whereas in the Netherlands, individuals will not hesitate to contest the decisions taken by these committees if they were not part of them and if they had not been consulted. They will do so without qualms, on the grounds that there was no search for consensus. It will be more difficult in a Dutch company, or in society in general, to impose the implementation of an IT tool or a method at all levels by a decision taken at the top of the hierarchy without consensus.

This obsession with consultation gives rise to palaver that takes a long time. Consulting to obtain everyone's approval is a time-consuming national pastime that pales in comparison to the efficiency of a structured and disciplined French-style organisation. The latter does not waste this time and can spring into action "at the sound of a whistle", as in the army. However, we remember that the French, who want to control everything upstream and who prioritise the quality of long-term sustainable solutions, had to first devote a lot of time to studies and analyses that were as broad and synthetic as possible. Some study and ponder among experts, while others palaver in society.

Enhanced mobility

Since managerial skills can be applied to any position in a company, and the manager does not need to master new technical skills in a field when changing, mobility within the company, or elsewhere, is enhanced. The recovery times for moving from one position to another are shorter, and changes of position are more frequent.

Risk taking

Risk-taking is encouraged because it is seen as fostering innovation, not as a mistake that led to failure. In any case, the responsibility for an attempt that did not produce the expected results will be shared, because the decision will have been consensual. Everyone knew.

In France, it took the formalism of an inter-professional agreement at the national level to try to break its negative connotation by establishing a "right to make mistakes". You can't change your nature. The French, incorrigible thinkers who cannot launch themselves without first analysing, need a legal right to protect themselves, or to encourage themselves. The Dutch, favoured by a society that will have educated them to do so, are doers who act first, then look to see if it works or not, and how to improve the situation so that it eventually passes. Something that is frowned upon in France, it is not uncommon to promote someone after a failure, because they will have taken the risk and shown that it did not work in that direction.

Silo organisation

Short-term responsiveness, individual autonomy, a taste for innovation, and a spirit of initiative are mixed and crystallised in organisations of small autonomous groups within large groups. They gain speed of decision-making and implementation without depending on other teams that do not have the same objectives. They free themselves from the slowness of thinking, the heaviness of studies and administration that the French love, while depriving themselves of overall coherence and greater sustainability. They will lack the structure, hierarchy and discipline to design and implement major state development programs that have made France's reputation, in the nuclear or aeronautics sectors for example. But they excel in research and innovation in a pragmatic spirit that benefits daily life, and of course, in trade, like their renowned international companies such as Shell or Philips, the latter being called the "Société Royale Philips" ("Koninklijke Philips N.V."), like their royal national airline KLM ("Koninklijke Luchtvaart Maatschappij").

In France, this independence that materializes in autonomous and reactive local cells, in "silos", is not viewed favourably. In the country of centralisation and control, of egalitarianism and precaution, such provisions are perceived as threatening to the state edifice or the company. It would then be necessary to bring these overly independent elements into line and hierarchy. This has always been the case throughout history, whether for France or for the Netherlands, each having adopted a divergent mentality and principles.

> « *The Dutch attitude could be compared to a spouse in a couple who believes that by remaining independent, he gains flexibility, speed of execution and adaptation, and that he thus contributes to the development and longevity of the couple.*»[79]

---

[79] *Un champs de Lys et de Tulipes, Les cultures française et néerlandaises, terreau du Groupe Air France KLM*, Jérôme Picard, The BookEdition.com

Professional role playing game

The primacy of private life, which does not allow itself to be invaded by time-consuming work, as well as the protest allowed at work without fear of personal resentment, is indicative of a real split personality that the French have difficulty conceiving. The Dutch adopt an attitude at work that is reminiscent of role play, as in a play where the actors take on the behaviour of a fictional character that they are not in their private life.

Just like a doctor or a psychologist, a good leader will be professionally engaged in his work, but personally detached. You have to know how to evaluate, decide and communicate, always politely and while preserving the motivation of the teams, but without letting your personal affect speak, without taking into account your emotional state. The Dutch have this ability to be able to keep themselves personally detached from their professional commitments, by putting aside their emotions and without fear of appearing impersonal or hypocritical, more than the French whose professional life encroaches considerably on their private life. For the latter, the two spheres, professional and private, are not clearly separated as in the Netherlands, but rather merge into a single sphere in which the person and the function are closely linked. They transpose their personal behaviour that they have in their private life, which means that they tend to take professional remarks as personal attacks. Whereas a Dutch person only takes on a very distinct role at work, whose script written for his function he plays like in a play.

The Dutch therefore leave their true personality at the locker room when they come to work. They play the score assigned to their position, which they will change overnight when they change positions. Similarly, rivalries and confrontations will not prevent them from going for a drink after work with those they have fought against, and whom they will not prevent themselves from finding very nice otherwise, and whom they can hang out with in their free time. This is what allows the Dutch to conduct tough negotiations without personal feelings. They will never fear damaging their personal image and self-confidence, which remain carefully protected in the private sphere. For them, there is a clear difference between doing, the work that one has to do, i.e. "playing", and being, the person one really is.

Business + pleasure = « bleisure »

Something that is hard to imagine for the French, who regret it very much, there is nothing wrong with having fun and flourishing at work. The Dutch practice "Bleisure" completely legally. When they are traveling in a sunny country, that is to say far from their own, they will not hesitate to shorten a working day to go for a walk and enjoy their evening in the sun. They will also extend their business trip to enjoy, at their own expense of course, a leisure weekend before returning home. This is a normal and justified practice that they do not hide, while the French will see it as a dishonest, even illegal, way of taking advantage of the system.

Administrative simplicity

In France, it is an oxymoron, the word administration being necessarily synonymous with complexity and heaviness. Its labor code, which has 3,600 pages, including 675 pages of legal articles, the rest being made up of comments and judgments of all kinds, grows by 100 to 200 pages per year![80] And what is true at the state level is just as true at the business level, where collective agreements only add to the problem.[81]

In the Netherlands, individual autonomy, initiative, efficiency and responsiveness take precedence over concern for employee protection. The state trusts companies to delegate rules negotiated locally directly with employee representatives.

---

[80] *Le Figaro économie, 20 avril 2015*
[81] *La « Loi travail » discutée en 2016 en France vise à corriger ces excès.*

Work less to save more time

Nearly half of Dutch people work part-time, compared to less than 20% in France, which puts the Netherlands far ahead of Sweden or Germany. This choice concerns the whole of society at all levels of the hierarchy, not just workers, technicians or office workers. This choice is justified on the one hand, by the high cost of nursery places for young children who must therefore be collected early in the day, or kept at home a few days a week, and on the other hand, by the government's desire to share work in order to reduce unemployment. It is indeed a permanent balance between professional and private life that this Nordic-inspired company favours. In the Netherlands, the average working time is 30 to 32 hours per week.

Additionally, working more leads to high tax rates which can quickly become discouraging.

The "construction vacation" [82]

For the sake of efficiency and organisation, most construction companies close at the same time during the summer period ("BouwVakantie"). This allows employees and craftsmen to take their vacation, but also not to delay construction sites when a trade is missing while the others want to work. For 3 weeks each year in summer, nothing is built, developed or renovated in the Netherlands.

Retirement at 67

Seeing life expectancy and the age of the population increasing, with a birth rate stagnating at a level not allowing generational renewal since the 1970s (1.57 children per woman compared to 1.87 in France), the Dutch have therefore already raised the retirement age from 65 to 66 in 2014. It stands at 66 years and 7 months in 2022, 66 years and 10 months in 2023 and

---

[82] « BouwVak »

will increase to 67 years in 2024 and 2025. From 2026, the legal pension age may be further revised upwards if life expectancy continues to increase.[83]

Show yourself worthy through work

Christianity has marked earthly life and work with the seal of trial and punishment, reserving the deliverance of a worthy life for the afterlife. Indeed, the word "travail" (work) comes from the Latin "tripalium", which was an instrument of torture made up of three stakes, on which the victim was suspended, like on the cross made up of two stakes. Work, without being torture these days, would always be a source of discomfort and torment.

On October 31, 1517, the monk Martin Luther (1483-1546) posted his famous "theses" against the door of the church of Wittenberg in Germany to denounce the sales of indulgences by the pope and by the Catholic clergy, which he considered otherwise entirely corrupt. In doing so, the German monk overturned the way of thinking about the world and God. It was no longer by doing good on Earth that man could hope to earn his salvation, but by working. Having already received divine grace through the fact of a birth granted, which attested to the divine esteem attributed to all, men had to then show themselves worthy of it through their efforts and their work throughout their lives.

> It was no longer a question of earning one's salvation to redeem an original fault for which each individual bore the guilt by the fact of their birth, but of showing oneself worthy of the divine grace from which everyone benefited at birth, of fulfilling oneself a debt and a duty throughout his life.

With 18% Protestants, including Calvinist denominations including the highly respected royal family, compared to 2% in France, Protestantism is not the majority religion in the Netherlands, any more than Catholicism is in France with 48%.

---

[83] *https://ec.europa.eu/social/main.jsp?catId=1122&langId=fr&intPageId=4993*

However, it is the Protestant work ethic that predominates in all layers of society, its pronounced entrepreneurial spirit being commonly considered as one of the pillars of national prosperity.

Another relationship to work

The social movement in France in 2023 against the increase in the retirement age from 60 to 64 has caused incomprehension in the Netherlands. "So, you French don't like work?» This question, which is not a reproach towards lazy people, on the contrary denotes the difference with which the Dutch view work in their lives. The question could have been "So, you French don't like your lifestyle?". It denotes a very different way of life that the French have never managed to adopt.

There is a completely different balance between work and private life in the Netherlands, which means that one's perception of one's occupation, and one's life, is radically different. Work is more appreciated, there are fewer complaints about it. Hours are shorter in a day. We start earlier, it's true, and, at the cost of a shortened lunch break, we also finish earlier than in France. Peak times for returning to transport begin at 4:00 p.m., then around 5:30 p.m. the offices are empty. Here the simulacrum of work by being present at the end of the day does not exist. If hours are extended to complete a task, we will be more concerned about an inefficiency in the method, which will have to be corrected in order to get home on time. In addition, the separation between professional and private life is clearer. The Dutch thus devote a large part of their time to training and leisure activities, generally in the evening, without experiencing an overload of activity or the feeling of a double day weighing down. Part-time employment is very developed, by necessity when you have children, because you have to be able to take care of them when they also leave school earlier than in France, around 3 p.m. or 4:00 p.m. With the COVID health crisis, working from home, which was already very developed, has only become stronger. At work, as we have already mentioned, relationships are less hierarchical and are more peaceful and less tiring. We change employers more easily and more often than in France, income is greater there, and the social recognition that results from it is also greater. In short, constraints seem to be better accepted when you have the freedom to organise your time, your day, your week, and your life.

Getting rich through work

Unlike Catholics, money is not taboo among Protestants, for whom getting rich through work is an essential value. Personal work gives earned money a certificate of honesty, and claimed avarice respectability.

Since the merger of the French flagship company Air France with its Dutch equivalent KLM in 2004, employees of both companies have been confronted with these cultural and ethical differences. One anecdote among others is edifying. Air France had signed a software purchase contract for its own use, including a discount for itself, but also for KLM, in the event that the latter would later purchase the same software. For its part, KLM had signed another contract for other software, but with a singularly different clause. If Air France were to purchase this other software, KLM would be entitled to a retroactive discount for itself alone. Each had followed its principles, equality for Catholics and prosperity for Protestants.

The disclosure of this affair caused a stir that was also a perfect illustration of the cultural differences within the two communities that were confronting each other. Unlike the Dutch, the French took the affair badly, as if they could not take responsibility for their own behavior, while their Dutch colleagues, who had no intention of harming and had caused no harm to their partners, did not feel found wanting. In accordance with their principles, they saw neither greed nor injustice in it.[84]

---

[84] Un champs de Lys et de Tulipes, Les cultures française et néerlandaises, terreau du Groupe Air France KLM, Jérôme Picard, The BookEdition.com

"I will maintain", national motto

The motto of the Netherlands "I will maintain » (« Je maintiendrai » being kept in French), originally to safeguard the United Provinces[85], still illustrates today this spirit of unwavering resistance, first facing the sea to defend territorial conquests[86], but also to defend his positions on principle. The Dutchman is permanently on the defensive while the Frenchman demands on principle. The difference between these two attitudes of protest lies in the active and initiative-oriented character of the Dutchman, turned towards action and the future, while the Frenchman remains immobilised in the claim and the complaint, often out of concern for equality, which figures centrally in his national motto "Liberty, Equality, Fraternity". By nature, the Dutchman steps up to defend himself, to "maintain" tirelessly. He will do it without thinking, without embarrassment and without malice.

Taxes, return on investment

Dutch citizens do not mind paying some of the highest taxes in Europe. We often hear it said, even by foreigners living in the Netherlands, that the return of taxes is visible in services and in the organisation of society. The feeling of paying for nothing while receiving little in return seems less present in this country than elsewhere.

Taxed from the first euro

The Dutch pay income tax from the first euro they earn. Of course, the scales are progressive, the sums claimed remain measured according to income levels, but sufficient for everyone to be aware of their real and direct participation in the State budget, which in fact becomes that of all individuals.

---

[85] *Voir Chapitre X , Epilogue*
[86] *Voir Chapitre VII, Le combat séculaire contre la nature*

It is remarkable to note that the Dutch react immediately to announcements of public measures and expenditure by evaluating them in relation to the increase in taxes that they will entail.

Guilty debt

Likewise, everyone knows the country's level of debt, which is commonly measured by the debt that weighs on the head and wallet of each citizen. We can recall that France's debt in 2024 amounts to €3,000 billion for 67 million inhabitants, which represents a debt of €45,000 per inhabitants. It amounts to €450 billion in the Netherlands, which has 17.5 million inhabitants, which represents a debt of €25,000 per inhabitants, or around half that of the French.

The word "debt" translates in Dutch (as in German), as "schuld," which also refers to responsibility or guilt for wrongdoing. For example, "het is mijn schuld" means "it's my fault" or "I'm guilty." It is easy to understand that individuals from a Protestant culture do not like this very much.

Massive taxation on automobiles

Only foreigners do not pay to be able to drive on the highways in the Netherlands. Residents must pay a high annual road tax, depending on the weight of their vehicle. For a family car weighing more than a ton, you will need to count on 1200 euros per year. The bill climbs further for SUV vehicles which are generally much heavier.

When purchasing, you will have to pay an additional tax that does not exist in France (the BPM), in addition to the Value Added Tax (VAT). The taxation of a new vehicle may thus represent between 30 and 40% of the sale price of the vehicle.

Fuel taxes are higher than in France, especially for diesel.

Insurance with excess

Health insurance is compulsory as in France. However, for several years it has been managed by private companies which offer insurance contracts similar to those for cars. Depending on your income and age-related risks, you can choose more or less extensive coverage, at variable prices depending on the guarantees. The basic package, which costs €1200 per year, guarantees free access to the general practitioner, with a deductible of €300 for access to the specialist. But at this price, dental care will not be reimbursed.

Health retirement

Health insurance will give anyone who has contributed during their life a pension from the age of 67, independent of any professional activity. This "health" pension, or state pension, is therefore added to that earned through work. This guarantees people who have not been able to go to work, because they are busy at home and with their family, for example, to be able to receive a basic pension whatever happens.

VII. Health, life, then death

★ *The Dutch know the secret of the magic potion.*

★ *Health expenses must be managed like others.*

★ *The Dutch are responsible throughout their lives, with dignity until their death.*

★ *In the Netherlands, death, like birth, is not considered an illness. This must happen to everyone, and it would be useless to try to protect yourself from it by vain and illusory persistence.*

Paracetamol, the secret of the magic potion

Access to a specialist doctor is strictly regulated and limited by the general practitioner. It is impossible to access it directly and personally, without a reference letter from the general practitioner.

In addition, he will limit prescriptions and medications to the strict minimum, first prescribing paracetamol in reasonable quantities to calm the discomfort caused by the illness while waiting for it to disappear on its own, if it is benign. Additional examinations are also restricted. Dutch culture, of Calvinist and Protestant inspiration, considers illness and pain, as long as they remain bearable, as something natural that one must know how to endure.

Anti-antibiotics

Antibiotics are almost banned, they will only be prescribed in cases of vital necessity. It is rightly considered that individuals must challenge their immune system by regularly confronting it with infections. They will emerge strengthened and better protected subsequently, which I was able to personally verify upon my arrival in the Netherlands and throughout my stay. I have rarely been sick.

Without antibiotics, the body itself must fight against the infection for a few days, at the cost of fatigue and certain discomfort. It will be possible for any employee to stay bedridden at home for up to 2 weeks without a medical certificate. However, he can expect checks to check the patient's ill state.

Protocol prescription

Medication prescriptions follow a strict and mandatory protocol. The doctor will prescribe the cheapest generic drug first. If side effects, which should prove to be bothersome appear, the doctor, who will be consulted again, may possibly prescribe another one that is more expensive but more comfortable for the patient. Only if the medicine still does not give satisfaction from a medical point of view, then we can have access to the most expensive and most effective brand.

No fluorescent green crosses

In France, in the heart of villages, towns and shopping centres, pharmacies make their signs in the shape of fluorescent green crosses shine and flash like lighthouses in the middle of the storm. These emergency beacons seem to reassure the French, a people naturally worried about their health. Nothing like this in the Netherlands where people, with a less anxious constitution, do not worry unduly. Pharmacies do not stand out from other businesses, they can be discreet, or even difficult to locate. It is not necessary to signal them since each has its own captive clientele who must necessarily know where to go to obtain their medications. It will be impossible to go elsewhere to obtain medication without a prescription.

Dropper pills

The pharmacist has access to the online medical prescriptions of any patient who comes to buy medicine from him. Only half of the required quantities will be delivered initially, the other half will be delivered halfway through recovery, if necessary. The quantities of pills are counted to the nearest unit, in an unmarked white box, labeled with the patient's name and dosage. Generic drugs are used without knowing the name of the manufacturer.

Generic comfort medications, including the famous paracetamol, or other anti-inflammatories, are available over the counter in drugstores.

One shall ask before going to the emergency room

Except in serious cases or accidents, you cannot go to the first aid service for a problem that could be treated by the attending physician. You must first call on the phone to assess the situation. If necessary, the hospital will send an ambulance or specially equipped bikers with emergency equipment.

In the emergency room, patients eligible for immediate care will be sorted from those who will be cordially but firmly sent home.

The general practitioner is not a psychologist

The doctor, general practitioner or specialist, is not a psychologist who listens to the patient's stories and anxieties. He will not relieve his worries and give him his diagnosis without pitying him or comforting him excessively..

This attitude of speaking about the facts directly, without extending into a long discussion, could be considered by a French person as a lack of listening or compassion. This is an important cultural difference that can leave a bad impression and lead to a sloppy or unreliable diagnosis. French patients, thus surprised and skeptical, who repeat the consultation in France, then note the same diagnoses among French colleagues. The level and quality of medicine are very similar in the two countries, while the listening and attention given to the patient are completely different.

However, in the case of serious pathologies, such as cancer, doctors follow a very different protocol and way of announcing the illness to the patient, devoting much more time, attention and sensitivity. In these serious cases, the patient will then receive the comfort and attention they need.

Your newborn may die

A few days after his birth in January 1996, our newborn son suffered a sudden bout of fever during the night. His whole body had swollen, taken by an oedema which blistered him on all sides. We rush to the emergency service, where the baby is taken from our arms without formality to be immediately taken care of. We waited, distraught, in a room with dim lighting, it was perhaps 2 or 3 a.m., between « dogs and wolves » when fatigue combined with anxiety, when the doctor summoned us. What we were about to hear was going to petrify us. Calmly, he explained to us the situation we were facing. If the infection our baby suffered from was of viral origin, it was likely that he would not be able to survive it given his young age. If, on the contrary, the infection was of bacterial origin, probably nosocomial contracted in the hospital where he was born a few days before, he could survive if the antibiotics took effect. The frankness of the doctor, who wanted to respect the parents' right to know the truth, and the obligation in which he found himself to tell it to us, plunged us unceremoniously into the culture of the country like a cold shower. Our child, who fortunately survived, received every attention and benefited from the most professional medical services. We have no complaints about the competence and effectiveness of Dutch medicine. But we came out of this misadventure completely stunned by the cultural shock.

I had plans, too bad, I have to die...

For the second time in a row in two days, we went to the emergency room. But this time, noting that the red patches of skin were progressing dangerously towards the knee, which indicated the ineffectiveness of the prescribed antibiotic, the doctors decided to hospitalise my wife while waiting to be able to identify the bacteria responsible for the infection. Isabelle found herself bedridden in a room with two other patients her age, that is to say in their fifties. While visiting her, I listened with her, totally amazed, to the conversation one of these women was having with a friend. Her cancer having reached an incurable stage, she took note of it with a seemingly impassive realism.

> « *Of course I had plans, we planned to travel to Asia. But now, I have to cancel, I'm going to die. We all have to die one day.* »

The intern, who had just arrived, only confirmed the hopeless situation. It was only when he declared that the infusion feeding was going to be stopped, because it had become useless, that the patient, until then apparently impassive in the face of her fate, took offense and cried out loudly that she didn't want to hasten her death! We remained petrified in the face of the drama that was playing out straight before our eyes..

Death at the Museum

In 2019, after years of work, the natural science museum "Naturalis" in Leiden opened its doors to the public in a brand new building, with futuristic shapes that promises an exceptional journey into the fantastic history of life on our planet. In such a spaceship, the museum takes visitors on an immersive experience rather than a static and dusty academic presentation. Accompanied by my friend, who is a fan of fossils, megalodon teeth and other trilobites, we climb aboard with curiosity. On the way to the experience.

Indeed, we enter a world with changing ambient lighting, covered with animated and sound wall projections. The animals and visitors are immersed in a cinematic environment that succeeds in producing its effects by enlarging the environment beyond the walls. We let ourselves be transported, admiring the mysterious and vibrant life that envelops us like explorers discovering a forgotten world. We approach the last floor which offers an ode to life, to its extraordinary fertility, by exposing in abundance the genital appendages that nature uses, in the animal as well as plant world, to reproduce. The extraordinary variety of shapes and colours makes the visitors smile who are won over by the comical experience. We thought we would end the experience in this light-hearted way, when we noticed the last stage of the journey that we had to cross: death.

The entrance to the corridor was dominated by large premonitory letters:

"Death is inherent in life; it allows it to regenerate."

In a dark corridor with no escape, under glass bells were arranged the remains of animals that death had paralysed in its immobility. At the end of the row, a last bell was empty. The children could then slip underneath to reveal their hilarious head, the last trophy in the hunting board of the eternal cycle of life and death. The parents, without any hesitation, then took the photo of their child thus immortalised. "Stop moving and laughing, you're dead! ». The two French sexagenarian that we were, understood a little haggard, that the end of the experiment was coming soon. We went out, end of the show.

Let's talk about death

A friend of my wife, who has lived in the Netherlands for 30 years where she raised her three children, was recently diagnosed with stomach cancer, which had to be operated on and treated quickly, and from which she is cured today. She confided to me that having been able to talk about illness and death without taboo on various occasions during all the years she lived in this country, before falling ill, had diligently prepared her to face them.

« When we are confronted with it, we face the enemy better, because we are less terrorised. What is unknown and hidden is scary, and fear doesn't help. »

Personalised funeral ceremonies

One of my partners at the fencing club in The Hague was struck down by a devastating cancer in her early sixties. During the assaults, she demonstrated an extraordinary passion for her age. Her unfailing enthusiasm and good humour did not allow her to survive. On the day of her funeral, all her partners, in white fencing uniforms and gloves, masks held at their hips, lined up with dignity on each side of the coffin to honour her with the fencers' salute, sabres drawn. Her partner had put on her favorite piece of classical music.

Years later, my neighbour was also to succumb to cancer. For the ceremony, her family gathered around her coffin, to hang a garland of beautiful, turgid tulips, bursting with colours.

No therapeutic relentlessness

In hospital or at home, when an elderly person is visibly at the end of his, or her life, the tendency will be not to initiate special care in an attempt to prolong his, or her life by a few months. This will save wasted effort, unnecessary expense and suffering. This approach reflects the fatalistic mindset of the Dutch population, but not that of non-natives, immigrant populations, or international expatriates working in international organisations..

In the Netherlands, death, like birth, is not considered an illness. This must happen to everyone.

Don't revive me

Our neighbour, a former forensic pathologist in the gendarmerie, had seen too many patients resuscitated after cardiac arrest find themselves in a state of severe mental and physical deficiency, to risk suffering the same fate. He carried with him with his papers, a card which stated in large letters "DO NOT

REANIMATE". Some people wear the instruction as a pendant around their neck.

Goodbye, now I want to die

New arrivals, barely settled in our new neighbourhood in the Netherlands, we received a visit from a neighbour who came to say goodbye to us. Suffering from incurable cancer in the terminal phase, he came to say goodbye, in all simplicity, with remarkable calm and detachment, and with great courage, it seemed to us. Two days later, he was euthanised.

> *The Dutch are keen to determine, as much as possible, the time and conditions of their end of life. They want to be able to decide for themselves when and how to die, most often at home, when the situation is hopeless for them. Doctors owe the whole truth to autonomous individuals who demand respect and dignity.*

It must be kept in mind that euthanasia remains strictly regulated by law, and that doctors assume their responsibility. The patient's wishes will be compared with medical reports and testimonies from trusted people. A doctor can never recommend euthanasia on his own initiative, any more than a patient can obtain it alone of his own free will.

In March 2019, the Covid 19 pandemic broke out, which mainly hit the elderly and those suffering from pathologies reducing their immune resistance. To patients who had to go to intensive care to be put to sleep, the doctor had to specify what the chances of survival were. In the case of the elderly, these being weak or even non-existent, many Dutch people decided to end their days at home without illusory respiratory assistance.

The historic legalisation of euthanasia

In 2002, the Netherlands became the first European state to decriminalise euthanasia and assisted suicide. What seemed at the time to be a breakthrough as sudden as it was revolutionary in the eyes of other European countries, was in fact the culmination of 30 long years of illegal practices, changes in mentality in a constantly evolving society, and court judgments, who were trying to adapt to it. It is through their particular approach to social issues that the Dutch were able to reach such a broad consensual agreement on such a sensitive subject [87].

Unlike France where the debate mainly concerns ethical, moral, religious and dogmatic questions, the Dutch take into account the evolution of mentalities and practices actually desired by society, and will focus the entire discussion on procedures, protocol and supervision of implementation to best adhere to this reality and morals.

30 years of illegal practice

The law of April 1, 2002 was significant in the evolution of mentalities, the attitude of patients and the practices of doctors themselves, as well as the constructive and pragmatic approach to the judgments rendered. If this law put an end to three decades of illegal practice of euthanasia, both by individuals and by doctors throughout the country, it was indeed the culmination of a long process of adaptation of rules and laws to the evolution of morals and mentalities in society. This law cannot therefore only mark an outcome, nor close a debate which would have been settled once and for all. It was only an additional step, certainly significant, in a process of evolution and adaptation of a society that was progressive by nature. This evolution is still underway today, 20 years after the adoption of the law.

For 30 years, Dutch society was shaken by cases of illegal, and therefore criminal practices, which each time set a precedent. At each new trial, the judges evolved their interpretations and their rulings according to changing mentalities.

---

[87] *Laurence Petit, consultante Akteos, regards interculturels*
https://regards-interculturels.fr/2019/05/debat-fin-de-vie-aux-pays-bas/

In a society where the individual is better considered within his community and by political parties, patients and doctors presented judges with a fait accompli, charging the legislative system to draw the lessons that were necessary following the evolution of mentalities.

It is in line with this approach, pragmatic and non-doctrinal, that the new legislation of 2002, unprecedented and pioneering at the time in Europe, wanted to protect the medical profession which was already practicing assisted death in an unofficial and illegal manner for many years. From now on, doctors who accompanied their patients to death could no longer be prosecuted, provided that all the practical criteria laid down by law for the implementation of the end of life were strictly respected.

Cases and trials [88]

1973, The Postma affair, or shortening life in the terminal phase

A doctor administered a lethal injection of morphine to his terminally ill mother, following her repeatedly and clearly stated requests to end her life. On this occasion, the court defined the conditions, all necessary, according to which shortening a life was legally admissible:

- a terminally ill patient due to an incurable illness or accident
- unbearable physical or mental suffering
- clear demands to end one's life
- carrying out the operation by a doctor

---

[88] *Nederlandse Vereniging voor een Vrijwillige Levenseinde (NVVE)*
https://www.nvve.nl/informatie/euthanasie/de-euthanasiewet/totstandkoming-van-de-euthanasiewet

1981, The Wertheim affair, or assisted suicide

A person helped another person commit suicide by obtaining a lethal drug and administering it to her. The "patient" was an alcoholic woman, having experienced a succession of tragedies since her childhood, who lived in isolation and who thought she had cancer. On this occasion, the court examined the conditions according to which an assisted suicide became legally acceptable, that is to say not punishable, in opposition to the penal code of the time:

- It did not occur in terrible conditions for the environment and for the person
- It was not possible without the help of others
- The decision could not be made by a single person and always involved at least one doctor who would prescribe the medicine to be used.

1983 The Schoonheim affair, or shortening life

A general practitioner ended the life of an elderly woman following her express and sincere request, by administering a lethal injection. For the first time in the history of Dutch law, euthanasia, as described by art. 293, was proven, but was considered not punishable because it satisfied the precise criteria for ending one's own life in an acceptable manner and which are:

- need for help from a third party
- carefully considered request on the basis of permanent suffering of the applicant
- greater care taken both in the assessment of the question and in the assistance itself

> *The court took into account the evolution of mentalities, the right to self-determination to decide to end one's life being increasingly accepted in Dutch society.*

1993 The Chabot affair, or psychological pain alone

A physically healthy woman ended her life using medication provided to her by her psychiatrist. He concluded that she suffered from depressive symptoms, without presenting psychiatric disorders, that is to say without suffering from mental illness. For years, this woman had endured psychological suffering following marital problems, her divorce, and the death of her two sons. After attempting suicide herself, she finally contacted a psychiatrist.

Until then, justice had never had to make a distinction between physical and psychological suffering. Mental suffering had always been easily associated with a proven somatic or psychiatric illness, which was not the case for this woman who suffered psychologically without having a physical or psychiatric illness..

> *In its verdict, the court avoided the question of whether the woman was ill in the psychiatric sense of the term. It only mattered to him that his suffering was real, unbearable and without hope of remission, and that his request for help was formulated freely and deliberately, which met the classic requirements of jurisprudence in matters of euthanasia. Judges therefore do not consider the cause of suffering, and the absence of psychiatric illness, as important or significant.*

For the first time, the suffering endured was considered, without being linked to a proven illness.

2000 The Brongersma affair, or life becoming unbearable

In April 1998, a former senator ended his life using medication provided to him by his general practitioner. The senator had no serious physical or psychiatric conditions, but his life had simply become unbearable.

As with the Chabot affair ten years earlier, the central question for the court was whether this case involved unbearable suffering without hope of remission. While there was no consensus on a narrow or broad definition of intolerance of suffering, the court opted for a broad definition. Furthermore, in the absence of any prospect of improvement or change, the court ruled that the situation could therefore be considered hopeless. All the requirements of diligence having been respected, the court recognised that the doctor had rightly invoked the force majeure clause. The proven offense was not punished, and the suspect was released from any legal proceedings.

However, the public health ministry, which doubted that "being tired of life" or "wanting to end life" amounted to unbearable and hopeless suffering, appealed the decision.

> *The Court declared the attending physician guilty, without however punishing him, because it considered that the discussion on the justification of assisted suicide, in the case of suffering unrelated to illness, was still in its initial phase in society.*

A deadly virus? do not panic ..

At the very beginning of the pandemic, the French media immediately fell into panic and anxiety. Journalists in France then devoted the entire evening television news to the pandemic, the catastrophic situation in emergency departments and the skyrocketing mortality rate. The media had become anxiety-producing machines that terrorised the poor French people whom this media relentlessness had transformed into frightened victims without discernment and without judgment. In a very theatrical and dramatic announcement, the French president announced "a state of war" throughout the country, to a population reluctant, it is true, to the containment measures which deprived them of a certain freedom.

In the Netherlands, on the contrary, journalists devoted only 15 minutes of the evening television news to the pandemic, with factual information without emotion, with facts and figures, and this without terrorising the spectators. Then they discussed the other usual national and international topics for the remaining 40 minutes.

The Dutch Prime Minister announced in a style devoid of grandiloquence which inspired calm and seriousness, the new restrictive measures to a population which submitted to them in a disciplined manner, at least in the early days.

He then spoke specifically to adolescents and students during a subsequent press conference which was specially dedicated to them, in order to show them compassion and understanding, they who were going to be particularly affected in their student life. He appealed to their sense of responsibility as reasonable young adults.

In France, it was necessary to discipline people during confinement by giving them exit notes like for recess at school. In the Netherlands, nothing was obligatory by law or decree, everyone could go out whenever they wanted, as far as they wanted, as long as they did not meet anyone on the way and that they respected the imposed distances.

If my time has come ..

Compared to the members of my family and the elderly people I knew in France, my neighbours in their seventies and eighties did not panic in any way.

With a coolness that would make the Frenchman that I am pale, they declared that they wanted to follow the barrier measures, but not to fear the virus. If they were going to get sick, it was their time.

For these elderly people it was not a question of rushing towards death, all of them scrupulously followed the distancing measures, and many no longer left their homes. Solidarity at that moment was very important. For people who could do their shopping themselves, supermarkets set up time slots reserved only for those over 70. Home deliveries were also widely used.

It is a high price for the younger generations

In the early days of the pandemic, Dutch academics questioned the lockdown and the expected negative consequences for the economy. They asked without taboo the question, absolutely heretical in France, of comparing the survival of already elderly people with the price to pay and the destruction of the jobs of young workers, often having families to support. We were far from "Whatever it takes"…

VIII. The age-old fight against nature

★ *The Dutch are the conquerors of the sea. They are a people of builders whose threatened territory requires them to be constantly on the alert. By necessity as much as by nature, these people act and take measures to cope in life constantly.*

★ *The Dutch have been protecting themselves from nature for centuries. They tame it more than they protect it.*

★ *Rising ocean levels are not the problem. The storms are.*

A people above ground

Lost in the mists of the North Sea, in the cold and muddy marshy areas of the Rhine delta, with no other natural resource than common peat, the extraction of which only caused the subsidence of the land even lower beneath the sea level, the emergence, literally and figuratively, of a community that conquered much of its territory by pushing back the ocean by force, to become the most powerful nation in Europe at its peak of a golden century in the 17th century, can only be due to an extraordinary strength of character.

Due to a lack of resources and space to live, these peoples of the Rhine delta have built their community and their prosperity literally above ground. They have forged a temperament made of courage and stubbornness, a true vital wealth for these people from the swamps.

Very early on, the Batavian and Frisian peoples had no other choice to survive than to strengthen their land to stay above the swamps and to venture out to sea to fish and trade, in order to improve their daily lives. not very favorable. Then the Rhine delta became the crossroads of maritime traffic and commerce in Europe, which made the Dutch the obligatory importers and exporters of Northern Europe, while reinforcing their innate temperament for trade and negotiation, as well as their ability to explore solutions and alternatives to get out of a difficulty that stands in their way.

A people of builders

The struggle of the Dutch people against the waters is ancestral. It has continued to define the geography of the country as much as the proactive mentality of these people who can never let their guard down and must constantly build to protect themselves.

The danger of being submerged by the waves is constant, as is the need to undertake often titanic work. Uninterrupted centuries of resistance to the natural invader have made the Dutch builders, not of empires, but of an entire country. It shaped their view of the world around them.

The predicted disaster

In 1951, hydraulic engineer Johan van Veen, an expert in water management in the Netherlands, warned the government of the weaknesses of the flood protection system by pointing out the vulnerability of dikes and dams. His warnings were not heeded by the authorities.

In 1953, a storm in the North Sea of rare violence, combined with high tides, succeeded in destroying the dikes on the south-west coast of the country. The disastrous flood that followed caused the deaths of 1,800 people, severely damaging agricultural lands and towns in the region. My neighbour was born precisely at this time, in a neighbouring polder to the north of the flooded areas. His father was unable to attend the birth because he had to remove the corpses of the drowned animals from the fields. The catastrophe was seen as an invasion and aggression of the nation.

The country reacted with a counter-attack plan on a national scale, codenamed "Delta Plan", a real Maginot line facing the sea. The whistleblower Johan van Veen, whom no one wanted to hear, was responsible for coordinating the design, planning and work of the Delta Plan.

The Maginot "Delta" line

The Delta Plan was civil engineering undertaking, which included a complex system of dams, dikes, canals and enormous pumps. The plan was developed in several lengthy stages, but well prepared by careful planning and extensive research. The project, which began in the 1950s, spanned several decades. The first facilities of the Delta Plan were inaugurated by Queen Juliana on October 4, 1960. This date marked the end of the first phase of the plan, which included the construction of the works and dikes of the southwest islands and the Zeeland region. The inauguration ceremony took place at one of the main dams of the Delta Plan, the Eastern Scheldt Dam, in the presence of thousands of people, including engineers, workers, politicians and foreign dignitaries. This inauguration was a historic moment for the Netherlands, it was widely publicised throughout the world.

Today, the Delta Plan is still considered one of the most ambitious and successful engineering projects in the world. It is continually improved and strengthened to this day to face the challenges of climate change and increasingly frequent and intense storms. The plan benefits from a state-of-the-art monitoring system, including satellites, radar, pressure sensors and drones to monitor water levels, winds and waves.

> *The titanic undertaking of the Delta plan, as well as its implementation over several decades in a vast military organisation, certainly denote the voluntarist spirit and the pugnacity of the Dutch, who can never lower their guard in their resistance against the sea and waters.*

Protect yourself from nature

We easily understand that the permanent threat and the incessant work for which the Dutch people excel out of vital necessity, have also forged their mentality and their relationship with the natural elements.

> *The Dutch, in an ancestral and instinctive way, protect themselves from nature more than they preserve it. They need to tame it rather than protect it.*

In today's era of global warming, rising ocean levels and brutal climate change across the world and Europe, the Dutch cannot fall into pessimism, desolation or anxiety. For them, and this for centuries, they know that they will have the country and the living space that they will have been able to conquer and preserve, literally, against winds and tides. The saying goes that "No one can fight nature" except the Dutch.

Global warming and rising sea levels

Today, alarmist speeches of submersion by rising waters hardly cause fear, much less panic. If there is a country in the world that is well prepared for this because it has been fighting against engulfment for centuries, it is the Netherlands.

The IPCC[89] regularly proposes different scenarios concerning the increase in temperatures and its consequences. The preferred scenario today represents an increase of 4.5 degrees Celsius by 2100, which translates into a rise of 1 meter in sea level as the worst-case upper limit. In the previous assessment report in 2010, scientists anticipated an elevation of 93 cm, which has therefore just been re-evaluated by an additional 10 cm.

The problem is not just rising water levels, for which the country has been preparing for decades. The problem that is emerging today is that of the violence of storms and precipitation, the frequency and intensity of which are increasing considerably with the warming of the planet's atmosphere.

On the country's coasts and at the mouths of large rivers, sea level is only one element that can cause a sharp rise in water levels in front of the dikes. In fact, we must add high tides, powerful offshore waves, storms, as well as local effects such as increased precipitation in Central Europe which swells the great rivers of the Rhine and the Meuse. At the mouths of large rivers, these effects combine, with on one side, the sea which rises up the rivers, and on the other, the increased flow coming from the interior of the land, which causes the phenomenon of "high waters". Dutch civil engineering thus calculates a probable "high water" level resulting from the simultaneous combination of all these factors, at 4.60 m above sea level.

---

89 *IPCC Intergovernmental Panel on Climate Change*

Elevation of dikes

With the risk of rising water levels, the Dutch undertook work in the 2010s to raise the level of their protections all along their coasts. Without procrastinating, they sacrificed the view along the boulevard which bordered the beaches of the village of Katwijk, by building high artificial dunes there. No one will be able to contest or oppose the work. Overnight, villas and restaurants were moved and rebuilt further away, the boulevard blocked and the waterfront pushed back. Between 2015, the start of the work, and 2019, the village and its seafront which made its reputation, changed its appearance, something quite usual in the flat country, which is under permanent construction. Under the new dunes built on the seafront, a parking lot with a futuristic design was created which won the "Rhineland Architecture Prize" in 2015, a biennial prize rewarding the best building in the Rhineland.

All dikes on the North Sea front have already been raised to 7 meters above sea level, so well above 4.60 m in the case of "high water". They could be even more so if necessary.

Delta plan barriers activated in December 2023

In December 2023, storm Pia caused chaos in Europe. For the first time since its construction, the storm barrier of the "Maeslantkering" on the Meuse, one of the structures of the delta plan, was activated. This dam is made up of 2 monumental gates in an arc, 22 meters high and 210 meters long. When open, the doors are stored on dry land at the sides of the bank. A computer automatically triggers its closure during an impending high tide that exceeds the Amsterdam Normal Water Level (NAP[90]) by more than 3 meters. In 2007 and 2018, the barrier had also been closed during previous storms, but at a reduced closure level to

---

[90] NAP "Normaal Amsterdams Peil", Amsterdam Normal Level, reference sea level 0 (average level) measured in Amsterdam

test the systems. This time in 2023, it was the first alert in a real situation, causing the complete closure of the structure.

Breakwaters on the closing dike

The north of the country is completely closed by the famous closing dike "Afsluitdijk", which is in fact a giant 32 km long dam closing the southern inland sea "Zuiderzee" and protecting the polders of the surrounding provinces. It is the centrepiece of the work carried out under the direction of engineer Cornelis Lely between 1927 and 1933. The closing dike can contain a water rise of up to 10 meters. This therefore largely compensates for the estimated elevation of 4.60 m in the case of "extreme waters". The remainder, up to the crest height of 10m, aims to limit the excess of breaking waves to a sustainable quantity. This dam faces the waters of the North Sea, a veritable corridor several hundred kilometres wide, channeled to the east by the coasts of Norway and Denmark, and to the west by those of England. Storms coming from the north, which are more and more frequent, hit the country's coasts head-on. Breaking waves at high water could reach around 4.5 m, which is an extreme wave height, but they would be contained by the sea wall twice as high.

Against the power of the breakers, the closing dike is currently reinforced by breakwaters in the shape of concrete starfish, measuring several meters wide and weighing 6 tons each. They fit into each other to form a protective framework along the entire northern side of the dike.

Reconstruct the original landscape

Between the village of Wassenaar and that of Katwijk in the province of South Holland, a small forest of bushes and small shrubs had developed over time in the middle of the dunes facing the sea. One might have thought that these trees helped to secure the dune, a barrier against the water.

In 2010, it was decided otherwise. In order to recreate the original landscape, all the trees were uprooted, the soil scraped and left bare, until the original lunar-looking landscape was recreated. It is true that we also had to take care to preserve the filtration capacity of the dunes which collect drinking water in this location.

"Zandmotor", the sand engine

The fine sandy beaches, which stretch for tens of kilometres along the North Sea, have been subject to strong currents and constant erosion for centuries, causing them to recede inexorably. The Dutch do not hesitate to replenish entire beaches by pumping sand offshore to dump it on the coast.

In this relentless fight, Dutch civil engineering has been attempting an unprecedented manoeuvre since 2011. It involves using the currents' own forces to replenish the sand on the beaches along the coast. Near the city of Rotterdam, on a long eroded coastal strip, pump boats and machines have built from scratch a gigantic deposit of sand pumped from the sea. An artificial crescent-shaped island of 130 hectares made up of sand and gravel has risen from the water, about 1.5 km from the coast. Subjected to coastal currents, the sand from the deposit is eroded and carried along the coast towards the north, to be deposited further on the beaches which are thus reconstituted. The objective of this island is therefore to allow nature to use its power and redistribute the sand on the coast, in such a way as to strengthen the natural defences against storms and floods.

Construction of the island began in 2011 and was completed within a year. Since then, the "sand motor" ("Zandmotor") has been regularly monitored and studied to assess its effectiveness. Once again, this Dutch coastal engineering project is considered a model of innovation combining modern construction techniques with an environmentally friendly approach. Dutch civil engineering has never more deserved the term "brilliant"..

Civil engineering also does archeology

The artificial "sand engine" island, which adjoins the coast, has also become a tourist attraction for beach and water sports enthusiasts as well as for fossil hunters!

While walking at low tide on these stretches of sand, and scratching the touches of shells, I was able to pick up for myself the blackened and hardened phalanges of a large prehistoric animal, probably coming from the foot of a mammoth or an auroch. A friend, an amateur palaeontologist who showed me around, explained to me that around 10,000 years ago, Great Britain and continental Europe were connected by an immense plain known as "Doggerland", today now buried under the North Sea. By pumping sand from the bottom of the sea and dumping it on the artificial island of "Zandmotor", Dutch engineers have brought back the fossilised remains of terrestrial animal life that disappeared 8,000 years ago.

Under construction, days and nights

Everywhere in the country, even in the most remote towns, we are rerouting the tracks, we are digging canals and tunnels, we are strengthening the dikes, we are constantly changing and transforming the urban landscape, whose tracks will always have a tendency to sag on loose, sandy ground. All buildings are necessarily built on concrete stilts which go deep into the ground like in Venice. The cycle paths are paved with bricks which can easily be removed for constant upgrading. Dutch civil engineering shows impressive dynamism.

> *The construction sites never stop, they work day and night, with an organisation worthy of a large-scale permanent military operation across the entire country.*

> *The Netherlands is both Hercules with his prodigious strength who undertakes colossal works, and Sisyphus condemned to roll his rock perpetually.*

Raccoons

This atavism to channel and control nature materialises at the individual level through the meticulous maintenance of gardens and the household, a subliminal guarantee of security and comfort. Nature must be scraped and pruned everywhere.

The Dutch cannot imagine nature as anything other than well-kept. They do not understand nature if it is not transformed and developed by the hands of man.

A clean but polluted Switzerland

The whole country is generally very well kept, well organised and clean. The Dutch, a people of builders, have the genius for well-thought-out urbanisation, which provides, in a small space, roads, sidewalks, cycle paths, rows of trees, without forgetting of course the essential and picturesque canals. Everything is well thought out and meticulously arranged, like a reduced-scale construction of a small village populated by playmobils, or like a painting by the painter Brueghel filled with houses and small characters moving in all directions in a doll-like setting.

However, this cleanliness is only apparent. Although well organised, the country is today polluted by agricultural and flower farms which constitute a leading export industry on a global level. This tiny country on the globe has developed intensive agricultural production to become one of the leading exporters in the world.

Now is the time for de-pollution and sanitation. In order to reduce soil pollution and nitrogen dioxide emissions, it is estimated that half of the farms will have to be closed in the coming years, which poses a major problem for the economy, and especially for society. The farmers defend themselves and have regrouped into a political party tinged with populism, the "Farmers & Citizens Movement" ("Boeren Burgers Beweging BBB"), which has just taken the lead in the provincial elections of March 2023 in a landslide. electoral tide. We are witnessing in the Netherlands, as in many European countries, the confrontation of an urban population, sensitive to the themes of ecology and the preservation of nature, against a rural population which stakes its survival, even if it means continuing to pollute such a small space. The cleanliness and de-pollution of the country are at this price.

The harbour of the future

The Netherlands was built on the delta of the Rhine and the Meuse, and became the main port of Europe there. Maritime trade is the flagship industry of this small, strategically placed country. The deep-water port of Rotterdam has expanded since the 1960s in successive stages, to guarantee it reception capacities equal to the largest ports on the planet, such as Shanghai, Singapore or Antwerp. The latest extension, the "Maasvlakte 2" project, emerged from the sea with, as one might expect, extraordinary measurements: 11 kilometres of dikes, 3.5 kilometres of quays, 560 hectares of basins, 700 hectares of new industrial spaces, 24 kilometres of roads and 14 kilometres of railways… After five years of work, the site was opened in 2013 under the name "Port of the future" to be ready to welcome the super tankers of 2035.

A "FutureLand" museum at the entrance to the area was created to allow the public to discover "what it looks like when everything is big, when everything is gigantic! In FutureLand you experience the development of the new port area of Rotterdam with your own eyes. Maasvlakte 2, the most modern container terminals for the largest ships in the world, but also the latest offshore developments. Let yourself be surprised by digitalisation or the development of promising forms of new energies.»

Offshore wind power, the construction site of the century

The Dutch have seized the problem of global warming and the development of renewable energies in which Europe is engaged, to open the next project of the century, that of offshore wind energy. The incentive to initiate a fundamental reorganisation is once again pressing in the collective culture of a people inclined to undertake large-scale civil engineering programmes.

The next period in the fight against the sea and nature is the development of enormous offshore wind energy potential. The mills of the Middle Ages which dried up agricultural lands and polders, today again become crucial in protection against nature in the form of offshore wind farms.

At the end of the port of Rotterdam[91], on vast land newly reclaimed from the sea to accommodate the giant tankers of the future decade, the gigantic open-air construction site for the assembly of giant offshore wind turbines has opened, whose height (260m) from the water surface to the end of a wing, is close to that of the Eiffel Tower (320m). Dozens of masts and giant wings are lined up on the ground along the quays as far as the eye can see in an accumulation of material worthy of the logistics of preparing for the landing in Normandy. The giant wind turbines are assembled vertically like rockets that are prepared for takeoff, then taken out to sea, on specially designed barges, where they will be attached to columns secured to the bottom under the sea. For several years, the skyline in Rotterdam and Amsterdam, as well as along the coast, is covered with fields of offshore mills. It is a national company which is as well known in the Netherlands as the Ariane rockets taking off from the Kourou spaceport are in France.

---

[91] *Maasvlakte II*

IX. The end of innocence ?

★　*The harmony of social life in the Netherlands could be compared to an old-fashioned innocence, now threatened by the challenges of our modern age.*

★　*Do delinquency and violence, immigration, political assassinations, the rise of populism call into question the apparent carelessness of this permissive, but nevertheless very organised society, which above all likes to live in harmony?*

★　*For decades, far from being late for a crisis, the Dutch have been at the forefront of societal mutations and transformations, well ahead of France..*

Times change, as always

Seen from France, conflictual and anxious, Dutch society gives the impression of having reached a point of stable balance, balanced by moderation, tolerance and compromise. We admire the ability of the Batavian to have succeeded where the French struggle in repeated strikes which break out before any negotiation, in the problems of integration of populations of foreign origin and the communitarianism which results from it, in the polarisation of the debate politics, in the urban violence of social protests, in the opposition, criticism and systematic denigration practiced by political parties. We must concede to the Dutch a certain serenity and a sweetness of life which does not speak its name, but which makes those who claim to follow the so-called French "Art of Living" green with envy. Seen from France, we quickly come to envy this state of harmony by predicting that the Netherlands, which protect itself from the waters and the outside world behind their dikes, will not be able to hold out for long in the face of the increasing dangers that each era modern carries with it. We tell ourselves that this time, the challenges they face will overcome their illusory defenses and take away their innocence from another era.

In truth, the Dutch people have been dealing with developments and fluctuations for centuries, and this is completely natural. They consider the world around them as a vast ocean, moving and changing by nature, in the middle of which they must know how to float and navigate. For decades, the Dutch, far from being behind in a crisis, have been at the forefront of societal mutations and transformations, well ahead of France.

They have developed a remarkable ability to constantly adapt to times and new challenges that inevitably arise, without losing their soul and their identity. They consider crises and changes as the normal course of history and life. Then they get to work.

The crises of the 1980s

In the 1980s, budgetary austerity and the rise of individualism brought their share of challenges that seemed to undermine the Dutch good life.

Delinquency and crime

This permissive society was faced with a spectacular increase in delinquency and crime due to drug trafficking, to the point that insecurity and repression had become the primary concern of citizens. The speeches, usually measured and balanced, hardened to demand more law and order. The government coalition of the moment adopted "zero tolerance" against crime.

This apparently permissive people, who wanted more than anything to live in harmony and security, reduced their tolerance to zero to become very strict in terms of maintaining order and fighting crime.

Furthermore, the government coalition did not neglect prevention by creating jobs for the inactive, and by offering social reintegration programs to delinquents. This approach, pioneering at the time, but which sparked some debate, nevertheless made it possible to reduce the crime rate in the country.

Social assistance and accountability

Furthermore, the role of the welfare state was called into question when social protection encouraged a growing number of people to declare themselves partially or totally unfit for work, and thus become prematurely inactive. This period was marked by a strong mobilisation of civil society, trade union organisations and political parties to find solutions to these well-identified problems. The debates dealt with solidarity and equity, the foundations of the welfare state, while seeking to reconcile the demands of competitiveness and flexibility of the globalised economy. It was proposed to strengthen solidarity between generations and promote mutual aid between citizens to reduce poverty, exclusion and precariousness, while advocating for a reduction in social benefits and increased individual responsibility. to encourage initiative and autonomy.

We then put in place activation and reintegration policies for the unemployed, as well as professional and continuing training to enable workers to adapt to economic changes, while undertaking reforms to reduce public spending and rationalise administration. , particularly in the field of health and pensions.

Immigration and integration

It was clear that the multi-cultural society was only an ideal far from reality, and that it was weakened by communitarianism and a ghettoisation of foreigners who grouped together in neighbourhoods where unemployment and violence were rife.

The Netherlands was one of the first European countries to implement a policy of cultural diversity and integration, rather than assimilation or cultural homogenisation. The government implemented a policy of tolerance and multiculturalism, recognising the cultural diversity of the country and encouraging the integration of immigrants.

It was necessary to promote equal opportunities for all Dutch citizens, regardless of their ethnic origin, and to promote the participation of cultural minorities in the social, economic and political life of the country: Dutch language learning programs for immigrants, recognition of dual nationality, establishment of quotas for ethnic minorities in the public and private sectors, and promotion of cultural diversity in education and the media. This policy was continued and strengthened throughout the 1980s, although with mixed results.

Ecology

The Dutch were very early confronted with pollution problems, due to the density of their population and the number of vehicles in circulation in such a small country, but also by the development of intensive agriculture. In addition, the Rhine delta brought pollution of German, French and Belgian origin to their banks, and the exploitation of natural gas from the northern deposits caused energy consumption and the resulting pollution to surge.

The Dutch have long been aware of the degradation of their natural environment, and sought to provide answers, which positioned them at the forefront in matters of ecology.

As early as 1988, Queen Beatrix urged her fellow citizens to become aware of the urgency of the problem of pollution in her Christmas address which she dedicated to ecology. It caused awareness followed by strong public mobilisation. A sustainable development policy was put in place, with a series of measures to promote more environmentally friendly modes of production and consumption.

In 1989, the Dutch government adopted its "National Environmental Plan", which set ambitious goals for limiting air, water and soil pollution, protecting biodiversity and promoting energy. renewables. The Netherlands was already at the forefront of the fight against climate change, with the establishment of a greenhouse gas emissions trading system in the 1990s. This system, a pioneer in Europe, allowed companies to negotiate and sell emission rights between themselves, with the aim of reducing emissions overall. The Dutch system[92] was considered one of the most advanced and ambitious. at the time. It was strengthened over the years, with the introduction in 1995 of a tax on CO_2

---

[92] *"Environmental Quality Decree"*

emissions in the Netherlands[93]. From 1995, this system served as a model for the creation of a European market. carbon and the establishment of the European Union emissions trading system [94].

Thus, the Netherlands was the first country to introduce a system for regulating greenhouse gas emissions. Their experience helped shape EU environmental policies in this area.

At the political level, ecology had therefore become a central issue in public debates and gave birth to ecological political movements, such as the Green Party (GroenLinks) which was founded in 1989 and which obtained good electoral scores in the years that followed. Traditional parties integrated environmental issues into their programs, notably with the creation in 1989 of a Ministry of the Environment and Public Health.

Awareness of the deterioration of their environment in the 1980s sparked strong mobilisation in the Netherlands, which adopted an ambitious and pioneering sustainable development policy in Europe.

The crises of the 2000s

Cybercrime and ecology

The country still faced problems of air pollution, waste management and reducing greenhouse gas emissions. While statistics showed an overall decline in delinquency and crime in the Netherlands, cybercrime appeared in the 2000s with new practices against which it was necessary to find solutions.

---

[93] *Introduction of the carbon tax in Sweden and Norway in 1991, in Denmark in 1992, in Finland in 1997, in the United Kingdom in 2001, in France in 2014 (Contribution Climat Energie CCE) but which was canceled in 2019 following demonstrations by yellow vests.*

[94] *EU ETS*

Political assassinations

The sudden appearance of political assassinations in a peaceful society was a shock and a major challenge. In 1986, South African anti-apartheid activist Dulcie September, who lived in Amsterdam and worked for the African National Congress (ANC), was assassinated in Paris. In 2002, right-wing populist Pim Fortuyn was assassinated by a far-left activist in Hilversum, while he was campaigning for the parliamentary elections and openly criticising immigration and Islam. This assassination caused an earthquake in Dutch society, which was accustomed to absorbing and mitigating blows.

> « *Our democracy has lost its innocence. The Netherlands has changed. The thread has broken.* »[95]

In January 2044, the deputy headmaster of a school in The Hague, Hans van Wieren, was shot in the head by a young man of Turkish origin.

In 2004, the director and essayist Theo van Gogh, a fierce critic of Islam and director of a controversial film on the condition of women in this religion, was assassinated in Amsterdam by an Islamist. Although the country has not experienced a large-scale attack like those that occurred in France or Belgium, these assassinations were exceptional and striking events which caused strong emotion throughout the country.

After Pim Fortuyn's death, his political party, the LPF, won a number of seats in Parliament, but quickly descended into infighting and scandals, losing most of its seats in the following elections. The assassination of Theo van Gogh sparked debates on immigration, freedom of expression and the tensions that Muslim communities aroused. Reactions to the assassination were mixed, with peaceful protests on one side but also acts of violence on the other.

---

[95] *Melkert, chef du parti travailliste, 7 mai 2002*

Thus, by the end of 2004, intercommunal tensions were particularly high and xenophobia had reached an unprecedented level. Few people still dared to publicly criticise Islam. The assassination of Theo van Gogh had a chilling effect on freedom of expression, even in the Netherlands, where speech had always been free.

That same year, VVD MP Geert Wilders left his party to found the Wilders group, which would soon become the far-right PVV party. Its aim was clear: to occupy the political space left vacant by the death of Pim Fortuyn.

The ostrich policy?

The Netherlands, so peaceful until then, found itself on the brink of an unprecedented ethnic confrontation. The sacrosanct "living together" was threatened. The existence of distinct communities in society was then publicly called into question. The traditional organisation of society into watertight "pillars" had led to the formation of a Muslim bloc, where individuals were taken care of "from birth to the grave", without going through the Dutch identity melting pot or being encouraged to mix with the native population. The famous Dutch tolerance also seemed to be affected. The Dutch realised the harmful side effects of a coexistence based on mutual ignorance. The freedom given to each community to live according to its own rules was more of an ostrich policy than a true model of integration. It became urgent to build bridges between these communities that evolved in parallel without really mixing.

> *Instead of blocking the growing Muslim community, Dutch society focused on empowering them. Instead of continuing to isolate them, they needed to be integrated, with commitments on their part to adhere to the country's values.*

The Balkenende II government took a hard line against crime and implemented a strict immigration policy, accompanied by much more restrictive integration measures, including a "civic integration obligation" (inburgeringsplicht).

A Moroccan mayor in Rotterdam

Secretary of State for Social Affairs between 2007 and 2008 in the Balkenende government, Moroccan Ahmed Aboutaleb, a member of the Labour Party, was appointed mayor of Rotterdam in October 2008 by the Queen, on the proposal of the city council. He thus became the first Muslim mayor of Maghreb origin to head a major European metropolis, in one of the bastions of populism in the Netherlands. His ability to calm inter-community tensions, particularly after the assassination of Theo van Gogh, had been praised by many political figures. He also attracted strong criticism, particularly from Geert Wilders and the radical right, who criticised his dual Dutch and Moroccan nationality.

> *His clear and firm positions on civic engagement made him famous. "Leave if you don't like freedom." In January 2015, following the Charlie Hebdo attack, Aboutaleb castigated jihadists by inviting them to "fuck off" to Afghanistan, or Sudan, if they did not want to respect the democratic values of Western societies. "The Charlie Hebdo attack forces Islam to question itself!" he said in an interview with a French newspaper[96], in which he asked Muslims to sincerely embrace the constitution of the rule of law to better ensure their place in society.*

The popular Ahmed Aboutaleb left office in October 2024 to applause and thanks from his community, after 15 years of remarkable service. His term is widely considered a success. Under his leadership, Rotterdam has become safer, with a significant decrease in crime rates. He has been able to pursue a firm policy against extremism and radicalisation, while promoting dialogue and integration, demonstrating a rare political talent. His strong leadership, pragmatism and ability to unite a cosmopolitan

---

[96] *l'Express, 17 février 2015*

city like Rotterdam have made him one of the most respected mayors in the Netherlands.

None of these crises eroded the Dutch people's commitment to tolerance and their visceral rejection of violence. On the contrary, it reinforced their intolerance of any form of extremism. Their conception of society, entirely focused on maintaining a harmonious "living together"[97], has never been eroded by the blows of crises and the emergence of a multi-ethnic society.

The crises of the 2020s

The current 2020s were not short of new crises which were added to the old ones. There were, in continuation of the endemic problem of drug trafficking which has only continued to develop, death threats from the Moroccan trafficking network, the "Mocro Mafia", against the chief of staff Mark Rutte in 2021, then against Crown Princess Catharina Amalia in 2022, which has since deprived her of a normal student life with her friends. This situation has only reinforced the popularity and affection that the population has for its royalty, embodied here by a young girl prevented from studying and living simply like the others.

In 2019, Dutch farmers triggered a large movement of protests against drastic measures aimed at closing half of the country's livestock farms, to reduce polluting emissions of nitrogen dioxide (Stikstof). In March 2023, the peasants' political party "Citizens' Peasant Movement" (Boeren Burgers Beweging, BBB) won the provincial elections hands down, ahead of all other parties. This victory, as unexpected as it was resounding, could not have been possible without the aggregation of protest votes from another part of the population, exasperated by two affairs which offended the very principles of their life in society. Once again, the crises revealed how the Dutch understand the world, without calling into question their spirit of tolerance and their liberalism.

---

[97] « Samenleving », voir chapitre « La vie en société »

Groningen gas and destroyed houses

The first affair, known as "Groningen Gas"[98], dates back to the exploitation of natural gas in the north of the country in the 1990s, and which gained momentum in the 2000s and 2010s. The exploitation of a field natural gas located in the province of Groningen, started in 1959 and operated since then by the company NAM[99] (Nederlandse Aardolie Maatschappij), caused earthquakes which damaged many houses in the region. Around 100,000 households were affected, and around 1000 families had to leave their homes due to the damage suffered. Since the first lawsuit filed in 2015 by a family from the town of Appingedam against the operating company NAM, many other plaintiffs have joined the legal proceedings to try to obtain compensation for the damage suffered. As of the date of the provincial elections in March 2023, no compensation had yet been granted to the victims. However, in January 2020, the Dutch government announced an agreement between NAM and the victims for global compensation of up to 1 billion euros. But since then, the case has become bogged down in numerous expert opinions and counter-expertise, parliamentary reports and legal battles during the courts.

This affair touches a sensitive chord in the Dutch mentality. Despite a good nature displayed in society, the Dutch people nonetheless feel a certain national pride for their country, small in size, but international in scope due to its economic success. This success was made possible in part by the financial windfall from the northern gas fields, but also by their commercial talent, and above all by their ability to create dialogue and understanding between employers and employees, which they are as proud in the eyes of the world as of their tulip exports.

This famous Dutch-style dialogue and consensus is based on a fundamental axiom: trust. All the former

---

[98] *Groningen gas field*

[99] *Joint venture between Shell and ExxonMobil*

leaders of government coalitions were appreciated for the trust that could be placed in them, and certainly not for their charisma, which most lacked, unlike French politicians who carved out a media profile thanks to their eloquence and verve.

It was often said to compare the two Dutch politicians: "Rather the experience of Balkenende[100] than the charisma of Gerd Leers.". Indeed, Balkenende did not have one, but the trust he aroused was such that "we could have entrusted him with his own wallet, he would have returned it with interest". He was fully trusted to manage state affairs, that is to say, to represent and defend individuals.

The affair of the damaged houses in Groningen had taken a turn going against the trust placed in the politician. All of a sudden, we saw the State turn against its own citizens by sending them lawyers who doubted the good faith of the victims and pleaded against them. The State had become an adversary, trust was broken. Mark Rutte, the current prime minister at the head of his fourth government coalition, was accused of being incapable of resolving a crisis that had lasted too long. Too many promises and actions that did not follow through, which has become unacceptable in the minds of many.

This affair also reawakened the intolerance of the Dutch towards abuses of power which threaten individual freedoms. The financial power of the operating company NAM, accumulated thanks to the gas deposits of which the Dutch know the importance for their economy, turned against them and betrayed both their confidence and their pride. Many citizens cannot bear to see a company that has become a national flagship turn against them. Could we imagine the national airline KLM shamelessly cheating its passengers? The Dutch feel a certain shame in seeing their state and society fighting against the deprived inhabitants of

---

[100] *Prime Minister of 4 government coalitions from 2002 to 2010*

Groningen, while leaving them in need without wanting to compensate them.

The family allowance affair

Another case recently came to shock the sensitivity of the Dutch and their distrust against abuse of power against citizens. The so-called "family allowances" scandal (Toeslagenaffaires) broke out in 2019, when a whistleblower, Pieter Omtzigt, a tax service official, revealed that charges had been wrongly brought against parents accused of family allowance fraud. Brutally, these individuals were forced to repay, without question, large sums of money, which for many would have been impossible for them. Indeed, a parliamentary investigation confirmed that the accusations were unfounded for most of the families charged.

The population could not bear to see the tax services unfairly harass families, some of whom were faced with serious financial problems. Noticing the lack of capacity to provide for their children, social services even went so far as to remove child care from some poor families. Here again, trust was broken when the administration turned against its own citizens. This affair caused great excitement among the population, who noted their helplessness in the face of the excesses of a bureaucracy whose dysfunctions they could not tolerate. The State has still not officially recognised its fault, nor apologised to the accused. Due to the complexity of the computer system, we do not envisage a possible settlement before the 2030s.

These two cases will remain, as long as they are not resolved, a thorn in the trust that the Dutch place in their government, and which remains fundamental in their eyes. Pieter Omtzigt resigned from the ministry and launched his political party, the "New Social Contract" (Niewe Sociale Contract NSC) which obtained 20% of the votes in its first campaign during the legislative elections of November 2023 to renew the resigning coalition.

The rise of populism

The victory of the "Citizens' Peasant Movement" party (Boeren Burgers Beweging, BBB) in the provincial elections of March 2023, then the resounding victory of the far-right party (PVV) of Gerd Wilders, which came first in the legislative elections of November 2023, attest to the indisputable rise of populist parties, like other countries in Europe, such as Italy, Austria or Sweden. The French media, accustomed to the French presidential majority regime, and eager for sensationalism, forget to present these events in the context of proportional elections specific to a parliamentary regime, as the Netherlands has known for generations. They neglect to mention the need to form a government coalition, which necessarily implies compromises, and above all, they do not report the notorious shift in the program of the far-right party (PVV) for these elections, which openly abandoned all its extremist dogmas to only deal with crises that affect the daily life of the population, such as the housing crisis, the health system for the elderly, and above all, the crisis of migrants whose influx totally exceeds capacities reception of the country.

The far-right PVV party did not come out on top in the elections by playing on its traditional extreme and provocative program, which gave it its business when it was in opposition and could criticize at all costs without endorsing no responsibility. On the contrary, the PVV provoked support by explicitly abandoning its caricatured themes of exclusion and Islamophobia, such as the ban on the Koran, the Islamic veil or the closure of mosques. He chose very concrete problems that Dutch society has been facing for some years, namely an acute housing crisis and problems in the health system, in particular the care of elderly people with dementia. The caricatured attacks against the European Union were also relegated out of the program, to allow the party to no longer limit itself to the sterile role of the opponent, but to adopt the responsible attitude of a political party which wants to take into account hand the daily problems of the Dutch.

Above all, at the end of 2023, the far-right PVV party has not won anything yet. It certainly comes first in the ranking of seats obtained (37), but far behind the majority of seats (76) that the future coalition will need to have a majority in the parliament which has 150. Geert Wilders, the head of the PVV must therefore find another 39 additional seats to form the coalition and be able to govern. That is to say that he will probably be in the minority, or tied, within his own coalition.

In countries with proportional elections and government coalitions, the party that comes out on top in the elections is still far from being able to govern. If he does so, it will be at the cost of a coalition, in which he will not be in the majority, or tied, and the compromises that will result. Of course in France, the news of the PVV's relative "victory" in the Netherlands was staged to cause a sensation. It was analysed through the prism of the French majority electoral system, and its notable absence from the practice of the government coalition..

The government coalition system, which means that a single party has never been able to govern alone in the Netherlands since the end of the Second World War, necessarily creates responsibility for political figures who can no longer remain in the political opposition, and a dilution of ambitions by the compromises necessary for the formation of a coalition. In the Netherlands, there is no President or single-headed government made up of a single majority party, but a coalition "Cabinet" of which the leader, the "Prime", is only the representative.

That being said, despite the well-known moderating effects that a coalition necessarily exerts on all its participants, the Dutch were still shocked by the results of the legislative elections of November 2023, and the first position thus obtained by the far-right party PVV.

A natural force of adaptation

Far from being an outdated innocence threatened by the challenges of our modern age, the Dutch mentality represents a natural force of adaptation. In short, the Dutch have sought to respond to these multiple challenges by mobilising their capacity for innovation, dialogue and compromise, in a context of rapid change in their society and their economy.

With an unwaveringly progressive and pragmatic temperament, the Dutch protect themselves from ideological or conceptual fantasies that would hinder their responsiveness to crises. They take the changing world as it comes to them, and act accordingly.

Each crisis will be an opportunity for them to reveal this very particular national character: a serious, hardworking and enterprising country, where originality is often required. In the end, they will always have been able to transform and evolve while preserving their identity.

Set a good example

It is consideration in social relationships, discussions and negotiations, the respectful tone of political speeches, the constant concern for harmony and balance in community life, as well as the empowerment of individuals, which will help the integration and calm of populations of foreign origin. Conversely in France, the aggressive behaviour of demonstrators, the animosity and acrimony of political speeches, the vehemence of the media and social networks, the polarisation of positions, the systematic challenge to authority, the propagation sick with anxiety through television, all this can only set a bad example and amplify the problems more than it can alleviate them.

Compared to Dutch society, French society seems incapable of accepting a changing world and the need to adapt to it. It is not the Dutch who risk losing their innocence, but rather the French who have never known it, and who have been struggling for a long time in a state of permanent nervous and conflictual crisis.

X. At the roots of political culture

★ In countries with a Protestant culture, the scandal is not so much the wealth of others as the poverty of all.

★ The Declaration of the Rights of Man and of the Citizen of 1789 was rewritten in 1948, adapted to the concerns of contemporary times.

★ Rather than egalitarianism, more guaranteed rights and dignity for individuals.

Human Rights: 1948 rather than 1789

France swears by its Declaration of the "Rights of Man and of the Citizen," which it drafted in 1789. Since then, a later declaration, the European Charter of Fundamental Rights of 1948, has prevailed everywhere else in Europe today. This new charter responded to the concerns of the post-World War II era.

Inspired by the American Declaration of Independence of 1776 and the spirit of the Enlightenment, the French Declaration of the Rights of Man and of the Citizen of 1789 marked the beginning of a new political era. Its first and founding article is:

"Men are born and remain free and equal in rights. Social distinctions can only be based on common utility."

After the horrors of the Second World War, the international community brought together a committee of legal experts, including the Frenchman René Cassin, to draft a new Universal Declaration more suited to the concerns of the modern era. It was adopted by the United Nations General Assembly in 1948.[101] The first article of the 1789 Declaration will be rewritten as follows:

"All human beings are born free and equal in dignity and rights. They are endowed with reason and conscience and must act towards one another in a spirit of brotherhood."

This article omits the notion of "common utility" and establishes the individual as a being "endowed with reason and conscience," which grants them autonomy. It also attributes to them a "dignity" of their own. While the first article of the 1789 Declaration did not concern itself with this, mention is made here of social relations and human interactions, which today embody the famous "living together" of the Dutch. Individualism is exercised "towards one another" in a spirit of "brotherhood." All of this

---

101 https://www.humanium.org/fr/normes/declaration-universelle-droits-homme-1948/

reflects profound conceptions and differences in the organisation of society compared to France.

Individual law above national law [102]

The Declaration of 1789 guaranteed rights to individuals as citizens. The definition and guarantee of these rights are therefore conditioned by belonging to a particular State and subject to its power. This Declaration thus establishes the French State and its authority.

In contrast, the Declaration of 1948 conceives of man in a more realistic way than the philosophers of the Enlightenment did, by recognising a profession, a family, a homeland and a religion, which it does not intend to govern. All these affiliations are considered as so many dimensions prior to and independent of the State. This Declaration aims to ensure the protection of man against the abuse of state power and dictatorship.

> *It seeks to protect individuals directly by imposing the primacy of human rights over national law and by offering them, if necessary, supranational protection. International law establishes a supranational moral order with universal vocation.*

Dignity rather than the wealth of others

In 1789, the problem in France was that of the undue wealth and power of the aristocratic classes, confronted with the emergence of the bourgeoisie in a revolutionary context of class struggle. The French Revolution was first a reaction against the inequality of political rights. It was about sharing power with the bourgeois and popular classes, affirming the existence of a people and its freedom within a nation embodied and defended by the State.

---

[102] *https://www.lesalonbeige.fr/les-differences-entre-les-droits-de-lhomme-de-1789-et-ceux-de-1948/*

In 1948, the problem was that of the ravages of poverty and exacerbated nationalisms that had led to dictatorships, war, terrible destruction and monstrous genocides. It was the urgent affirmation of individual rights and the inalienable dignity of each person, sealed in democratic principles.

Excellence rather than arrogance

J. Attali describes the after-effects of this French spirit inherited from the Declaration of 1789.

> « *French culture, for which the scandal is wealth and not poverty, therefore differs from countries with a Protestant tradition for which it is exactly the opposite: the scandal is poverty. In fact, many people in France then confuse competence and arrogance, excellence and privileges, elitism and favouritism. Because we end up denouncing all success, even if it comes from work, as being the translation of an undeserved privilege: as if all success were necessarily the translation of an undue privilege.* »[103]

The Dutch certainly do not denigrate excellence, without however making it an end in itself.

Le libéralisme anglo-saxon

The Nordic countries of Protestant inspiration refer more readily to the spirit of the 1948 declaration, which is less part of a logic of class struggle than of freedom, the guarantee of rights and individual dignity. The Anglo-Saxon countries consider as cardinal values the four freedoms decreed by the American president Franklin Roosevelt in his speech on the State of the Union in 1941 :

1. freedom of speech
2. freedom of religion
3. freedom from want

---

[103] J. Attali https://www.attali.com/societe/arrogance-et-excellence/

4. freedom from fear

In Anglo-Saxon countries, free and undistorted competition is seen as a fundamental protection for individuals, allowing them to undertake, produce, buy and sell, with equal opportunities.

XI. At the roots of Protestant culture

★ *Luther or the theological Reform*

★ *Calvin or Economic reformation*

★ *Henry VIII or State reformation*

Luther: Theological Reformation

On October 31, 1517, the monk Martin Luther (1483-1546) posted his famous "theses" on the door of the church in Wittenberg, Germany, to denounce the sale of indulgences by the Pope and the Catholic clergy, which he also considered entirely corrupt. In doing so, the German monk was going to shake up the way of thinking about the world and God. It was no longer by accomplishing good works on Earth that man could hope to gain his salvation, but by working. Having already received divine grace by the simple fact of his birth, attesting to God's esteem for him, man then had to prove himself worthy of it by his efforts and his work throughout his life.

> *It was no longer a question of earning one's salvation to redeem an original sin for which each individual bore the guilt by the fact of his birth, but of showing oneself worthy of the divine grace from which everyone benefited at birth, of paying off a debt and a duty throughout one's life.*

Lutheranism spread to the northern regions of Germany and as far as Scandinavia. From an economic point of view, this new dogma did not advocate a progressive society: the economy was still to be based on agriculture. Lutheranism is today very present in certain regions of Germany and Scandinavia.

John Calvin: Economic Reformation

Unlike Luther, who denounced the dominant Catholic religious doctrine of the time, the French-born pastor John Calvin (1509-1564) proposed a new conception of society and economic activity. His reform, launched in 1541, had a major impact on the advent of a small-scale capitalism of the middle and urban classes, breaking with the agrarian economy. Craftsmen and merchants could, through their activity, hope to make a profit, albeit moderate, as could lenders and bankers, by lending capital providing a profit carried over from period to period. Even peasants could try to lighten the burden of working the land by contributing their meager savings.

Work, instead of being a punishment, became a praiseworthy occupation to improve one's lot, even a vocation. Honesty, rigor and application to doing the work well were thus elevated to the rank of virtues.

> *Economic success in this world is considered a divine blessing, and thrifty thinking, combined with profitable use of resources, becomes a duty prescribed by Christian morality.*

Calvinism spread mainly in Switzerland, where Calvin resided, in the Netherlands, and also in France.

Henry VIII: State Reform

In England, the Reformation would result in a radical break with the Vatican, when Henry VIII declared himself head of an independent Anglican Church in 1534. This break was motivated by fundamentally new conceptions for society. First of all, there was the "equalisation of the conditions of man". By placing the faithful on an equal footing with their clergy, the Reformation abolished sacred categories, such as that of priests. Furthermore, the break with Rome meant that there was no longer any structure above the States, nor any supranational organisation. The Churches became independent of each other, thus obtaining their autonomy to act and think. This was all that was needed for individuals to benefit from it too.

> *The faithful themselves were no longer seen as submissive and obedient subjects to the dominant religious doctrine, but as active participants in the religious life of their church and, above all, of their community.*

This new conception of earthly society and its economic activities, as well as of the individual within his community and his relationship to the afterlife and to death, have remained cultural and political foundations. Despite the virtual disappearance of religious practice, the Reformation and its implications remain deeply rooted in the mentality of the Nordic countries of Protestant tradition, particularly in the Netherlands.

Tolerance, to support without approving

The etymology of the word "tolerate" reflects well the origin of the notion of tolerance as it began to appear in the writings of Protestant theologians of the 15th century, and especially in Martin Luther, who was the first to use the word "tolerance".

> *The word "tolerate" comes from the Latin "tolerare," which means "to bear" or "to endure." It reflects the idea of putting up with and enduring something, even if one does not agree with it or fully approve of it.*

At the time, the concept of tolerance carried the negative connotation of "to bear," without implying any sympathy or approval, as was to become the case later. On the contrary, Luther, by using the term "tolerance," expressed his frustration and discontent with those who opposed his ideas or the nascent Protestant Reformation. By "tolerance," he prepared himself to bear and endure the criticism of his opponents, without, however, being willing to accept or respect it.

> *At that time, the use of the term "tolerance" meant the endurance that had to be armed to face opposition. It certainly did not reflect a lenient attitude towards the diversity of religious beliefs.*

God does justice, one does not kill each other

The difference, however, with the fanatic religious spirits, lies in the fact that Luther, and later the Protestants of the United Provinces, left it to God to punish deviant behaviour contrary to divine principles.

Since salvation was granted by faith in God, not by human works or efforts, and therefore certainly not by the sale and purchase of indulgences, the doctrine of "faith alone" (sola fide) made each person responsible for his actions before God, who was responsible for judging and punishing. And since no one could escape death, no one ultimately escaped divine justice.

The principle of toleration, which was that of enduring without accepting, associated with the idea that men do not have to render divine justice in their society in place of God, was the basis of an organisation structured in "pillars", separating religious communities and their practices, without them authorising themselves to kill each other. This organisation, which made it possible to evacuate violence, ensured the pacification of a country fragmented into multiple cultural and religious communities [104]. It would later become known as 'pilarisation' and become characteristic of Dutch society as a whole.

Tolerance becomes more tolerant

Religious tolerance, as we understand it today, was developed later, especially during the Enlightenment, by philosophers and thinkers such as John Locke, Voltaire and Baruch Spinoza. These philosophers advocated the separation of church and state, freedom of conscience and a tolerance that became charitable and benevolent towards different religious denominations, and towards others in general. This new altruistic tolerance was to become part of the political and cultural identity of the Dutch people.

The "pilarisation" of society

In the late 19th and early 20th centuries, Dutch society followed these principles of tolerance to the extent of allowing Catholic and Protestant communities to live as they wished, without forcing them to fit into a common national mould. It was

---

[104] Néerlandais, *Lignes de vie d'un peuple*, entretien avec Fouad Laroui, Ateliers Henry Dougier

then tolerated to live separately, each on their own in their respective community, without this being seen as an attack on the unity of the country. On the contrary, separation and compartmentalisation, respecting the religious freedom and free expression of each, thus honoured the fundamental principles of the Constitution [105] that allow peaceful coexistence and social harmony to be maintained. The total respect for the customs and traditions of each religious group led to an extreme partitioning into communities, which were called "pillars". Each pillar had its own institutions, schools, political parties, trade unions and social organisations. Individuals were identified and affiliated to a specific pillar, with interactions between the different pillars being limited. "Pilarisation" was therefore not without a certain social segregation. It divided the whole of Dutch society along confessional lines into distinct religious, political and ideological cells.

The end of the pillars

In the 1960s and 1970s, the Netherlands experienced the social, cultural and political transformations which swept the European continent and which quickly brought an end to the model of pilarisation.

This is the basis for social protest and questions, the traditional structures of society and reclamation, plus individual freedom and equality in the domains of politics, culture, sexuality and civil society. The norms of tradition lie in religion and in morality and questions about the profit of individualism, tolerance, spirit and emancipation of women. Together with the society of diversifying culture and ethnicity, with the arrival of immigrants and coming mainly from Morocco, Turkey, Indonesia and the former Dutch colonies. The religious communities are homogeneous, so they reflect the "pilarisation" and disparity in their rapidity.

---

[105] Articles 6 (liberté de religion) & 7 (liberté d'expression) de la Constitution "Grondwet voor het Koninkrijk der Nederlanden »

The political reforms reflect the electoral systems and the political structures for favouring a representative and diversifying and encouraging the political participation of the citizens, independent of their religious affiliation. And these decades are transformations based on the pilarisation system that characterises the Dutch society, which is also a matter of openness, pluralism and individuality.

A conservative island in a progressive country

Today, there is a whole region, which crosses the country diagonally from the southwest to the northeast, nicknamed the "Bible Belt" (Bijbelgordel) and is characterised by a still strong influence of Protestant orthodoxy, where religious precepts play a central role in daily life. The region is often seen as an enclave of religious conservatism within an otherwise largely secularised Dutch society. It is home to conservative Protestants from the Reformed churches, who practise fundamentalist beliefs and interpret the Bible literally. Religious conservatism is matched by a pronounced social conservatism, with the inhabitants of the belt generally opposed to social developments such as abortion, same-sex marriage, the dissemination of media content deemed contrary to their beliefs and, more recently, vaccination against the Covid-19 virus.

This region stands out in a country that is otherwise rather progressive.

A legacy in advance

By nature, Catholicism is hierarchical and universalist, Protestantism is pluralist. Every Catholic is supposed to submit to the authority of the one true Church, while a Protestant can, if necessary, found his own Church. Religions and their worldviews are very much a reflection of the men who created them and the societies they wanted to build according to their culture and the organisation of their life in society.

Our modern societies are no longer organised around books and printing, which allowed the dissemination of Luther's theses in Europe, but around global digital communication networks, and soon artificial intelligence. A hierarchical and centralised culture is no longer suitable for a world that demands experimentation and individual initiative, which can no longer and no longer wants to "let itself be ordered from above". Today, when we need to be responsive and develop an ability to adapt, a mindset inspired by Protestantism is more appropriate. Modern times will irresistibly make French society a "neo-Protestant" country. Of course, it will not be enough to mechanically turn the buttons and sliders of an economic model. A transformation will take place that will affect national identity, deep culture and mentalities, undoubtedly under the impetus of the younger generations who are taking the place of the older ones.

Dutch society, of Protestant origin and naturally progressive, has inherited a head start.

XII. At the roots of historical culture

★ *Founding Guilds*

★ *A Two-Headed Republic*

★ *The Invention of Tolerance, Freedom of Worship and Thought*

★ *Advanced Urbanisation and Education, the End of the Rural World*

★ *The Huguenot "Brain Drain"s*

It is men who make their history

It is easy to invoke specific facts, isolated from the moving flow of history from which they were extracted. It would be futile to try to escape the perpetual movement that never stops and that constantly transforms societies and men. Why should a particular historical episode have more significance than the subsequent events that followed with as much force and influence on our modern era? Historians, and especially politicians, cannot resist the temptation to pick up scattered arguments and characters to support the writing of a national novel as they please.

> *It is even more difficult to evoke the history of conflicts and incessant alliances between European countries, which, far from distinguishing them from each other, has made them similar in this vast shared European chronicle. All European countries share the same history with their neighbours, allying or confronting them since the time of the Roman Empire, as have all peoples and nations in Europe for two thousand years.*

If the historical reasons remain ambiguous, mentalities and cultures are symptomatic, as if history were only the pretext for the expression of the specific genius of a people and the responses it provides to events, as if stubbornly, every people shaped its own history and its own society no matter what. So much so that, instead of trying to explain the present through historical episodes that took place centuries ago, we would be more inspired to identify the cultural and behavioural constants that history has revealed, without being the cause.

Although close neighbours in Europe, alternately enemies or partners, the Netherlands and France have each followed and established radically different societies throughout history. The Netherlands is the country of the aggregation of small polders conquered from the sea, where everyone has their say and feels responsible for the compromise found to allow the community to survive. A country in which villages, towns and regions necessarily had to get along, because none of them was strong enough to achieve their ends by remaining isolated.

On the other hand, France was the country of large regions that could be self-sufficient, each the size of the Netherlands. They were conquered by a central authority that would always be concerned with controlling the desire for independence. Never, since the conquests of the Parisian royalty and the establishment of the absolute monarchy, has France been able to change its centralising and oppressive model. Whether it was the royalty of Charles VII to oust the English, the absolute monarchy of Louis XIV, the French Revolution in the name of Public Safety, Napoleon I for the Empire, the Bourbons for the Restoration, then all the Republics up to the fifth, each successive regime will have suffered the previous conquests as a threat to its very existence. The central power will have systematically reinforced the structures of state control left in place by the previous regime, with the aim of increasing their efficiency in order to ensure its political survival.

In the case of both countries, it would be the geography, the territories and the intrinsic culture of a people that would have, in the end, made the history of a country more than the historical events that were only episodes.

> *In the Netherlands, a need for solidarity and peaceful unification within a larger group has given rise to a society that has preserved autonomous regions, but which share a sense of responsibility towards the community thus constituted. Conversely, in France, the existence of autonomous regions the size of the Netherlands and having no vital interest in allying with each other, except under the effect of the will of conquest and domination of one over the others, has given rise to a centralising and coercive system aimed at authoritatively maintaining a grouping.*

It is not history that made France, but the French, or rather those who held central power in Paris, who maintained French society at all costs in a centralising and highly hierarchical structure. It is not because France experienced absolute monarchy that it is centralising, but because it never ceased to be so under the threat of dislocation. In European history, France appears to be a unique case compared to its German, Spanish, Italian and, of course, Dutch neighbours.

Historical precursors

Geography shapes the temperament of a people more surely than the historical events it faces. We will nevertheless endeavour to extract from the flow of wars, events and eras that history has carried across the continent, what could have shaped the Dutch temperament, what allowed its emergence, sometimes apparently rapid, but most often resulting from a slow maturation over the centuries, and which has inevitably distinguished it from other European countries.

The invention of tolerance in politics, the formation of a commercial oligarchy and an early form of republic with a sharing of powers, freedom of thought and expression, the constitution of a global maritime empire, the creation of the first joint-stock company and the first stock exchange, a communitarianism pushed to the extreme in society… Nothing less than all this has made the Netherlands, for better or for worse, true precursors throughout history.

Autonomous and prosperous guilds

Merchant guilds were associations of merchants and traders formed in the Middle Ages (12th–15th centuries) to regulate and protect their economic interests. They were often organised by city and grouped together merchants from the same sector or industry. They had the power to set professional rules, regulate prices, control the quality of products, and limit competition. They were also responsible for training and apprenticing new members of the profession.

When Charles V's son Philip II of Spain inherited the Netherlands after his father's abdication in 1555, he took control of it as the new ruler, as well as his kingdoms of Spain and Naples. He applied the same policy of centralisation and religious intolerance towards Protestants, without considering that he was in the country of guilds and merchant cities that reached their peak precisely from the 14th to the 16th century.

In these regions, composed of prosperous merchant cities with a tradition of autonomy and self-governance, the guilds exercised considerable political influence. This urban and merchant tradition encouraged the establishment of a republican political system (1581-1795), led as in Venice by a merchant oligarchy.

The invention of "tolerance" in politics

In 1579, the United Provinces promulgated the famous "Act of Toleration"[106], a real societal time bomb that would become the founding act allowing the construction of a society adept at religious diversity and freedom of expression, a small preserved island surrounded by ever more absolute monarchies and ever more conquering emperors in Europe.

Far from being inspired by altruism or true human tolerance, this Act was originally a purely political treaty aimed at promoting peace and unity between provinces deeply divided by burning religious issues, in order to put an end to the conflicts between them. It was necessary to establish peaceful coexistence between the different faiths present in the region, in particular the Calvinists and the Catholics. In the midst of the war against powerful Catholic Spain, it was a question of strengthening the alliance between all the separatist Dutch provinces by allowing them to concentrate on their common fight against the Spanish invader. By allowing freedom of religion and ensuring the protection of the rights of religious minorities, the act aimed to secure the support and loyalty of the Catholic provinces of the

---

[106] *Egalement connu sous le nom de « Placard de Tolérance », signé dans la province d'Utrecht*

south towards the Protestant provinces of the north, and to enable them to embrace the cause of independence for the United Provinces.

> *The Act of Toleration was originally a peace treaty to make war better.*

Far from being a measure of religious tolerance, the Act of Toleration granted freedom of worship to Calvinist Protestants and Catholics, but not to other religious groups, such as Anabaptists and Jews, who were not included in this protection.

Thanks to the creation of a republic 200 years before the French Revolution, the Act would soon find fertile ground to transform into true tolerance in society and foster the emergence of freedom of thought and expression. Thanks to the Republic, the Act of Toleration would escape its initial limitations to become the constitutional foundation guaranteeing freedom of worship to all subjects living in the Kingdom of the United Provinces, something that would long remain unthinkable elsewhere in Europe.

The act of abjuration, refusal of absolute monarchy

In the midst of the war against Spanish domination, the Provinces rejected the authority of the King of Spain and proclaimed their independence by "The Act of Abjuration"[107] of 1581. This act, which founded the Republic of the United Provinces from 1581 until the invasion by French revolutionary troops in 1795, occurred in the context of the struggle for independence, religious tensions between the Provinces that hindered the union against the occupier, oppression and persecution.

In rising up against the authoritarian domination of the Spanish absolute monarchy in 1568, the rebel Provinces were careful not

---

[107] *Plakkaat van Verlatinghe*

to inflict on themselves another potentially absolute and tyrannical monarchy. They were careful not to choose a hereditary king, but only a political leader and a military leader in the person of William I of Orange-Nassau. They sought to establish a political system establishing greater participation and greater representation for the citizens, which thus guaranteed a counter-power. These were the foundations of the Republic of the United Provinces, which was to become a pioneering model of republican government in Europe at that time.

A republic 200 years before France

Without being able to speak of the egalitarian and social democracy that the Nordic countries embody today, the United Provinces set up from 1588 [108], two centuries before the French Revolution, a tentative republic governed by elected representatives rather than a hereditary monarch, within a confederation of autonomous provinces, each with its own governance and laws. This represented an early form of federalism, with a limited central government and extensive powers granted to individual provinces. Long before democracy, this system, which still ignored the plebs, divided affairs between the patrician families of the upper middle class and merchants, and those of the aristocracy and nobility. Each of the seven provinces had its own government, which functioned as follows: a "pensionary", who dealt with civil and economic affairs, as well as "foreign" policy, and a "stadhouder" in charge of military affairs. The provinces were placed under the preeminence of the richest of them, Holland, whose government was located in The Hague, the federal capital of the republic.

The division of power balanced the tensions and rivalries between the supporters of the royal nobility, especially the Orange family, which supplied the warlords, and the republican merchants. The balance did not yet prevent violent outbursts, as in 1672 in The Hague, when a mob of raging Orangists (royalists) massacred its

---

[108] *Période de la République néerlandaise, de 1588 à 1795*

"pensioner" Johan de Witt, whose statue today stands on the "Buitenhof" square opposite the parliament and the statue of his rival William III of Orange-Nassau, on the "Binnenhof" square.

Freedom of thought and expression

The establishment of the Dutch Republic in the 16th century naturally helped to ensure the application of the Act of Toleration and promoted freedom of thought and expression. This freedom became the exorbitant and extraordinary privilege granted to any immigrant coming to settle and work in the Republic. The Republic being a confederation of autonomous provinces each with its own governance and laws, which fostered a more open and tolerant climate towards new ideas and intellectual personalities. Unlike other royal courts in France and Europe, the United Provinces were not subject to a single sovereign or a single institution exercising rigid control over the arts, sciences and thought. The Dutch provinces and their two-headed governance were relatively autonomous political entities, each city having its independence, which guaranteed freedom of thought throughout the kingdom. The United Provinces were soon recognised as a place where thinkers and artists could express themselves freely, question established ideas and pursue their work without fear of persecution. The environment was therefore particularly conducive to the emergence of new and controversial ideas, scientific progress and important cultural developments.

Young explorer sets his country on an adventure

Born in 1563, Jan Huyghen van Linschoten, who is little known today, is the one who, through his personal initiative, laid the foundations of the Golden Age of the Netherlands, the 17th century during which Holland experienced an exceptional boom and global expansion for a small country. He did so in a typically Dutch way: individually, with an adventurous, enterprising, curious, methodical and pragmatic spirit.

Born in the fishing village of Enkhuizen, he wanted from a very young age to "see and travel to exotic countries, in search of adventure"[109]. As a young teenager, he followed his brother to Spain, to Seville, where he stayed for four years, before going to Lisbon, Portugal. At the age of 20, fluent in Portuguese, he managed in 1583 to get hired as an assistant to the Catholic Archbishop of Goa, in the Portuguese colonies in India. For this curious and bold spirit, it was the ideal observation post within a major trading post in the already developed Portuguese trade network. Goa was at the crossroads of maritime routes through which thousands of ships passed each year. Having access to a wealth of information on the activities of the Portuguese, in particular the reports of the merchants and long-distance navigators who made substantial profits with even more distant countries, such as Japan, the young and shrewd Jan began to copy them meticulously.

In 1587, the archbishop died during a voyage back to Portugal, forcing Jan to also set off back to Europe. He did not die, but was shipwrecked in the Azores, another Portuguese maritime post, in the Atlantic Ocean. He was stuck there for two years, which he used to study again, just as scrupulously, the movements of the Portuguese ships that were sailing to and from the Americas.

He eventually reached the Netherlands, but only stayed long enough to embark on an expedition led by the famous Willem Barentz in search of a legendary, but still chimerical, sea passage to Asia via the northern hemisphere. The expedition ran into icebergs blocking the way north of the Scandinavian coast, and had to turn back.

Finally confined to his home, Jan van Linschoten decided to publish a book of his observations in 1595, aptly titled "Travelogues of Portuguese Navigation in the Orient," in which he compiled information obtained from the navigators, missionaries, and traders he had met, as well as copies he had

---

[109] *Ecrits personnels de Jan Huygens van Linschoten*

made while working at the archbishopric of Goa. He produced a five-volume work on Madagascar, Mozambique, Aden and Arabia, Bengal, Burma, and Borneo.

> *Apart from the picturesque descriptions of the fauna and flora, as well as the customs and habits of the natives, the book is distinguished by the precision of the information relating to the exploitation of resources in the colonies and the lucrative trade of the Portuguese empire. The abundance of wealth and the practical organisation of its exploitation are detailed in a precise and explicit manner, as an incentive to come and help oneself.*

The book immediately caused a sensation among the merchant and trade class of Amsterdam, who launched their first long-distance expeditions, scrupulously following the enlightened advice and precise information of Jan van Linschoten. This was the starting point for the establishment of the immense Batavian maritime empire.

Precursors of shareholding and capitalism

Within a decade, a multitude of maritime trading companies had sprung up. Piracy, scurvy, and shipwrecks made business very risky, and many of these companies survived only a single expedition. Merchants from Amsterdam and Rotterdam competed fiercely, which eroded their profits. While Great Britain had just created its "British East India Company" or BEIC[110] in 1600, which would inevitably intensify competition against the Batavian merchants, the Dutch government decided to do the same and created its own company in 1602: "Dutch East India Company"[111] or VOC. The new company, which brought together all the ships and resources of the small pre-existing trading companies, granted itself a 21-year monopoly on all Batavian trade east of the Cape of Good Hope[112]. All independent trade in

---

[110] « *East India Company* » *EIC puis* « *British East India Company* » *BEIC*

[111] *Vereenigde Oost-Indische Compagnie VOC*

[112] *Afrique du Sud*

the eastern seas was forbidden. But the profits from membership were potentially enormous, with participating merchants taking their share of the vast revenues while paying only negligible taxes. To facilitate the participation of investors, large and small, the United Provinces invented shareholding capitalism.

It is now accepted that the VOC, due to its financial structure and size, was the creation of the first public limited company by participation, i.e. by shares, of such magnitude in the world. The Dutch are considered to be the inventors of modern capitalism with the establishment of shareholding on the scale of a multinational company.

Investors could buy shares in the company to receive profits. Each person could thus invest as they wished and hope for a profit proportional to their investment. Shareholding thus allowed a whole class of the population, less well-endowed than the rich merchants, to obtain income. Dividends generally reached 10 to 15%, sometimes even 25% [113]. It was this capitalist concentration of small and large investors that made it possible to finance the VOC's large-scale maritime expeditions and commercial activities.

Better than the English

The English had founded their British East India Company (BEIC) in 1600, two years before the Dutch East India Company (VOC) was founded in 1602. Both companies were pioneers in using the shareholder structure to finance their commercial activities.

However, the Dutch VOC was much larger and more influential than the English BEIC. It was the largest trading company of the time. Its shareholder organisation and governance were more developed and sophisticated than the English model. The VOC introduced several innovations in its operations, including the issuance of shares that could be traded on a stock exchange, i.e.

---

[113] Mourre, *dictionnaire encyclopédique d'histoire*

the development of a liquid market for shares, and the regular distribution of dividends to shareholders. These practices were crucial to the development of capitalism and the financial system from the 17th century onwards, including the establishment of the first stock exchanges. The VOC also introduced innovations to manage the distribution of risks among investors and the dissemination of financial information.

Long before the French

The emergence of capitalism in the Netherlands fostered the economic flourishing of their "golden age"[114] whose peak was between 1650 and 1670, at the very moment when the French were trying to catch up by creating their own companies in the 1660s: the "Compagnie des Indes Orientales" and the "Compagnie des Indes Ouest". Created late, they were far from enjoying the same success.

In France, world trade and colonial expansion in the 17th century were launched late in a completely different national context that was less conducive to business, by state policies put in place by Louis XIV supported by commercial companies.

> *In the Netherlands, it was the individual initiatives of explorers and traders that had launched the movement 60 years earlier, with no other policy than the spirit of enterprise and free competition. This multitude of merchants was then grouped together within a state structure that respected the participation of its members while encouraging other investors to join. This was the shareholding and the first company of global scope.*

Urbanisation, education and interior scenes

In the 17th century, the United Provinces experienced a dazzling economic and urban boom, contrasting with a France

---

[114] « Gouden Eeuw »

that was still largely agricultural. While French society remained structured around vast rural estates and a landed nobility, the Dutch developed a way of life centred on the city, trade, and education. This gap is reflected not only in the social and economic organisation of the two nations, but also in their artistic expressions, particularly through painting.

In the France of Louis XIII and Louis XIV, the economy was largely based on agriculture. The minister of Henri IV, Maximilien de Béthune, Duke of Sully, illustrated this reality when he stated that "plowing and pasture are the two breasts of France". The majority of French people still lived in the countryside, in a world where access to education was limited, particularly outside aristocratic and ecclesiastical circles.

Conversely, the United Provinces experienced exceptional urbanisation. From the end of the 16th century, Amsterdam, Leiden and Rotterdam became nerve centres of international trade, attracting merchants, artisans and intellectuals. In 1675, around 60% of the Dutch population lived in cities, a figure much higher than that of France. This urbanisation was accompanied by a high level of education: the literacy rate was among the highest in Europe, thanks in particular to the development of schools and printing. The United Provinces were a centre of knowledge, attracting thinkers and scientists from all over Europe, such as Descartes who stayed there for a long time.

This urbanisation and education had a profound influence on artistic production, particularly painting. Unlike France, where art remained mainly in the service of the aristocracy and royal power, Dutch painting was also aimed at a cultivated urban bourgeoisie. Johannes Vermeer perfectly embodies this development. His paintings, such as "The Reader at the Window" or "The Girl with a Pearl Earring," depict scenes from everyday life, highlighting the interiors of bourgeois homes and the importance of education, reading, and commerce. The interiors depicted by Vermeer and other painters of the Dutch Golden Age (Pieter de Hooch, Gerard ter Borch) reflect a world where the domestic space becomes a place of culture and refinement, reflecting an urban and commercial society. These works bear witness to a society where the values of work, education, and commerce shape everyday life, in contrast to the persistent rurality of France.

The Huguenots' "brain drain"

The United Provinces exerted a real magnetism at the time, attracting entrepreneurs, merchants, thinkers, artists, in short, all the talents that Europe had at the time. The flight of the Huguenots from France to Northern Europe, and in particular the United Provinces, contributed greatly to their economic and cultural development. Driven out by the revocation of the Edict of Nantes in 1685, these French Protestants found refuge in a country that guaranteed freedom of worship, thought and expression. This vast exodus was akin to a real "brain drain", where skilled artisans, merchants and intellectuals fled France for more tolerant and prosperous lands. While the United Provinces benefited from this influx of skills and capital, France sank into decline, weakened by the wars of religion and the incessant conflicts under Louis XIV. This phenomenon, comparable to a powerful "soft power" in favour of Hollande, contributed to strengthening its influence and its dynamism, at the very moment when France was losing a precious part of its economic and intellectual elite.

Spinoza, Descartes... and so many others

In the 1590s, Spinoza's (1632-1677) parents, Sephardic Jews of Portuguese origin, fled the Inquisition. They naturally found refuge in the Netherlands. Although the Jewish community was not explicitly mentioned and protected by the Act of Toleration, it was nevertheless able to live peacefully in this environment conducive to the practice of religion and freedom of thought. It was in this community that Spinoza was born, grew up and was influenced by the ideas and values that shaped his philosophical thinking.

After leaving France, René Descartes (1596-1650) arrived in the Netherlands in 1628, first in Amsterdam, then in Deventer and Utrecht. He lived in the United Provinces for most of his life (21 years) where he continued his philosophical and scientific work and wrote his most important works, such as his famous "Metaphysical Meditations" [115].

Philosophers and scholars include Pierre Bayle (1647-1706), a philosopher and writer who fled France for Rotterdam in 1681. His Dictionnaire historique et critique influenced the Enlightenment with its defence of religious tolerance and freedom of thought, and Jean Le Clerc (1657-1736), a theologian and philosopher who was exiled in Amsterdam. Merchants and bankers include Jacques de la Court (1620-1680) and Pieter de la Court (1618-1685), two brothers from a prosperous Huguenot family who were influential in trade and economic policy. Pieter was the author of Interest van Holland, a key text of economic liberalism. There was also Jean de Labat (17th century), a wealthy Huguenot merchant who left France to develop his commercial activity in Amsterdam. Among the printers and publishers who revolutionized the dissemination of knowledge, we must mention Élie Luzac (1721-1796): Huguenot printer and publisher in Leiden, known for having distributed philosophical and political texts of the Enlightenment, notably those of Voltaire and Rousseau, Henri Desbordes (1649-1722), bookseller and publisher active in Amsterdam, who played a major role in the dissemination of reformed and rationalist ideas. Finally, artists and craftsmen were also numerous. We must mention Daniel Marot (1661-1752): architect and decorator, who introduced the French classical style to the United Provinces and worked for the court of William III of Orange, Jean Armand de Lestocq (1658-1721), Huguenot doctor who settled in Holland, then in Russia, where he became an advisor to Peter the Great, and Abraham de Bellebat (17th century), Huguenot goldsmith and engraver who settled in Amsterdam and developed his art there.

---

[115] Voir Annexe F, René Descartes le Hollandais

An entire enterprising, creative and thinking society had thus taken up residence in the north of Europe, in the United Provinces, far from royal absolutism and its persecutions. This was Holland's good fortune and a loss for France, which some historians consider to be the cause of its inevitable decline.

XIII.Epilogue

★ « *Je maintiendrai*", *the national motto in French!*

★ *René Descartes the Dutchman*

★ *Blue + White + Red = Orange!*

★ *The royal and national colour, of French origin.*

★ *The young Queen Wilhelmina coined the expression "The Little Queen"*

★ *A Dutch "lemon" who became a famous French car manufacturer*

★ *Why is "Babybel" cheese wrapped in red wax?*

★ *Should we say "Holland" or "The Netherlands"?*

Beyond profound cultural differences, the Netherlands and France share some historical anecdotes whose origin few people suspect.

« *I will maintain* »

Since 1815, « I will maintain » has been the national motto of the Kingdom of the Netherlands. It is still expressed in French (« Je maintiendrai »). It was the personal motto of William I of Orange-Nassau, governor ("stadhouder") of the provinces of Holland, Zeeland and Utrecht in 1559. He is considered "The Father of the Fatherland" by the Dutch, as he led the revolt of his people against the Spanish occupiers and led the Netherlands to independence. He was assassinated in Delft on 10 July 1584 by the Frenchman Balthazar Gérard.

> *While the French motto "Liberté, Égalité, Fraternité" reflects its Catholic inspiration and its disposition for egalitarianism, at the cost of a restricted individual freedom, the Dutch motto reflects the promise of the princes never to renounce the sovereignty of the Kingdom of the Netherlands. Today, it symbolises this spirit of survival and defence of the national territory against the waters, as well as the need for prosperity essential to this survival, resolutely turned towards the future.* [116]

Orange, national royal colour

In addition to the colours of their national tricolour, "red, white, blue" like the French flag, but arranged in horizontal bands, the Dutch are particularly fond of the colour orange, which is the colour of the royal family. Over time, holidays and national or sporting celebrations, the colour "Oranje" has become the popular national colour. They wear it for all sporting competitions and national celebrations alongside the country's flag. They do not hesitate to dress head to head in orange, to hang garlands of

[116] *Un champs de Lys et de Tulipes, Les cultures française et néerlandaises, terreau du Groupe Air France KLM, Jérôme Picard, The BookEdition.com*

orange pennants throughout the city, to repaint the facades and storefronts orange.

This colour actually comes from the name of the French town Orange located in the Vaucluse department in the Provence-Alpes-Côte d'Azur region, when in 1544, Guillaume, Count of Nassau, inherited the principality of Orange from his cousin , René de Chalon. The royal family then became the House of Orange-Nassau. Since then, the city of Orange has shared the same motto as that of William I of Orange-Nassau and the Netherlands.

René Descartes the Dutchman

René Descartes (1596-1650) is a key figure in French culture, philosophy and science, to whom he bequeathed his famous "critical spirit" which became the cornerstone of the French national spirit. What is forgotten to mention is that the development of his ideas and works took place in the Netherlands, the United Provinces at the time, where he lived for most of his life (21 years, died at 54). He was able to enjoy the tolerant intellectual atmosphere and political and religious stability there, and escape the religious and political conflicts that were ravaging France at the time and which drove away the Huguenots and thinkers. His extended stay in Holland, a country of freedom of expression and thought, allowed him to escape the Inquisition and thus encouraged the development of his philosophical and scientific works.

The "Little Queen" Wilhelmina

The end of the 19th century saw an immense popular craze for the bicycle throughout Europe, in France, in England, but also in the United States. In the Netherlands, the craze spread to all social strata of the population, including the royal family itself. Wilhelmina, who was Queen from the age of 10 in 1890 until 1948, used it in person to travel by bicycle in her kingdom. During an official visit to France in 1896, when she was only 16 years old, the French press affectionately nicknamed her "the little Queen". Since then, the French have continued to name their own bicycles "little queen."

Citroën, a Dutch lemon

André Citroën, the founder of the French automobile firm, was born in 1878 to a Dutch father Levie Citroen, and a Polish mother Masza Amelia Kleinman. He was the fifth and last child of Jewish diamond merchant parents, who left the Netherlands to immigrate to France in 1873. Upon settling in Paris, the family added the French diaeresis to the Dutch surname, changing Citroen to Citroën. The origin of this family name dates back to a fruit and vegetable merchant grandfather who bore the name Limoenman ("lime man") and who transformed it into "citroen" ("lemon"), undoubtedly more appropriate to his profession.

Today, the Dutch are fond of old Citroën cars like the DS and the legendary 2CV, which they assemble in kits, and with which they organise rallies in the country and in France.

The Dutch's affection for legendary historic cars is not limited to this French car model. It is also shared with the jeeps and motorcycles of the American army which landed in Europe during the liberation.

"Babybel" cheese with red wax

Since the Middle Ages, Dutch cheeses, notably Edam and Gouda, have been exported throughout Europe. Their waxed or paraffinised crust protects them from bacteria and ensures the preservation necessary at sea to withstand long navigations. The red colour of the wax comes from the wine in which the cheeses were dipped during the crossings.

Holland, the Netherlands or Nederland ?

Holland is just one of 12 provinces in the Netherlands.:

1. Groningen
2. Friesland
3. Drenthe
4. Overijssel
5. Flevoland
6. Gelderland
7. Utrecht
8. Noord-Holland
9. Zuid-Holland
10. Zeeland
11. Noord-Brabant
12. Limburg

It is therefore incorrect to refer to the country by the word "Holland" only, which was used until recently by the Dutch tourist office itself to promote the country's culture and folklore to foreign tourists. In order to extend the visits to the other provinces of the country, which also have a lot to offer, it was recently decided to abandon the typical name "Holland" and prefer "The Netherlands".

The term "Les Pays-Bas" or "The Netherlands" ("De Lage Landen" or "De Nederlanden"), and all denominations which are in the plural, are incorrect. It refers to the reunion of the Lower Provinces (or the United Kingdom of the Netherlands) after the Napoleonic Wars during the Congress of Vienna in 1815, and which brought together the current territories of Belgium, Luxembourg and the Netherlands, until 1830, the date of the Belgian uprising.

The Dutch are therefore the only ones to use the correct form, the singular name "Nederland", to designate their country, the other names having falsely retained the plural "Les Pays-Bas" or "The Netherlands".

XIV. Annexes

★ *Historical timeline.*

★ *"15 million people" A popular song, which became a national anthem to distinguish itself with humour, which says a lot.*

★ *An information campaign against polarisation and aggressiveness*

★ *René Descartes, the Dutchman*

★ *An almost crazy questionnaire to measure the morale of the population*

★ *Government coalitions since 1950*

A. Historical timeline

		Dates NL	Event and significance	Dates FR	Event in France
		1568	Start of the Eighty Years' War against Spain, led by William of Orange.	1572	St. Bartholomew's Day Massacre, persecution of Protestants in France.
		1579	Act of Tolerance, early steps towards Dutch religious independence.	1598	Edict of Nantes: religious tolerance for Protestants in France.
		1581	Act of Abjuration, declaration of independence of the United Provinces from Spain.	1590	Henry IV becomes King of France, consolidating power.
		1584	Assassination of William of Orange by the Frenchman Balthasar Gérard.	1584	Henry III faces France's religious wars.
		1585	Spanish capture of Antwerp, closing of the Scheldt River, leading to Amsterdam's spectacular growth.	1590	Siege of Paris by Henry IV, rise of Protestant power in France.
Golden century	Republic	1590	States General assume sovereignty of the Dutch Republic.	1598	Henry IV issues the Edict of Nantes.
		1595	Publication by Jan van Linschoten on Portuguese colonies, key to the future Dutch colonial empire.	1608	Foundation of Quebec by Samuel de Champlain, French expansion in America.
		1602	Creation of the Dutch East India Company (VOC), beginning of Dutch colonial trade.	1624	Start of French colonial trade in the Caribbean.
		1621	Creation of the Dutch West India Company (WIC), further colonial expansion.	1635	Establishment of the French West India Company.
		1625	Founding of New Amsterdam (later New York).	1608	Foundation of Quebec, France's American settlement.
		1629-1649	René Descartes settles in the Dutch Republic, writing his major works.	1637	Publication of "Discourse on the Method" by Descartes.
		1639	The Dutch Republic becomes the world's leading maritime power.	1661	Beginning of Louis XIV's reign, centralization of power in France.
		1648	End of the Eighty Years' War, official recognition of Dutch independence.	1648	Treaty of Westphalia: end of the Thirty Years' War, recognition of Dutch independence.
		1649	Descartes leaves the Netherlands for Sweden.	1650	Death of Descartes in Stockholm.
		1667	End of the Second Anglo-Dutch War, New Amsterdam exchanged for Suriname with England.	1667	Start of the War of Devolution, French expansion under Louis XIV.
		1672	End of the Dutch Republic, war with France and England.	1672	Louis XIV invades the Netherlands (Franco-Dutch War).
		1685	Revocation of the Edict of Nantes: massive arrival of French Huguenots in the Netherlands.	1685	Louis XIV revokes the Edict of Nantes, forcing Protestants to flee to the Netherlands.
		1795	The French impose a Constitution, modernizing civil status.	1789	French Revolution, abolition of absolute monarchy.
		1815	Congress of Vienna: creation of the United Kingdom of the Netherlands with Belgium and Luxembourg.	1815	Napoleon's defeat at Waterloo, end of the French Empire.
		1830	Belgian Revolution, separation of Belgium from the Netherlands.	1830	July Revolution in France, rise of liberalism.

Dates NL	Event and significance	Dates FR	Event in France
1839	**Treaty of London, recognition of Belgian independence.**	1830	Belgium gains independence after a revolution supported by France.
1848	**New liberal constitution, reduced monarchical power.**	1848	Revolution of 1848 in France, establishment of the Second Republic.
1917	**Introduction of proportional representation and state funding for private schools.**	1914-1918	World War I, German occupation of northern France.
1919	**Women granted the right to vote.**	1944	Women gain the right to vote in France after Liberation.
1953	Flood disaster in Zeeland, leading to reinforcement of dikes.	1954	Start of the Algerian War, end of France's colonial empire.
1982	**Abolition of the death penalty.**	1981	France abolishes the death penalty.
1991	Maastricht Summit, foundation of the European Union.	1992	France ratifies the Maastricht Treaty by referendum.
1995	**Fall of the Srebrenica enclave, massacre under Dutch UN protection.**	1995	Jacques Chirac elected president, France returns to NATO's military command.
1997	**Treaty of Amsterdam, strengthening of EU institutions.**	1997	France co-signs the Amsterdam Treaty.
2001	**Legalization of euthanasia, brothels, and same-sex marriage.**	2013	France legalizes same-sex marriage.
2002	**Assassination of Pim Fortuyn, rise of right-wing populism.**	2002	Jacques Chirac defeats Jean-Marie Le Pen in the presidential election.
2004	**Assassination of Theo van Gogh, tensions over freedom of speech.**	2015	Charlie Hebdo attacks in France.
2014	Malaysia Airlines Flight MH17 shot down over Ukraine.	2015	Paris terrorist attacks, rise of international tensions.
2023	Right-wing populist PVV wins Dutch elections.	2022	Emmanuel Macron defeats Marine Le Pen in the presidential election.
2001	Legalization of euthanasia, brothels, and same-sex marriage.	2013	France legalizes same-sex marriage.
2002	Assassination of Pim Fortuyn, rise of right-wing populism.	2002	Jacques Chirac defeats Jean-Marie Le Pen in the presidential election.
2004	Assassination of Theo van Gogh, tensions over freedom of speech.	2015	Charlie Hebdo attacks in France.
2014	Malaysia Airlines Flight MH17 shot down over Ukraine.	2015	Paris terrorist attacks, rise of international tensions.
2023	Right-wing populist PVV wins Dutch elections.	2022	Emmanuel Macron defeats Marine Le Pen in the presidential election.

B. Song "15 Million People"

In 1996, the song "15 Million People", originally written for an advertisement for the Dutch postal bank Postbank, broke the ratings charts and, reaching number 1 in the top 40, gained national fame.

Land of a thousand opinions
Land van duizend meningen

The land of sobriety
Het land van nuchterheid

All together on the beach
Met z'n allen op het strand

Rusk for breakfast
Beschuit bij het ontbijt

The country where no one lets themselves go
Het land waar niemand zich laat gaan

Unless we win
Behalve als we winnen

Then passion suddenly breaks loose
Dan breekt acuut de passie los

So no one will stay inside
Dan blijft geen mens meer binnen

The country resistant to condescension
Het land wars van betutteling

No uniform is sacred
Geen uniform is heilig

A son who calls his father Piet
Een zoon die noemt z'n vader Piet

A bicycle is not safe anywhere
Een fiets staat nergens veilig

15 million people
15 miljoen mensen

On this tiny piece of land
Op dat hele kleine stukje aarde

Who do not dictate the laws to you
Die je niet de wetten voorschrijft

Who leave you in their value
Die je in je waarde laat

15 million people
15 miljoen mensen

On this tiny piece of land
Op dat hele kleine stukje aarde

They don't have to go through the straitjacket
Die moeten niet 't keurslijf in

They leave you in their value
Die laat je in hun waarde

The country full of protest groups
Het land vol groepen van protest

No leader who is really the boss
Geen chef die echt de baas is

The curtains are always open
Gordijnen zijn altijd open

Lunch is a cheese sandwich
Lunch is een broodje kaas

The land of tolerance
Het land vol van
verdraagzaamheid

Not for the neighbour
Alleen niet voor de buurman

The big question that still remains
De grote vraag die blijft altijd

How does he pay his rent now?
Waar betaalt 'ie nou z'n huur van

The country that takes care of
everyone
't Land dat zorgt voor iedereen

No dog in the gutter
Geen hond die in de goot ligt

With nassi balls in the wall
Met nassi ballen in de muur

And no one eats dry bread
En niemand die droog brood eet

C. Comparison of cycle paths

	France	The Netherlands	% The Netherlands / France
Area	640 000 km^2	42 000 km^2	6 %
Population	68 million	17,5 million	25 %
km cycle paths	18 500 km	37 000 km	200 %
meter cycle path / inhabitant	27 cm	2,10 m	770 %
Number of bicycles	16 million	20 million	
Number of bicycles per inhabitant	0,2	1,17	

D. Monumental dikes and canals

North Closure Dike	30km, 80m wide
Eastern Scheldt barrier, Eastern Escaut Barrage (Delta Plan)	Composed of mobile barriers and fixed dikes. Total length: 9 kilometres. Number of sections: 65. Weight of gates: 480 tons each.
Haringvlietdam (Delta Plan)	Allows the control of water flow between the North Sea and inland waters. Total length: 4.5 kilometres. Number of gates: 17 large gates
Brouwersdam (Delta Plan)	Separates Lake Grevelingen from the North Sea, while being used as a transport and recreational route. Total length: 6.5 kilometres.
Maeslantkering, New Meuse Dam (Delta Plan)	Mobile barrier that closes automatically in case of storm to protect Rotterdam and the surrounding area. Length of the gates: 210 meters each, 22m high. Weight of the gates: 6800 tons each.
Veerse Gatdam (Delta Plan)	Separates Lake Veere from the North Sea. Total length: 2.8 kilometres.
Dunes	260 km
Dikes	3500 km, including 1450 km along rivers and streams which are dangerous.
Territory below sea level	26 %
Population living below sea level	65 %

E. Land below sea level

A third of the Dutch territory lies below sea level. By adding the areas that are less than one metre above sea level, we get half the country's surface area.

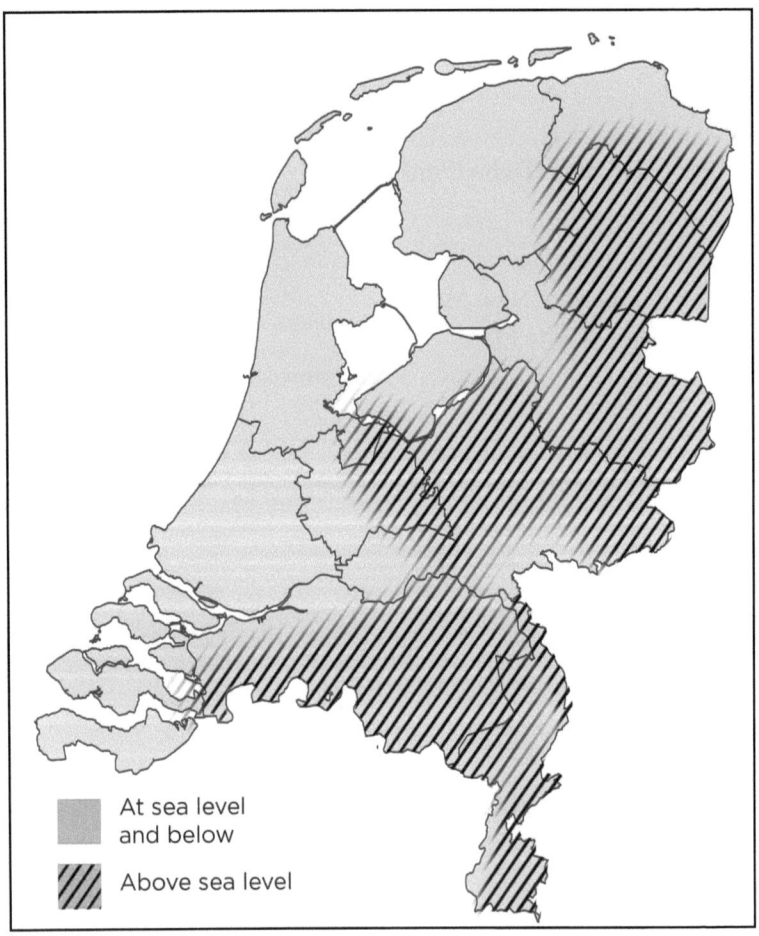

At sea level and below

Above sea level

F. The sectors of the education system [117]

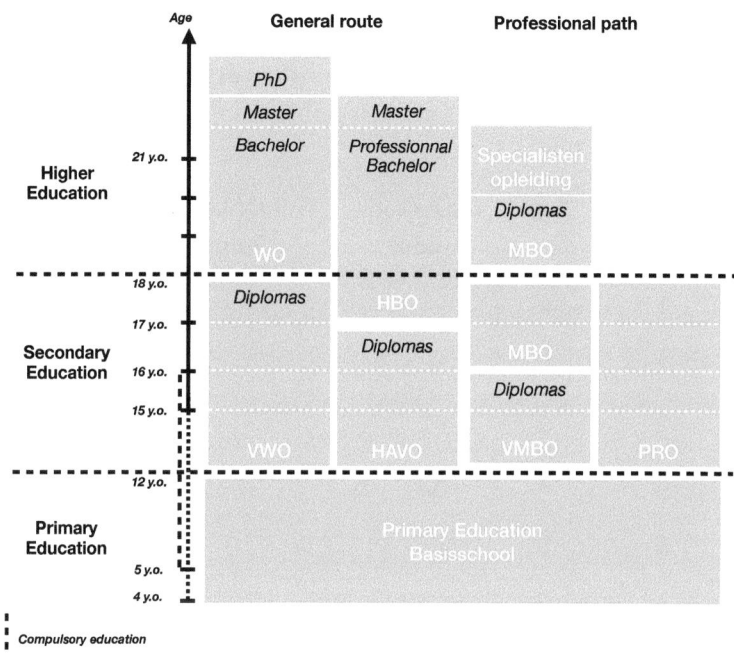

Basisschool: elementary School

VWO: voorbereidend wetenschappelijk onderwijs: pre-university secondary education

HAVO: hoger algemeen voortgezet onderwijs: general secondary education

HBO: Hoger beroepsonderwijs: higher vocational education

VMBO: voorbereidend middelbaar beroepsonderwijs: preparation for secondary vocational education

MBO: Middelbaar beroepsonderwijs: intermediate vocational education

PRO: praktijkonderwijs: professional learning

[117] *CNAM CNESCO Centre d'Etudes des Systèmes Scolaires*

G. School groups and classes

In the Netherlands, the orientation test occurs from the age of 11 in group 8, while it takes place at the end of the 3rd year in France at the age of 15. The results of the test are binding for the student who must then follow the orientation assigned automatically, the parents not being able to influence the decision.

Groupes in NL	Age	Classes in France	Guidance test & diplomas
1	4		
2	5		
3	6		
4	7	CP	
5	8	CE1	
6	9	CE2	
7	10	CM1	
8	11	CM2	CITO Toets
9	12	6 ème	
10	13	5 ème	
11	14	4 ème	
12	15	3 ème	Brevet des collèges
13	16	seconde	
14	17	première	
15	18	terminale	Baccalauréat

H. René Descartes « the Dutchman »

René Descartes (1596-1650) is a key figure in French culture, philosophy and science, to whom he bequeathed the "critical spirit" as the cornerstone of the French national spirit. What is forgotten to mention is that the development of his ideas and works took place in the Netherlands, the United Provinces at the time, where he resided for most of his life (21 years). He was able to enjoy the tolerant intellectual atmosphere and political and religious stability there, and escape the religious and political conflicts that were ravaging France at the time and driving away the Huguenots and thinkers. His extended stay in Holland, a country of freedom of expression and thought, thus favored the development of his philosophical and scientific works. Here is an overview of his life and works.

Youth and education (1596-1628)

• 1596: Born in La Haye-en-Touraine (France). Raised in a noble family, he received a classical education at the Jesuit College of La Flèche. Training in scholastic philosophy, mathematics and natural sciences. Studied law at the University of Poitiers (1616), but preferred to travel and take an interest in various fields of knowledge.

• 1618-1628: Service in several European armies (notably that of Maurice of Nassau in the Netherlands from 1618 to 1620) where he discovered scientific and mathematical ideas in connection with influential figures such as Isaac Beeckman, who inspired him to develop his scientific method.

Installation and major works in the Netherlands (1628-1649)

Descartes settled permanently in the Netherlands in 1628, attracted by the intellectual atmosphere, religious tolerance and political stability. It was during this period that he carried out most of his major works.

Philosophy: the method and foundations of knowledge

• 1637: "Discourse on Method". Written in French to be accessible to a wide audience. This text lays the foundations of his philosophical method: methodical doubt, which leads to the famous formula "Cogito, ergo sum" (I think, therefore I am). The tolerant environment of the Netherlands allowed Descartes to publish without fear of inquisition, unlike Catholic France.

• 1641: "Metaphysical Meditations". Work in Latin in which he deepens his ideas on the nature of reality, the body-mind duality, and the existence of God. This period marks his contact with the academic circles of the Netherlands (notably Utrecht and Leiden), which criticized and debated his ideas. The Netherlands, with its flourishing economy and pragmatic spirit, influenced his vision of a philosophy useful for everyday life.

Mathematics: birth of analytical geometry

• 1637: "Geometry" (in the appendix to the "Discourse on Method"). Descartes introduces analytical geometry, linking algebra and geometry through the use of coordinates (which will become the Cartesian plane). This discovery revolutionises mathematics by opening the way to differential and integral calculus. The Netherlands, where scientific printing flourished, allowed his mathematical works to be widely distributed in Europe.

Natural sciences and physics

• The laws of nature: He laid the foundations of modern mechanics by stating the first formulations of the laws of motion (precursor of Newton). In optics, he developed a theory of light and refraction. His Dutch environment, rich in technical innovations such as the astronomical telescope, nourished his work in optics.

- 1644: "Principles of Philosophy". Synthesis of his scientific and philosophical vision, influenced by Cartesianism debated in Dutch intellectual circles.

3. Final years (1649-1650)

In 1649, Descartes left the Netherlands for Sweden at the invitation of Queen Christina, who wanted to study philosophy. However, the harsh climate and his lifestyle disrupted by royal demands were fatal to him: he died in Stockholm in 1650.

I. Political parties

In the Netherlands political parties are:

Left parties:
- Left-wing working party **PvdA** (Labour Party)
- Left-wing socialist party, **SP** (Socialist Party)

The centrists:
- Progressive and pro-European Democrats **D66**
- Centre left, social democrats **NSC**

Right-wing parties, originally all Christian Democrats
- Christian Union, Reformed Political Party **CHU** (Christelijk-Historische Unie) - later merged into the CDA
- Anti-revolutionary party **ARP** (Anti-revolutionaire Partij) conservative and Calvinist, opposed to the revolutionary ideologies of the French Revolution and its ideals of secularization and secularism - later merged into the CDA
- Christian Union Catholic Party **KVP** (Katholieke Volkspartij,) - later merged into the CDA
- Christian Union **CU** (ChristenUnie)
- Right-wing Christian Union Catholic Democratic Party **CDA** (Christen-Democratisch Appèl)

The Liberals:
- Popular Liberal and Democratic Party **VVD** (People's Party for Freedom and Democracy)

The ecologists
- The Greens **GL** (GroenLinks)

Right-wing populists
- Forum for Democracy **FvD** (Forum voor Democratie)
- Farmers and Citizens Party **BBB** (Boeren Burgers Beweging)

Far right / radical right
- Party for Freedom **PVV** (Party for Freedom)

J. "Schoof" coalition formation process (July 2024)

To everyone's surprise, the November 2023 parliamentary elections put Geert Wilders' far-right or radical right PVV party in the lead. This party was rejected by many. This means that the process of forming the coalition – Explorer, Informer, Trainer – that followed was put to the test.

Parliamentary elections - November 2023: The Party for Freedom (PVV) won 37 seats, becoming the largest party. The VVD (liberal conservatives) won 25, followed by the NSC (centrist) with 20 seats and the BBB (rural party) with 14 seats. As usual, no party had obtained an absolute majority (76 seats). A first blockage appeared when the centre-left parties refused to negotiate with the PVV, citing its extreme positions on immigration and Islam.

The Explorer (verkenner) 27 November 2023: Ronald Plasterk was given the mandate to identify possible coalitions. A right-wing alliance between the PVV, VVD, NSC and BBB seemed viable but politically delicate. There was no shortage of initial disagreements, concerning Wilders' leadership and the migration agenda. The VVD and NSC opposed the idea of Geert Wilders as Prime Minister, judging his divisive image incompatible with stable governance. The PVV insisted on a drastic reduction in migration flows, which worried the BBB and NSC.

First informant – Ronald Plasterk (December 2023 to February 2024) had to negotiate a joint program. Disagreements intensified over migration quotas (annual reduction of 50,000 entrants requested by the PVV). The BBB demanded guarantees for farmers in the face of European climate standards. To ease tensions, the parties eventually agreed that Wilders would not be Prime Minister

Second informant – Kim Putters (February to April 2024) restarted the discussions by integrating a non-partisan mediator. A first compromise was the appointment of a neutral Prime Minister, acceptable to all parties. Former intelligence chief Dick Schoof was suggested as a candidate in March 2024. This was followed by a second compromise, an agreement on a "double priority": strict immigration and investments in the energy transition to satisfy the PVV and BBB respectively

Formateur – Richard van Zwol (May to June 2024) finalized the coalition agreement, entitled "For a secure and sustainable future", which was about 65 pages long and whose main commitments are: Drastic reduction of immigration (annual cap at 40,000). Gradual abolition of humanitarian asylum, except in strictly defined cases. Investments in rural infrastructure and the ecological transition. Labour market reform to boost employment. Portfolio distribution: Mix of politicians and experts. Wilders and the other party leaders did not take up any ministerial posts

Inauguration (2 July 2024) Dick Schoof presented his cabinet to King Willem-Alexander. The members of the government took the oath of office.

K. Government coalitions

Periode	Coalition	Premier	Parties
1950-1956	Drees I	Willem Drees (PvdA)	Labour (PvdA) and Catholic People's Party (KVP)
1956-1959	Drees II	Willem Drees (PvdA)	Labour (PvdA), Catholic People's Party (KVP) and Anti-Revolutionary Party (ARP)
1959-1963	De Quay	Jan de Quay (KVP)	Labour (PvdA), Catholic People's Party (KVP) and Anti-Revolutionary Party (ARP)
1963-1965	Marijnen	Victor Marijnen (KVP)	Labour (PvdA), Catholic People's Party (KVP) and Anti-Revolutionary Party (ARP)
1965-1966	Cals	Jo Cals (KVP)	Labour (PvdA), Catholic People's Party (KVP), Anti-Revolutionary Party (ARP) and Historical Christian Union (CHU)
1966-1967	Zijlstra	Jelle Zijlstra (KVP)	Labour (PvdA), Catholic People's Party (KVP), Anti-Revolutionary Party (ARP) and Historical Christian Union (CHU)
1967-1971	De Jong	Piet de Jong (KVP)	Labour (PvdA), Catholic People's Party (KVP), Anti-Revolutionary Party (ARP) and Historical Christian Union (CHU)
1971-1972	Biesheuvel I	Barend Biesheuvel (ARP)	Labour (PvdA), Catholic People's Party (KVP), Anti-Revolutionary Party (ARP) and Historical Christian Union (CHU) Christian Historical Union (CHU)
1972-1973	Biesheuvel II	Barend Biesheuvel (ARP)	Labour (PvdA), Catholic People's Party (KVP) and Anti-Revolutionary Party (ARP)

Periode	Coalition	Premier	Parties
1973-1977	Den Uyl	Joop den Uyl (PvdA)	Labour (PvdA), Catholic People's Party (KVP), Anti-Revolutionary Party (ARP) and Christian Historical Union (CHU)
1977-1981	Van Agt I	Dries van Agt (CDA)	Labour (PvdA), Democrats 66 (D66) and Catholic People's Party (KVP)
1981-1982	Van Agt II	Dries van Agt (CDA)	Labour (PvdA), Democrats 66 (D66) and Catholic People's Party (KVP)
1982-1986	Lubbers I	Ruud Lubbers (CDA)	Labour (PvdA), Democrats 66 (D66) and Catholic People's Party (KVP)
1986-1989	Lubbers II	Ruud Lubbers (CDA)	Labour (PvdA), Democrats 66 (D66) and Catholic People's Party (KVP)
1989-1994	Lubbers III	Ruud Lubbers (CDA)	Labour (PvdA), Democrats 66 (D66) and Catholic People's Party (KVP).
1994-2002	Kok I & II	Wim Kok (PvdA)	Labour (PvdA), Liberal Democratic People's Party (VVD) and Democrats 66 (D66)
2002-2003	Balkenende I	Jan Peter Balkenende (CDA)	Christian Democrats (CDA), Liberal Democratic People's Party (VVD) and Pim Fortuyn List (LPF)
2003-2006	Balkenende II	Jan Peter Balkenende (CDA)	Christian Democrats (CDA), Liberal Democratic People's Party (VVD) and Democrats 66 (D66)
2006-2007	Balkenende III	Jan Peter Balkenende (CDA)	Christian Democrats (CDA), Labour Party (PvdA) and Christian Union (CU)

Periode	Coalition	Premier	Parties
2007-2010	Balkenende IV	Jan Peter Balkenende (CDA), Wouter Bos (PvdA)	Christian Democrats (CDA), Labour Party (PvdA) and Christian Union (CU)
2010-2012	Rutte I	Mark Rutte (VVD)	Liberal (VVD) and Labour Party (PvdA)
2012-2017	Rutte II	Mark Rutte (VVD)	Liberal (VVD) and Labour Party (PvdA)
2017-2021	Rutte III	Mark Rutte (VVD)	Liberal Coalition (VVD), Democrats 66 (D66), ChristenUnie (CU) and Christian Democratic Appeal (CDA)
2021-2023	Rutte IV	Mark Rutte (VVD)	Liberal Coalition (VVD), Democrats 66 (D66), ChristenUnie (CU) and Progressive Party (PvdA)
2023-2023	Rutte IV	Mark Rutte (VVD)	Liberal Coalition (VVD), Democrats 66 (D66), ChristenUnie (CU), Christian Democrats (CDA)
2024 - ...	Gert Wilders I		Party for Freedom (PVV), Liberal Coalition (VVD), Peasants and Citizens Movement (BBB), New Social Contract (NSC)

L. Duration of coalition formation

When disagreements paralyse a coalition, or when a new one has to be formed following elections that reshuffle the cards, the current government coalition is closed and new negotiations for a new coalition begin again. These can even last months, up to 8 months for the last Rutte IV coalition (2021-2023)!

During these times of negotiations to form coalitions, it is democracy and parliamentary negotiation on all programmes that are working at full speed.

Coalition	Year	Duration of formation	Durée en months
Kok I	1994	95 days	3 months
Rutte I	2010	127 days	4 months
Rutte II	2012	54 days	2 months
Rutte III	2017	225 days	8 months
Rutte IV	2021	225 days	8 months

M. Rising sea levels

The IPCC proposes different scenarios for temperature increase and its consequences. Previously, we used to talk about "RCP" scenarios, but today we talk about "SSP" scenarios. For the safety of the country, the authorities are choosing the most likely scenario, previously RCP8.5, now SSP5-8.5. This represents an increase of 4.5 degrees Celsius by 2100 and now translates into a sea level rise of 1.01 meters as the worst-case upper limit. In the previous assessment report in 2010, Dutch scientists predicted a rise of 93 cm, which has now been raised by another 10 cm.

N. The strikes

	France	The Netherlands
2003	Teachers, Intermittent workers in the entertainment industry, Cultural sector (Pension reform)	
2004		Public transport
2006	Public transport (pension reform)	Nurses
2007	Refineries (pension reform)	
2010	Intermittent workers in the entertainment industry (unemployment & pension reform)	
2014	SNCF railway workers (pension reform)	
2018	Public transport, education, health (pension reform)	
2019	"Lawyers	Teachers
2020	Public transport, education, health (pension reform)"	Construction
2021	Intermittent workers in the entertainment industry (COVID)	Health, transport, education (COVID)

O. Demonstrations

	France	The Netherlands
2003	Pension reform	War in Iraq
2006	First employment contract CPE (high school students)	
2010	Pension reform	
2011		Social inequality
2012		Budgetary austerity
2016	Labor law	Rise of the extreme right, racism, xenophobia
2018	Yellow vests	
2019	Drop in income (farmers) Pension reform	Global warming (youth) Reduction of nitrogen emissions (farmers)
2020	Agricultural crisis (farmers)	Reduction of nitrogen emissions, reduction of livestock (farmers)
2021	Mercosur free trade agreement, Drop in sales prices, Reform of disadvantaged areas (farmers)	Imports of products (farmers) Reduction of nitrogen emissions (farmers) »
2022	Agricultural crisis (farmers)	Reduction of nitrogen emissions (farmers)
2023	Pension reform	

P. Riots

	France	The Netherlands
2005	Suburbs	
2007		Gouda
2010		Amsterdam
2018	Yellow vests	
2020	Suburbs and urban areas (COVID)	The Hague (COVID)
2021	Suburbs and urban areas (COVID)	Amsterdam, Eindhoven, Rotterdam (COVID)
2023	Suburbs	

Q. Campaign against polarisation [118]

In May 2023, in order to preserve "living together", in other words harmonious life in community, the SIRE association launched an information and action campaign to preserve a balance threatened by the rise of polarisation in public debate. The aim was to denounce its harmful effects, in particular the aggressiveness that it can induce in human relationships:

"Don't move away when polarisation is approaching".

The campaign aims to warn of the sneaky signs of bad relationships, and above all, it aims to give practical advice to be implemented by everyone in order to preserve good relationships between all.

"Nitrogen dioxide pollution, the policy of welcoming migrants, global warming or vaccination campaigns are sensitive subjects that can have a polarizing effect and that can separate people from each other. If this happens to your family members or a friend, the risk is to lose ties with your loved ones. Do you know what to do to avoid it? Do you think polarisation is jeopardising your good relationship? Visit SIRE.nl to find out what you can do when polarisation threatens.

First agree that you disagree with each other. If you know that you really won't agree, it is sometimes better to say: "let's agree to disagree". Then at least there is an agreement between you. You can then move on to another, less polarising topic.

The 10 attitudes to adopt to avoid the risk of saying something unpleasant.

1. A polarising discussion can quickly become very personal. You may disagree with the other person so much that

---

118 Sire.nl

you want to say something unpleasant. But when you're arguing with someone close to you, insults can have serious consequences and cause fractures that are hard to heal. Count to 10 if you feel that an annoying statement is starting to form. Take a deep breath. Or better yet, talk it out with each other. This will prevent you from having unpleasant words thrown at you.

2. Don't see the other person as someone who belongs to "that category ». In a polarising discussion, you can suddenly see the other person as the adversary. If you start saying things like "you're all..." or "you all want...", there's a risk that you'll no longer belong to the same group with the same bonds. If, on the other hand, you continue to see your cousin as your cousin or your girlfriend as your girlfriend, you're much more likely to have your bonds unaffected.

3. Accept that we are different. In a divisive discussion, you may sometimes be surprised at what someone thinks about a topic. But if you remember that we are all different, it is much easier not to fall out. Of course, you do not have to agree with each other's point of view. People differ, even people who are very close to you.

4. Ask why the topic is so concerning to the other person. To avoid drifting apart, you can ask yourself why the topic is so important to the other person, what is behind it? If you know why it affects the other person so much, you will be able to understand each other better. And sometimes you may even agree with the concerns that someone seems to have. You have found something that unites you.

5. Agree on how long you will talk about the topic together. A polarising discussion can become increasingly bitter the longer it goes on. So you can agree not to talk about it for more than a certain amount of time. For example, 10 minutes. During this time, both points of view are discussed, you listen to each other and explain if there are any questions. Then you drop it and move on to another topic.

6. Don't see a discussion as a competition. In a polarising discussion, you can of course try to convince the other person. But keep in mind that a discussion has no winners or losers. The one who wants to win stops listening to the other. Which only increases the distance. By talking and listening to each other, you don't move away.

7. Find out what you agree with. It is important to continue to listen to each other carefully in a discussion. Because in addition to the things you don't agree with, you will sometimes hear things that make you think: "That's interesting, there's something in that". Then maybe you can talk about it. This way, you will discover similarities in addition to your differences.

8. Name the close bond you have. A discussion on a polarising topic can drive friends and family apart. You can avoid this by naming what you mean to each other, what your bond is. "Hey, we may not agree... but you are still my sister." Or: "Okay, maybe we both see this very differently, but that should be possible, right, as good friends?" By naming your bond, you both realise that you have to take care of it first.

9. Let each other finish. Obvious and at the same time very difficult sometimes. A polarising discussion only gets fiercer if you keep interrupting each other. It is important that you both feel respected and heard. So, even if you have to bite your tongue sometimes, let the other person finish their sentences. Just make sure you give each other a chance to respond, without interrupting.

10. Calmly express that you are upset that you are so opposed to each other. Calmly say that you are having a hard time feeling so much distance when it comes to talking about this topic. For example, you could say, "It really bothers me that we are arguing like this… Can't we just talk more calmly?" So, both of you step away from the heated discussion for a moment and the distance will become smaller.

11. Stop discussing the topic for a moment. Stopping the topic for a while is a very effective way to calm things down. You have just let go of the debate for a moment, and you can come back to it together later. Who knows, you might end up having a good conversation again. And in the meantime, talk about something else.

R. Freedom of worship and expression in the Constitution

The Constitution of the Netherlands, officially called "Grondwet voor het Koninkrijk der Nederlanden" in Dutch, was adopted on 29 March 1814. However, it has undergone several revisions since then, including in 1848, 1887, 1917, 1938 and 1983. Religious freedom and freedom of expression have been enshrined in the Constitution since the 1848 revision, which guarantees and protects these fundamental rights.

- Freedom of religion is protected by Article 6, which recognises the right of everyone to practice their religion or beliefs, individually or in community with others, without discrimination.
- Freedom of expression, including the freedom to receive and impart information without prior censorship, is guaranteed by Article 7. However, certain limitations may be imposed for reasons such as the protection of reputation, the prevention of crime, or respect for the rights and freedoms of others.

Since then, these articles have been retained in the Dutch Constitution and are still in force today.

In France, freedom of religion and freedom of expression are also both enshrined in the French constitution.

- Freedom of expression is protected by Article 11 of the Declaration of the Rights of Man and of the Citizen of 1789.
- Freedom of worship is guaranteed by Article 1 of the French Constitution of 1958. Secularism is also a key principle in France, which guarantees the separation of state and religions.

Table of contents

I.   Another way of life   21

II.   Cultural paradoxes   31

III.   Youth, education and the Dutch temperament 41

VI. Work and politics   **159**

VII. Health, life, then death   **207**

XIV.Annexes 299

Table of contents 329

Selected bibliography 341

Thanks 343

Selected bibliography

★ **Un champ de Lys et de Tulipes**
Les cultures françaises et néerlandaises, terreau du Groupe
Air France KLM, Jérôme Picard, BookEdition.com

★ **Petites chroniques des Pays-Bas**
Plus totalement française, pas non plus néerlandaise, des
chroniques de l'entre-deux, Océane Dorange,
www.petiteschroniquesdespaysbas.com

★ **Canon van Nederland**
https://www.canonvannederland.nl/fr/

★ **Why Dutch are different ?**
A journey into the Hidden Heart of the Netherlands, Ben
Coates, Nicholas Brealey Publishing 2015.

★ **Les Néerlandais**
Ateliers Henry Dougier, Lignes de vie d'un peuple, Ateliers
Henry Dougier

★ **Voyage en Europe**
De Charlemagne à nos jours, François Reynaert, Fayard

★ **Histoire des Pays-Bas**
De l'antiquité à nos jours, Thomas Beaufils, Tallandier

Thanks

Many French people, living in the Netherlands, like me, but also native Dutch people, my acquaintances, my neighbours or work colleagues, whom I warmly thank, also contributed to this book.

In particular, Océane Dorange[119], Line and Peter Weizenbach, Margrit Sebek, Wilco and Véronique van Wee, Anne-Françoise Spoto, Sylvie Mellab, Cathy Barré, Gé Brussaard, Peter and Joost Noordermeer, André van der Sluis, and of course, my wife Isabelle, who raised our four children in the Netherlands without falling into a blissful admiration of Dutch society.

The testimonies and corrections thus collected reflect Dutch society since the 2000s.

---

[119] *Petites chroniques des Pays-Bas, Océane Dorange, www.petiteschroniquesdespaysbas.com*